# EN ROUTE

PUBLISHING

New York

# EN ROUTE

## A PARAMEDIC'S STORIES OF LIFE, DEATH, AND EVERYTHING IN BETWEEN

### STEVEN "KELLY" GRAYSON

Copyright © 2009

Published by Kaplan Publishing, a division of Kaplan, Inc.
1 Liberty Plaza, 24th Floor
New York, NY 10006

Library of Congress Cataloging-in-Publication Data

Grayson, Steve Kelly.
En Route : a paramedic's stories of life, death, and everything in between /
Steve Kelly Grayson.
    p. cm.
ISBN 978-1-4277-9971-5
1. Grayson, Steve Kelly—Anecdotes. 2. Emergency medical personnel—United States--Anecdotes. 3.Allied health personne—United States--Anecdotes. I. Title.
RA645.5.G736 2009
616.02'5092--dc22
[B]
                            2008048293


Printed in the United States of America


10 9 8 7 6 5 4 3 2 1

ISBN-13: 978-1-4277-9971-5

Kaplan Publishing books are available at special quantity discounts to use for sales promotions, employee premiums, or educational purposes. Please email our Special Sales Department to order or for more information at kaplanpublishing@kaplan.com, or write to Kaplan Publishing, 1 Liberty Plaza, 24th Floor, New York, NY 10006.

# CONTENTS

# DEDICATION AND THANKS

To all of my partners, past and present—this book is as much yours as it is mine. We know each other's favorite restaurants and kids' names. We know each other's wives and girlfriends, and for the most part we try not to mention one in front of the other. We complete each other's sentences, and we watch each other's backs. If you see yourself in here and don't remember the call, or you remember the call but somebody else was my partner, it's only because names, dates, and places have been changed to protect the innocent and the guilty, and to shield myself from the HIPAA monster.

To Kat Rickey and Lou Jordan, for believing.

To Susan LeJeune, for encouraging me to trust my own voice.

To Scott Millington: July 31, 1969 to July 26, 2005. Rest well, friend.

# Welcome to the Asylum

WHEN I FIRST started as an Emergency Medical Technician, I thought I had landed in an asylum and the inmates were running the place. The ink wasn't yet dry on my EMT-Basic card, and I didn't even have a uniform shirt on which to sew my new EMT patch. This didn't stop me, however, from purchasing every single piece of EMT equipment I could afford, and I brought them all with me that first night. If the opportunity presented itself for me to use my new window punch, or cut someone's boots off with my new trauma shears, I was ready.

I was riding with an outfit called Chennault Ambulance, a new service out of Fort Sperry, Louisiana. I'd tried several times to get an interview with StatMedic EMS, the big outfit in this area, but they refused to give me the time of day. These guys at Chennault were former StatMedic employees, and rumor had it that they needed more people. From the looks of things, I'd say what they needed were beds, and more room. There were EMTs sleeping on every horizontal surface in sight.

"Please pardon the mess," the owner, Linda Graham, told me apologetically as I waded through piles of invoices, supply catalogs, run tickets, and government forms of every description. "We just got started last week, and things are still a little hectic."

There was a man sitting on the living room floor amid an impressive pile of paperwork, and he looked up and smiled as we entered the room.

"This is my husband, Bob," Linda said, motioning for him to get up. "Bob, this is Kristy's friend, Kelly Grayson. He just got his EMT card, and he'd like to ride with us."

"The more the merrier." Bob smiled warmly, shaking my hand. "Has Linda given you the tour yet? Have you met everybody?"

"I was just about to do that," Linda replied, steering me into the den. There were two uniformed women sleeping on the couch and the divan. "Bobby Jean Sanders and JoAnn Graves," Linda whispered, pointing to each of them. "Yesterday, they drove our new ambulances from northern Arkansas to Baton Rouge to get them inspected, then turned around and drove back up here. Then they ran calls all night."

We tiptoed out of the den into the dining room. Along the walls, there were two folding cots with sleeping EMTs on them.

"Mickey Sanders and Marianne Fowlkes," Linda continued, pointing to each of them. "Mickey is Bobby Jean's son, and Marianne is a nurse. We've been working nonstop for the past two weeks," Linda whispered conspiratorially as she steered me back into the living room, "and everyone's exhausted. We made the decision to start our own service on a Friday, and we ran our first call the next Monday morning. It's been chaos ever since."

"How many trucks do you have?" I asked.

"Two," Linda answered proudly, "running twenty-four hours a day. They're both used, but they're dedicated to Chennault Parish exclusively." Linda went on to explain that everyone, with the exception of Mickey, was a StatMedic employee until two weeks ago. "We all got tired of spending our time out of town, running transfers in the city while our own parish was covered by an ambulance thirty minutes away," she said bitterly. "People up here don't need ambulances all that often, but when they do need them, they shouldn't have to wait almost an hour to get one. So, we started our own service. We don't know if we'll still be in business in six months, but we're damned sure going to try." She plopped down on the couch and sighed.

We spent the next few hours talking about my EMT course, what I used to do for a living, my family, and generally everything under the sun. About an hour into the conversation, I began to realize that I was being skillfully interrogated, and I wondered how many people they'd tag-teamed this way. It was the most thorough job interview I'd ever been subjected to.

At half past four in the morning, we were still talking when the phone rang. Bob, still sitting cross-legged on the floor, answered it. "The emergency line," Linda explained as Bob wrote down the particulars. "It looks like we've got a call." Bob hung up the phone and grinned.

"We're going to 412 Benjamin Franklin East," he said, beaming. "A lady having seizures."

"Let's go!" Linda exclaimed. "This will be your first call, won't it?" Before I could reply, she was out the door, waddling as fast as her short legs could carry her.

I sprinted for the rig, managing to jump in the back just before Bob roared off, spitting gravel from beneath the tires. The ride to 412 Benjamin Franklin differed from an amusement park roller coaster only in that I didn't have to pay for the ride and the roller coaster is far less rough. It was damned exciting, no doubt about it.

This is the real deal! I thought with growing excitement as Bob wove us quickly and unerringly through a maze of streets. This was what all the practice was for.

When we arrived at the address, I was the first person out of the truck. There was a man standing just outside the house, smoking a cigarette. He seemed remarkably unconcerned for someone whose friend or loved one was in the throes of a seizure. In EMT class, we were taught that seizures could be Bad Things.

"In there," he grunted, holding the door open. "Mama be seizin' again." Before I could walk inside, Bob bumped me out of the way.

"Let me go first," he said. "You help Linda with the stretcher." Disappointed, I trudged back to the rig and helped her haul the stretcher up the steep driveway. Linda just grinned at me. She could tell I was excited.

In the house, Bob was checking vital signs on a rather large black woman wearing a huge, flowery muumuu. There was a dark patch on the back where she had apparently urinated on herself. The woman wasn't seizing, but her breathing sounded horrible.

"Postictal," Bob said as if he expected me to know what that word meant. "Why don't you suction her and apply some oxygen?"

*Note to self: Look up the word postictal in Taber's dictionary at your next opportunity.*

I eagerly grabbed the suction unit and cleared the woman's airway, then applied a non-rebreather mask.

*Shouldn't we use an oral airway? I wondered. Maybe a bite stick, too? She's snoring a lot. Maybe if I just tilt her head back like this, it will—I'll be damned! It worked!*

Linda beckoned me over to help her lower the stretcher. I fumbled with the handles, but couldn't quite seem to make it work. The stretcher was nothing like the ones we used in EMT class. Linda saw me fumbling around and quickly squeezed the proper handle, and the stretcher promptly crashed down to its lowest position.

*Note to self number two: Learn how to work the stretcher, so you won't look like such a dumbass.*

"If you will get her legs, I'll get under her arms," Bob directed. "Just pick her up on my count and we'll put her on the cot." As he counted to three, I wrapped my arms around the woman's knees and lifted, soaking my polo shirt in urine in the process. Bob just smiled tolerantly as I looked in dismay at the yellow stain on the front of my white shirt.

*Note to self number three: Never get stuck with the lower body when you pick up someone who has pissed on herself, and carry a spare shirt in case you do wind up getting stuck with that job.*

I gathered the blood pressure cuff and oxygen bottle off the floor as Bob and Linda raised the stretcher. As I strapped the oxygen bottle on the stretcher between the patient's feet, without warning the stretcher collapsed to its lowest position, dropping the patient to the floor with a frightening crash. Shocked, I could do nothing but stare at Bob and Linda, who were both staring at each other.

"What did you do?" both of them asked each other, in unison. They shook their heads in denial and carefully lifted the stretcher again, taking pains to assure that the undercarriage was locked into position. They delicately rolled the patient to the rig as I trailed a safe distance behind, afraid to touch anything.

In the rig, Linda nodded toward a supply cabinet filled with intravenous supplies. "Spike a bag of saline for me, would you?" she asked, as she wrapped a tourniquet around the lady's arm.

*Somehow, I didn't think she wanted me to hurl the bag to the floor and do a touchdown dance. So what the hell did she mean?*

"Gimme that," Linda said impatiently, seeing my confusion. "Just get another set of vital signs."

I hurriedly complied, and quickly discovered that blood pressures are really hard to hear in the back of an ambulance. Linda was rolling her eyes and smiling.

After we dropped the patient off at the hospital, Linda bought me a Coke and showed me how to make up the stretcher. She favored tight creases in the sheets, and the straps folded just so.

"Are all seizure calls like that?" I asked her.

"Pretty much," she judged, grinning ruefully, "except for the part about dropping the stretcher. It is considered bad form to drop the patient. Remember that when you come to work for us."

"Am I coming to work for you?" I asked. "I don't recall anyone making a job offer. Besides, I didn't do very well on that call."

"You're green," Linda agreed, "but you don't panic, and you don't just stand around waiting for someone to tell you what to do. You're hired, if you want to be. We could use you."

What the hell, why not? I doubted I'd get along with the folks at StatMedic, anyway.

# I'm Clear, You're Clear, the Chihuahua Is Clear...

T HEY SAY THAT the measure of a man's intelligence is the degree to which he agrees with you. By that standard, Dr. Mark Brothers and I regarded each other as certified geniuses. Not that we interacted a great deal in the clinical environment; as a lowly EMT-Basic, I simply dropped off my patients at the hospital, bowed respectfully, and backed slowly away from his presence.

But this day was a different story. The all-powerful physician and the lowly EMT were on an even footing, because when it comes to Trivial Pursuit, I bow to no man. I am the King of Obscure and Arcane Facts. Mark Brothers, if not my equal, is at least good enough to sit at my right hand. We had been paired off as partners in a game of Trivial Pursuit, and we were spanking some serious ass. We were humiliating people. For six games straight now, we had run the board, winning with nary a question missed. For the past two games, it had been everybody versus us.

We were hanging out at the Fort Sperry station, celebrating Chennault Ambulance's third month of business, and things were looking good. Call volume was increasing, we'd upgraded our capabilities, and rumor had it that we'd even be getting paychecks any day now. Life was sweet. Since I'd been getting paid in promises, I'd moved into the Fort Sperry station to save money. The only drawback to living there was that I was perpetually on duty. Every morning, I woke up and stumbled to Bob Graham's office and knocked on the door.

"Am I on duty today?" I'd ask, and wait patiently as Bob became lost in thought, shuffling through the duty roster he keeps in his head.

"Yep," he invariably said. "We can use you." I would then obediently trudge to the bathroom, shower, and put on a jumpsuit. But I didn't mind. This stuff was so much fun, I'd have done it for free. (Well, actually, I was doing it for free at the time.)

The emergency line rang, interrupting our game and sparing the rest of the crew further humiliation at the hands of my M.D. partner and me.

"Cardiac arrest at 137 Owl Creek Road," Bob called. "Let's go."

I was Bob's partner. After two months spent as the attendant on most of our calls, our upgrade to EMT-Intermediate service had seen me demoted back to driver. I didn't like it; I was going to start paramedic school in two months, and I needed the patient-care experience.

"I think I'll ride with you on this one," Dr. Brothers mused as we got up from the table.

*Oh shit, just what I need.*

I said nothing, just sprinted to the rig with Dr. Brothers in tow. On the way to the call, I could hear him curse softly from the back as I made a few hard turns.

"Hang on, Doc!" I called unnecessarily. "Rough road ahead!" In the rearview mirror, I could see him hanging on to the overhead bar for dear life. "Why don't you toss the suction, the jump bag, and the automated external defibrillator on the stretcher?" I called back to him, adding, "and spike a bag of saline, too!" Bob looked over at me and grinned, shaking his head.

At the house, there was a woman doing CPR on a fiftyish man lying on the living room floor. Several other relatives were standing around sobbing quietly, and a hyperactive little Chihuahua was bouncing from the couch to the chair to the floor, yapping excitedly. The woman doing CPR was crying, and there was snot running from her nose, which she absently wiped away as Bob placed the AED on the floor next to the man.

"Ma'am," he asked gently, "what happened?"

The woman didn't answer, but just stared vacantly and cried, wiping her nose with her sleeve. There was a smear of bloody vomit on her lip. Delicately, I moved her to one side and handed her off to Dr. Brothers, who was standing around looking lost.

"Hey, Doc," I suggested, "why don't you find out what happened, and have someone gather up his medications? Hand me the suction before you go." Dr. Brothers hurriedly handed me the suction unit and escorted the woman into the other room, talking quietly to her. The Chihuahua snapped at my hand as I suctioned the vomitus from the man's mouth and Bob attached the AED pads. I swatted impatiently at the dog, who returned the favor by snapping at me again and growling ferociously.

"Uh, can one of you corral the dog?" I asked pointedly at the group of relatives standing nearby. A young woman, perhaps the victim's daughter, snapped out of her reverie.

"Sweetie! Stop that! Stop it this instant!" she scolded, snapping her fingers. "He's really a sweet puppy," she apologized.

*Sure, he is, lady. Why is it that every psychotic little ankle-biter has a name like Sweetie or Sugarpuss, instead of something that fits, like Tasmanian Devil or Charles Manson?*

For his part, Sweetie ignored her, jumping from the couch to his master's chest and back. Irritated, I batted the dog off the man's chest as I began chest compressions. I hit him a little harder than I intended, sending him somersaulting across the rug all the way to the fireplace. Sweetie bounced back up like nothing had happened, and contented himself with jumping back and forth from the couch to my back, nipping at my hair and shirt collar with each circuit.

"Sweetie!" the woman cried, anguished. "Please leave the nice man alone!"

I ignored them both, moving up to the man's head to ventilate as Bob pressed the analyze button on the AED.

"Shock indicated!" the AED announced.

"Everybody clear!" Bob shouted, looking at the AED and pressing the shock button...just as Sweetie completed another pinball circuit, landing squarely on his master's chest, right between the AED pads.

"Pop!" went the AED, accompanied by an agonized yelp and the stench of burning dog hair. Sweetie ricocheted across the couch and retreated for safer parts, yelping piteously all the while.

"What was that?" Bob asked, turning back to the patient with a frightened expression.

"If the dog wasn't in V-fib, he probably is now," I commented drily. "Apparently, 'clear' is not a command in his vocabulary."

The AED interrupted any further conversation by reminding us in its telephone-operator voice that the patient was still in V-fib and one of us should press the shock button. Bob just shook his head wonderingly and, looking at the patient this time, pressed the button again.

"Kachunk!" The defibrillator discharged, causing the man to arch his back in a prolonged spasm. Within a few moments, the man coughed and started breathing raggedly. Bob and I shared a triumphant look.

"No shock advised," the AED told us unnecessarily. "It is safe to touch the patient. Check breathing. Check pulse. If no pulse..."

There was no need to check breathing or pulse, or begin CPR, as the AED politely suggested. Dead people do not vomit and roll their eyes wildly. I quickly stuck the suction catheter in his mouth to clear his airway. Soon, the man was breathing better, but still coughing and retching. I switched the oxygen tank to a non-rebreather mask and placed it over his face.

"What happened to the dog?" Dr. Brothers asked as he escorted the patient's wife back into the room. "He came through here like his tail was on fire or something..." He trailed off as he saw our patient.

"Ma'am?" He nudged the woman, who looked up, startled. He just smiled, gesturing toward her husband. She gasped and kneeled at his side, sobbing again, but in a different way than before. The man said nothing, just closed his eyes and squeezed her hand as he coughed and sucked deep, shuddering breaths of pure oxygen. I took a little time gathering up our equipment. The woman continued to hold her husband's hand all the way to the ambulance, disengaging only briefly as we loaded him onto the stretcher.

Since Dr. Brothers was with us, Bob let me ride in the back on the way to the hospital. Dr. Brothers had a bit of trouble getting an IV. "Goddamn! Can you ask Bob to take it easy for the next couple of minutes?" he asked, frustrated. There was sweat dripping from his nose as he made his second stick at a vein.

"He is taking it easy," I told him. The ambulance was barely moving forty miles an hour, and I could see Bob's eyes in the rearview mirror, watching Dr. Brothers as he made his second, successful attempt. "Besides, we'll be at the hospital in two minutes."

Dr. Brothers had his eyes closed, concentrating as he auscultated heart and breath sounds. "Shit," he muttered disgustedly. "I can barely hear. Lungs sound clear, I guess. He may have a systolic murmur."

"They call it 'diesel engine,' Doc," I told him wryly. "Now you know why we palpate so many blood pressures."

"This machine doesn't even have a printer or a screen!" Dr. Brothers complained. "We need a real cardiac monitor, and some lidocaine, and maybe some dopamine..." He looked around in frustration for a drug box that wasn't there.

"We're not a paramedic service yet," I reminded him. "But the AED does have some interesting features. For instance, it has a voice recorder that activates when you turn the unit on. Where do you think we get the tapes you review?"

"You mean that?" Dr. Brothers asked, looking suspiciously at the AED.

"Yep," I confirmed with an evil grin, "everything is recorded for posterity, including Sweetie's electrocution."

"Good Lord," he breathed. "Well, at least no one will hear it but me."

"Well, we could make copies of the tapes before you get them," I mused. "Purely for record-keeping purposes of course."

"You do that," he threatened with a grin, "and I'll withdraw my recommendation for paramedic school."

# Papermedic

THERE WAS A ring-necked pheasant in the road, and Bob Graham seemed utterly fascinated by its presence. So fascinated, in fact, that he made me pull over so he could get a photograph of it, so I gingerly found a spot to pull over where we wouldn't get smeared by oncoming traffic. This stretch of road was known for its traffic fatalities. Bob eased out of the truck, creeping through the ditch to stalk his wary prey.

In a few minutes he was back, grinning triumphantly. "A ring-necked pheasant!" he exclaimed happily. "Do you know they're not native to this area?"

"They're not native to North America, period," I pointed out. "They were imported here from China sometime in the last century."

*Not to mention that there was a private shooting reserve and game farm less than a mile away. There is no wild pheasant population in north Louisiana, boss.*

"I know that," Bob replied, rolling his eyes. "What I meant was that they're not native here."

I just chuckled as he climbed back into the truck. He looked happy to be out of the office. Since we'd upgraded to paramedic-level service, he had spent the majority of his time as an office weenie. We had enough paramedics and emergency medical technicians to fully staff all the trucks, save one. That day Bob, who was an EMT-Intermediate, had decided we needed to be scouting for possible locations for a new station in the south end of the parish. I had been elected to chauffeur him around, partly because I was still waiting on the results of my paramedic exam and was not assigned to a truck that day, and partly because he was the boss and did not like to drive.

Bob had an unwritten rule that says the crew member with the lowest certification always drives. To my knowledge, the only time this rule had been waived was three weeks earlier, when I fell asleep at the wheel on a trip to Shreveport. I nearly wiped out the rig on a bridge abutment, so Bob drove for the rest of the trip while I attended the burn patient in the back.

My schedule had been more predictable of late, as had my paychecks. While I'd been in paramedic school, my work hours were best described as "every minute I'm not physically present in class or at a clinical site." The overtime pay had been quite welcome, and I'd actually been able to save enough money to buy a used Volvo.

At least once a week for the past six months, Bob or Linda had met me at the front porch of the Fort Sperry station after I'd driven home from paramedic class.

"Park your car and get your ass in bed," they'd say. "Your tag number and vehicle description are all over the scanner. Every uniformed officer in the parish is looking for the drunk in the tan Volvo." Staying awake had been increasingly difficult those days.

"I'm kind of worried about you falling asleep at the wheel lately," Bob said. His expression was mild, but there was something serious behind his eyes. This was not just an idle observation.

"I'm taking the Ritalin that Dr. Brothers prescribed," I protested. "It's working."

"No, it's not," Bob disagreed. "When I climbed back into the truck just now, you were asleep. Whenever you sit still for five minutes, you fall asleep. Plus, you snore like a chainsaw."

"So?" I retorted. "You snore, too."

"Yeah, but I'm not driving one of my ambulances on a daily basis," he pointed out. "I think you have sleep apnea, and I think you need to get tested. What happens if you fall asleep in the back with a patient?"

"I do my job," I stated flatly. "It doesn't affect patient care. I stay awake when I'm working on patients, and I only tend to doze off on long trips. That's why Dr. Brothers prescribed the Ritalin."

"I'm not comfortable with your driving," Bob repeated firmly. "And you will get a sleep study before I allow you to drive on a regular basis again."

Before I could frame a reply, the radio crackled and announced, "Nine-oh-two, Dispatch."

Huh? My employee number was 702. Actually, my employee number started out as something different, but ever since I accidentally drilled through the main oxygen tank while working on one of the rigs, I had been forever branded "Oh-two." At Chennault Ambulance, employee numbers were assigned according to certification level. Basic EMTs started with a seven, Intermediates started with an eight, and so on.

"Dispatch, seven-oh-two," I answered. "Did you have traffic?"

"Uh, correction, that's nine-oh-two," the radio announced clearly. "Your National Registry card and your temporary state permit just came in the mail. Congratulations." Bob clapped me on the shoulder happily, then looked quizzically at me as I pulled over and put the rig in park.

"Lowest certification always drives," I pointed out gleefully. "So get your ass over here and play chauffeur for a while. I need to get some sleep." Bob sighed, but switched places with me without a fuss.

"You're still getting the sleep study," he reminded me as he pulled away. "Try not to let your ego get any bigger than it is, Mr. Paramedic. I remember when you didn't know how to spike an IV bag."

# First Code

MICKEY SANDERS AND I were in Mason Ferry, the second day of a seventy-two-hour shift. I had been a paramedic for precisely nine days and I'd run precisely one call, a cardiac transfer to nearby Boothville. The patient had Activase, nitroglycerin, and heparin IVs running, in addition to his maintenance fluids. His vitals were okay, and he was essentially pain-free, if a bit dopey from all the morphine they'd given him.

The doctor told me the patient was having something called "anterior wall MI [myocardial infarction], possibly LAD occlusion." Apparently, the gold patch on my shoulder and the semi-intelligent look on my face had fooled this guy into thinking I knew what that meant. I, of course, nodded inscrutably and loaded my patient without further ado. We didn't cover twelve-lead EKGs in my medic class, but I'd started reading Dale Dubin's *Rapid Interpretation of EKG's*, and I was understanding it pretty easily, so I figured I was competent.

Halfway through the trip, the patient went into an idioventricular rhythm. Just before I started shitting my pants, I remembered something I'd been told about reperfusion arrhythmias. So I waited a few minutes, and sure enough he converted back to sinus rhythm. By the time we got to Boothville General Hospital, my guy was doing fine. I had just delivered my first patient in decidedly better condition than when I picked him up, and I'd accomplished this feat by doing precisely...nothing. I realize there's probably a lesson to be learned in there somewhere.

Anyway, that was the sum total of my paramedic experience to date. Exactly one year and nine days earlier, I became a Basic EMT. I had been working as an attendant for most of that time. Before we upgraded to paramedic-level service, I got a pretty good amount of direct patient-care experience. My employers and my instructors seemed to have confidence in me, but nothing compared to the confidence I had in myself. I was ready to go save some lives. Now, if somebody would just have the common courtesy to die I could show off my stuff!

Mickey and I were eating dinner in front of the television when someone knocked on the door. There was a man in a work uniform standing there on the porch. "Hey, are you guys the ambulance drivers?"

*Well, since there's an ambulance parked in the drive, yes, sir, I'd say that's a safe assumption.*

I let the "ambulance driver" comment pass unchallenged. This guy worked at a job where he had his name embroidered on his shirt. He was probably not bright or educated enough to know what a paramedic is. It suddenly occurred to me then that I had my name embroidered on my shirt as well. So what did that say about me?

"Yep, you got the right place. What can we do for you?"

"My wife said y'all were in the pink house," the guy said, looking relieved. The house we leased in Mason Ferry as our station was painted hot pink. It was distinctive, that's for sure. "Anyway, I was on my way home from work and I saw a truck in the ditch way up Highway 134. It was pretty banged up, so I figured someone needs to go check it out."

"Okay, sir, we'll do just that," I told him. "Thanks for telling us."

I motioned for Mickey to get up. He wasn't happy, but he'd get over it. This smelled like bullshit, but there also might have been something to it. What the hell, red beans and rice reheat pretty well anyway.

"Dispatch, Unit Two. We're en route to a reported wreck on Highway 134 north," I called in.

When I hung up the mike, my partner picked it right back up.

"Dispatch, Unit Two," Mickey radioed. "Could you notify the sheriff's office and have them send a deputy this way?" He looked at me and shrugged. "What the hell, it can't hurt, right?"

We rolled up Highway 134 toward Hadley, Arkansas, the strobes casting weird reflections off the trees. Once you get out of Mason Ferry, which doesn't take two minutes, this is a lonely stretch of road. Fifteen minutes out of town, we saw a truck in the opposite ditch. Not fifty yards up the road, there is a sign that says WELCOME TO ARKANSAS. The truck had obviously been wrecked. The windshield was starred, and it looked as if it had rolled over multiple times. The headlights were on and the driver's door was open.

"Dispatch, Unit Two. We're on scene."

We got out of the rig and checked out the truck. There was nobody around. Besides the body damage and the busted windshield, it was probably drivable. The keys were still in the ignition, and the switch was on. The cab was a mess, and there were several beer cans on the floor where they'd spilled out of an open twelve-pack. There were a few empties, and there were several more cans in the debris trail strewn behind the truck. I counted the cans and came up with ten unopened ones, still fairly cold. *I'll be damned. Somebody who actually had two beers!*

Our relative teetotaler was still nowhere in sight, however. We scanned the ditch, the woods, the opposite side of the road, everything. I'd just about decided that whoever wrecked his or her Chevy Silverado either walked home unscathed or caught a ride from someone, when Mickey called out.

"Uh, Kelly?" He was pointing his flashlight at something on the ground at his feet. I walked maybe a hundred feet to see what he'd found. Our driver had made his appearance.

The driver was lying facedown in the sandy ditch, a small puddle of blood seeping into the sand under his mouth. He was wearing the same type of uniform as the guy who'd notified us, and he was obviously dead. Mickey's shoulders slumped.

"Well, you'd better notify Chennault Parish Sheriff's Office that this is a fatality, and tell 'em to dispatch the coroner," I told him as he trudged back to the rig. "And bring me the cardiac monitor from the rig!"

There were headlights approaching from the direction of Mason Ferry. A truck pulled over on the shoulder and the driver got out. It was the guy who'd knocked on our door.

"Jesus Christ!" he exclaimed. "I work with that guy!"

"Can you tell us his name?"

"Naw, I don't know him all that well. He works in another part of the plant," our Good Samaritan told me. "Is he hurt bad?" My look told him what he'd rather not know. "Awwww, man!" he said, anguished.

He turned away slightly, mumbling under his breath. I couldn't tell what he was saying, but after a few words I realized it was a prayer. For some reason I was a bit embarrassed to overhear this, a man praying for the soul of someone he barely knew. It seemed vaguely unseemly to eavesdrop.

*Go ahead, brother,* I thought. *What you're doing is more than I can do to help.*

"CPSO says the coroner has been notified. He should be here in a little while," Mickey told me as he brought back the cardiac monitor. I intended to run an asystole strip for the coroner's report, our standard procedure.

As we rolled the guy over, the Good Samaritan gasped. The victim's face didn't look especially bad, but his mouth was full of blood, which was also oozing out of his nose and ears. The embroidered patch on his shirt said his name was Randy.

Mickey and I attached the monitor electrodes to Randy's chest and turned on the monitor. As expected, the rhythm was asystole, a long, un-broken stretch of flat line until...beep! I turned to Mickey, dumbfounded, and there it went again...beep! It was a slow idioventricular rhythm, may-be sixteen beats a minute.

*No way! This guy is dead! D-E-A-D, dead! What do I do now?*

Mickey cursed and sprinted for the truck. As usual, he wasn't slow in making a decision. Our protocols stated that as long as a rhythm exists, we work the code. Mickey knew this, and had gone to fetch the rest of our gear. It didn't occur to either of us to question the wisdom of the protocol.

"What is that? What does that mean?" our Good Samaritan wanted to know. I had forgotten he was there.

"It means that we're going to try to resuscitate him," I said bitterly. This was not how I'd envisioned my first cardiac arrest. "Do you know CPR?"

"Oh, God..." the man said as he knelt down next to Randy, starting chest compressions. He was praying out loud now. Mickey ran up, puffing, and handed me a bag valve mask. I tried my best to do a jaw thrust, but I couldn't ventilate through all the blood. I grabbed the portable suction and tried to clear the airway, but it didn't work worth a damn. It was a hand-operated, manual doohickey, which was about all our service could afford. It was the first time I'd ever used it on a real patient.

I cursed and dug through the bag for the laryngoscope kit. Mickey took over CPR from our Good Samaritan, who, under the circumstances, wasn't doing the best job anyway. I tried to intubate, but between the blood and the darkness, I couldn't make out a thing. I handed Mickey's flashlight to the Good Samaritan as I suctioned some more. I noticed the patch on his shirt.

"Here, Leon," I told him. "Hold the flashlight on his face."

Leon nodded dumbly and moved behind me with the flashlight. As I tried again to intubate, the beam played across Randy's face, chest, feet, and the surrounding ground. I looked over my shoulder, irritated, and saw that Leon was shaking like a crack baby. I grabbed his hand and pulled the flashlight down, resting it on my left shoulder.

"Hold it right there, Leon. You're doing good."

I still couldn't see anything.

It was useless. I couldn't get an airway, and we were working in the dark!

"How about we package him up and go?" Mickey asked, reading my mind. I nodded at him, and we quickly applied a cervical collar and rolled our patient onto a board. It could charitably be called spinal immobilization, if you were really charitable. We loaded Randy up quickly and rolled toward Fort Sperry Community Hospital, siren screaming.

*Okay, airway first. Get the tube, and then go with epinephrine and atropine down the tube. That will buy a few minutes until the next round of drugs; long enough to get an IV, maybe two. Open the IVs WFO, and start pushing the drugs, and...fuck! Who is going to do CPR while I do all this paramedic shit? Why in hell didn't I grab Leon instead of leaving him standing there in the ditch?*

I tried briefly to bag, but I couldn't get a good seal with the truck rocking the way it was. We were in a 1985 gas-burner Ford with a 351 big-block engine, and we were hauling ass. The truck was eight years old, and the suspension and steering had seen better days, but the engine still had plenty of go, and Mickey wasn't afraid to use it.

I grabbed on to the ceiling rail and hung on for dear life, digging through the cabinet for a pocket face mask. I spent the next few minutes with my head braced against the cabinets, doing basic life-support CPR. A state trooper passed us going the other way, all lit up with siren screaming.

*Where the hell was he ten minutes ago?*

I felt the truck slowing considerably as Mickey applied the brakes. We had to be coming into Mason Ferry, I thought, looking out the side window. But there was Fort Sperry Community Hospital! How in the hell did we go through Mason Ferry without me noticing? I hadn't even called in a report!

Mickey pulled in to the ambulance bay, parked, and hustled around to open the doors.

"We're gonna be in trouble," I told him as we unloaded the stretcher. "I forgot to call a report."

Mickey rolled his eyes and shook his head as we banged through the doors. Luckily, we had a welcoming party waiting. Dr. Brothers and two nurses were in the hallway. They had heard the radio traffic on the scanner and had anticipated our arrival.

Dr. Brothers looked at me with a displeased expression on his face as I breathlessly gave report. His expression softened a bit as he leaned over to auscultate an apical pulse. I looked down at my uniform and noticed that I was a mess. There was blood and sand ground into my shirt, which was partially untucked. I was dripping with sweat.

Dr. Brothers straightened up, shaking his head. "He's gone," he told us. "Let's call it at..." He paused, looking at his watch. "Nine-twenty P.M. Roll him in there until the coroner gets here," he said, pointing to a room. "I suppose someone should call the coroner and—"

"Shit!" I blurted, earning another disapproving look. "We already called him. He's probably on his way to the scene."

Dr. Brothers just shook his head and walked off. Later, he walked up to the desk where I was doing my report. He handed me a Coke. I was dreading what was about to come.

"Tough call?" he inquired politely.

"How could you guess?" I laughed nervously.

"Well, for one thing, you're still wearing bloody gloves, and there's a big dimple in the middle of your forehead that says "Wheeled Coach.""

"Sorry," I said, chagrined. I quickly stripped off my gloves and shot them into the biohazard can. "I guess I kind of fucked that one up, huh?"

"Yeah, you did," he replied evenly. "On the other hand, you got to make your mistakes on an unsalvageable patient instead of someone where a mistake might matter."

"Should we have coded that guy?" I asked him.

"Honestly, I wouldn't have," he replied. "But I wasn't there. The protocol says you should try to work patients who have organized rhythms, but you also have to use your judgment."

"I guess my judgment could use a little work," I admitted reluctantly.

"Well, we were told in medical school that good judgment comes from experience, and experience comes from bad judgment. So what did you learn from this?"

"That I can't do it all by myself," I reflected. "And that the book doesn't have all the answers."

Dr. Brothers nodded in approval.

"You might also want to wait until you know that the patient is actually dead before you request the coroner's services," he pointed out teasingly, then turned serious. "Look, you're good. Maybe you're too good. Everything comes easily to you, or I wouldn't have recommended you for a paramedic course with only three months' experience as an EMT. But talent alone won't do it. There's a big difference between confident and cocky." He playfully kicked my chair leg and walked away.

Outside, I found out that I wasn't the only one getting counseled.

Mickey was talking to the state trooper who'd passed us, Brian Hemphill. The conversation was loud, profane, and somewhat one-sided.

"What in the blue fuck did you think you were doing? Do you have any goddamn idea how fast you were going?" Brian raged. Before Mickey could answer, Brian continued his tirade. "One hundred thirty miles per hour, that's how fast you were going! You rotten little pissant!"

"I was going eighty-five miles an hour," Mickey replied, not very convincingly.

"Eighty-five? *Eighty-five?*" Brian spluttered, incredulous.

"My speedometer goes to eighty-five, and that's what the needle said," Mickey said just a little smugly.

"Don't you play games with me, Michael David Sanders! I got you on radar at one-thirty! What the fuck makes you think you can handle that speed on these roads?"

"I've driven that fast before," Mickey pointed out.

"That was in a brand-new police cruiser with good tires, suspension, and steering, not a 1975 high-top ambulance!"

"Actually, it's a 1985 model," Mickey corrected him, grinning.

"Let me tell you something," Brian growled menacingly as he grabbed Mickey's collar and pulled his face to within an inch of his own. The smile slipped from Mickey's face. "I don't care if I changed your fucking diapers. I don't care if I taught you how to play baseball. If I ever see you pull a stunt like that again, I will personally whip your little ass, and then tell your daddy, who will then whip your ass, too. And I will personally see to it that you are kicked off the sheriff's reserves! Do you read me, son?" he asked as he shook Mickey like a terrier shaking a rat.

"Yes, sir," Mickey said meekly.

Mickey Sanders was a third-degree black belt in tae kwon do. He had thirty pounds and three inches on Brian Hemphill, and he was twenty years younger. But you could see in his eyes that at that moment he believed that Brian was perfectly capable of stomping a mud hole in his ass and walking it dry. I believed it, too. Brian shook him once more for good measure, and then stalked back to his cruiser, still fuming.

I said nothing as we got in our rig. Mickey started it up and paused for a moment, then grinned at me unconvincingly. "Had him eating out of the palm of my hand," he declared.

"Sure, you did, partner," I replied sarcastically. "You had him right where you wanted him."

# Show and Tell

GOOD MORNING, EVERYONE! First of all, I'd like to thank Mrs. Johnson, your health teacher, for inviting us to speak to you today. My name is Kelly Grayson, and I'm a paramedic with Chennault Ambulance, and this is my partner, JoAnn Graves. Say hello to everyone, JoAnn! You'll have to excuse my partner, she's a bit shy."

"Mrs. Johnson has asked us to speak to you this morning and to show you our ambulance, so I guess I'll begin by taking a few questions. So who's first? You there, the young lady in the front with blond hair. What was your question?"

"What is a paramedic, sir?" she wanted to know.

"Good question! A paramedic is the highest level of emergency medical technician. There are three EMT levels in Louisiana—Basic, Intermediate, and Paramedic."

"What's the difference?" her friend asked.

"Well, length of training, mainly. An EMT-Basic has about 150 hours of training, and Intermediate has about 240 hours, and a Paramedic has upward of 1,000 hours of training. I get to do all of the cool stuff you see on *Rescue 911* and shows like that."

"How is a paramedic different from a nurse?" a black kid in a Tommy Hilfiger shirt inquired.

"Well, nurses work in a hospital, and we primarily work outside of a hospital. We work under more extreme conditions, too. The thing I like is that we can do more than most nurses without asking for permission from the doctor, like a nurse does."

"So you get paid more than nurses?" the kid pressed.

"No, I'm afraid not. We're not paid that much, actually."

"So how much does a paramedic make?" a jock in a football letterman's jacket asked.

"Well, a lot depends on where you work. I make about thirty-six thousand a year, but I have to work lots of overtime to make that much. But most paramedics, and I think JoAnn would agree with me on this, aren't in this profession for the money. They do it out of a desire to help people. We get paid in job satisfaction."

"How much does your ambulance cost?" the same kid asked.

"Well, it depends on how fancy your ambulance is. The one we have here today costs about fifty thousand dollars. The equipment in it costs about thirty thousand more, I guess."

"What's the grossest thing you've ever seen as a paramedic?" a cheer-leader wanted to know. Everyone else leaned forward in anticipation.

"Well, that's hard to say. I'm usually working too hard at a scene to pay much attention to things like that. What seems gross to you may not seem that bad to me, so it's hard to say. Some things look gross, but aren't really life-threatening. It's hard for me to pick out one particular call."

"How fast does your ambulance go?" another kid asked. Predictably, he was wearing a Dale Jarrett NASCAR shirt.

"Well, the ambulance I'm in now goes about ninety-five, although we rarely drive that fast. State law doesn't restrict how fast we can drive, as long as we show due regard for the safety of other motorists. Our company policy, however, states that we can exceed the posted speed limit by no more than fifteen miles an hour during an emergency response. So if you ever talk to my boss, I've never driven my ambulance faster than seventy miles an hour.

"Well, Mrs. Johnson is signaling me that my time is up, so I guess I'll wrap things up by saying thank you once again, and I hope you all enjoy your homecoming. If you will file out to the gym doors to your left, JoAnn will give you a tour of the ambulance."

Afterward, as JoAnn and I drove back to Mason Ferry, I asked her, "So, how did I do?"

"Great," she answered in her smoker's rasp. "If I didn't know you, I'd say you actually knew what you were talking about."

# Is It Me, Or Is It Drafty in Here?

IF I DIDN'T sleep, or eat, or take the time to shit, shower, and shave, no one would ever get sick. My instructors taught me this axiom, but I didn't believe it until I started working as a paramedic. I was reminded of it on this particular day, however, because I was standing in the shower with shampoo in my eyes when the pager tones went off.

"Unit One, respond Priority One to Riverview Convalescent Home, room C12, for an unconscious person," the pager crackled.

I cursed and hurriedly rinsed the soap out of my hair. At least the water was warm. In the Fort Sperry station, if you turned on the hot water in the kitchen sink, the water in the bathroom went instantly cold, a plumbing quirk that Mickey Sanders exploited at every opportunity.

I stepped out of the shower, shook the water from my hair, and hurriedly try to get dressed. My luck seemed to be running at zero, because my underwear and T-shirt were lying on the floor near the shower and got soaked by the spray. I could hear Mickey cranking the truck outside, so I just pulled the jumpsuit on sans shirt and stomped my naked feet down into my boots.

At Riverview, the call turned out to be a false alarm. The lady was not unconscious, but the nurse acted as if she were going to die at any minute. Our patient did have a slightly low blood pressure, and she was running a fever, so I took the time to start an IV on the way to the hospital. Judging from the urine in her Foley that looked like pulpy orange juice, I'd say she had a urinary tract infection.

At Fort Sperry Community Hospital, we dropped our patient off in the emergency room and hung out at the desk, flirting with the nurses. I must be have been throwing out a pretty good line of bullshit, because they all seemed to be buying it. Mickey considered himself the stud, but for some reason that day I was getting all the attention.

Leaning forward with my elbows propped on the counter, I talked about anything and nothing, enjoying the rapt attention of a growing crowd of nurses. They all blushed and laughed at my jokes, and some of them were quite obviously checking me out. I was enjoying myself immensely, basking in all this newfound attention, when Dee Walters, the ER charge nurse, beckoned me closer.

"Were you in the shower when you got this call?" Dee asked with a naughty glint in her eyes.

"As a matter of fact, I was." I grinned ruefully, rubbing my still-wet hair to demonstrate. "Why do you ask?"

"You didn't put anything on under your jumpsuit, did you?" Dee pursued, stifling a giggle.

"Well, I... how the hell do you know that?" I demanded, looking myself over. The entire crowd of nurses collapsed in peals of laughter.

"Because," Dee chortled, "when you lean forward like that, we can see all the way through your jumpsuit. We've been wondering when you would notice a draft or something."

Blushing furiously, I looked down to find that the front slash pockets of the jumpsuit afforded an unobstructed view of the family jewels. Anyone standing beside me could get a clear view.

*Oh, my God! Okay, don't panic. If you bolt and run, that will only make things worse. Just casually stand up and back away from the desk. Say your good-byes, and whatever you do, don't put your hands in your pockets. Cool, casual, and unperturbed—that's the way to play it.*

"Well, ladies," I said in as smooth a tone as I could muster, "on that note, I'll just go back to the station and finish getting dressed."

"Hey, man, you look a little flushed," Mickey smirked. "Is it too hot in here for you?"

"From the looks of things," Dee observed, her eyes sweeping me up and down and pausing significantly on my crotch, "I'd say he's cold. *Really* cold."

My pride abandoned me at this point, and I fled the ER and the uproarious laughter of the nurses. Over the next two weeks, damned near every nurse at the hospital asked me to model my jumpsuit.

# Misdemeanor Credit Card

IT WAS A boring day. It was late afternoon and we hadn't rolled a tire. We'd amused ourselves for most of the day with an all-out, take-no-prisoners war using rubber-band guns. The day before, Rob Daigle and I had discovered a display of six-shooter rubber-band guns at Wal-Mart. Being the consummate professionals that we were, who would never dream of horseplay in the workplace, we immediately bought two each.

Earlier, we'd ambushed Linda Graham with a barrage of rubber bands. We caught her at her desk, totally unprepared, and ran her into the supply room screaming for mercy. Unfortunately, there was some collateral damage in the ambush—two innocent sheriff's deputies caught a few stray rubber bands.

Eventually, Linda managed to escape the supply room under guard of two sheriff's deputies with revenge on their minds. I'd spent the last six hours peeking around every corner. Earlier in the morning, we'd gone to Wal-Mart for more ammo, but they were sold out. (The clerk wanted to know why the hell every uniformed person in Chennault Parish had to buy a rubber-band gun.)

Later in the day, two deputies responded hot north of town. According to the scanner, they were headed to Simmonsville for a man waving a gun.

"Wonder if it's a rubber-band gun?" Rob mused.

Before I could reply, the scanner grabbed our attention. Chuck Lawton, CPSO 312, was screaming for help. "Dispatch, 312! Get me an ambulance right now! Highway 25 at Satterly Farms! 302 wiped out! He got hit head-on! Dispatch, hurry up on that ambulance!"

Unit 302 was Dave Springfield, a deputy and good friend. He and his partner, reserve deputy Jeff Norman, had caught us in a rubber-band drive-by a couple of hours earlier.

Rob and I hit the ambulance at a dead run. We were already turning onto North Main when we got the dispatch call.

"Unit One and Unit Three, respond Priority One to Highway 25 North at Satterly Farms. Sheriff's deputy involved in a head-on collision." Unit Three was responding from Barton Corner, so Rob and I would beat them to the scene by several minutes.

"Dispatch, Unit One. Get Priority Air Flight en route, scene flight to Highway 25 North." Priority Air Flight was the flight service out of Shreveport. It was a twenty-minute flight to Chennault Parish. If we were lucky, we'd have Dave extricated just about the time the bird arrived.

"Unit One, ten-four. Be advised Fort Sperry Fire Department is en route." There were several vehicles with dash flashers in our rearview mirrors. Apparently, we weren't the only ones monitoring the scanner.

As we arrived on scene, there was a compact car straddling the centerline. At least, I'm assuming it was a compact car. It looked as though it had been through a car crusher. Springfield's cruiser was down in a steep ditch, straddling a drain culvert. Two deputies were helping Jeff Norman up the steep bank.

"Rob, go check out Norman. I'll check Dave. Get a firefighter if you need some help."

Deputy Dave Springfield was pinned behind the wheel, screaming at the top of his lungs. From looking at the cruiser, I had no idea how Norman managed to get out. Springfield's cruiser was crumpled like an accordion. The back dash was butted against the back of the front seat. The cage was demolished, and the backseat was just...gone. Neither airbag had deployed, and the steering wheel was bent like a taco. There were at least ten inches of dash intrusion, maybe more. Amazingly, the driver's window was intact.

Chuck Lawton was reaching through the driver's rear window, between the cage and the B-pillar, holding a paper towel to Dave's forehead. Chuck had blood up to his elbow, and he had the thousand-yard stare.

"We were doing at least eighty. He didn't even have time to hit his brakes. The other guy just crossed the line and hit him..." Lawton's voice broke and trailed off.

"Chuck. Chuck. He's alive, okay? We'll take care of him." Another thought occurred to me. "Chuck, where's Cujo?" Unit 302 was a canine unit, and Cujo was Dave Springfield's partner. If he was in that backseat, he was dead.

"He's at home... Dave left him... had Jeff Norman riding with him today..."

"Chuck, get my jump bag from the rig, okay?" He looked at me, focused as if seeing me for the first time, then nodded and headed up the bank. I punched Dave's window and reached in and held his head. "Hey, Dave? It's Grayson. We're gonna get you out. Just hold still."

"My fucking legs! God, it hurts! You gotta give me something!"

"Dave, we can't give you anything right now, okay? Let us check you out, and we'll cut you out of here as soon as we can."

"Just get me out! Jesus, this hurts!" His legs were folded under the dash. From the looks of things, both femurs and tibias were broken, maybe in more than one place. Maybe his pelvis as well. Colby Graham, Linda's son, hustled down the bank to me. He tossed me my equipment vest. He was also carrying the jump bag from my rig.

"Bobby Grisham's taking Jeff Norman to the hospital," he informed me. "Rob is driving him. They're working on him. Randall Murphy is working on the guy from the other car. What do you need from me?"

"Help me with Dave. Take C-spine for me. I've got to find a way to get to him."

I looked up the bank. There were cars backed up for several hundred yards, blocking both lanes. I shouted up to Chuck Lawton, who was standing near the open door of his cruiser, speaking on the radio.

"Hey, Chuck! Clear some of these cars out for me, okay? Priority Air is on the way, and I need a landing zone!"

I worked my way around to the trunk of the cruiser and punched the rear window. I couldn't even get to the passenger side of the car—it was straddling a culvert, and standing in the ditch on that side would put the window over my head. Colby Graham was much shorter than I was, and it was all he could do just to reach Springfield. The car seemed relatively stable, so I climbed onto the trunk. Of course, punching the safety glass of the rear window just left a neat little hole and spiderwebbed the rest of it. Frustrated, I kicked at the glass until it buckled, and managed to pull it out of the frame.

I shimmied across what was left of the back dash and grabbed Dave's neck from behind. The extrication crew was setting up their gear, and Colby wiggled into the car beside me. As small as he was, he could make it all the way into the front passenger seat.

"Colby, get his vest off and check out his chest. Try to get some oxygen on him."

"Now?" Colby asked quizzically. "What about his legs?"

"I can see what's wrong with his legs, Colby! We're not gonna be able to extricate him in the next few minutes, so let's get some oxygen on him and get a line started."

Colby nodded his understanding and began to cut Springfield's uniform shirt off while I bandaged the nasty cut on his head. The fire department was just starting to cut the driver's door off. I could hear the snarl of the Hurst tool and the groan of tortured metal. Colby managed to get Dave's shirt and ballistic vest off, and we were gratified to find no serious chest injuries. (As if the screaming at the top of his lungs didn't tell us his breathing was okay.) I guess a ballistic vest protects you from more than just bullets.

As Colby slid a non-rebreather mask over Dave's head, I grabbed his right arm and palpated a quick blood pressure. It was okay, about 140 systolic, but his heart rate was 120. Colby tapped me on the shoulder and handed me a spiked bag of saline.

*You're reading my mind, kid. You need a pat on the back when this is over.*

Colby was a First Responder, and about as sparky as a kid can get, but he was doing well. I slipped a 16-gauge into Dave's right arm and taped it down. It wasn't pretty—just three wraps with three-inch tape—but it was effective. (The neat little chevrons I was taught to make in medic school pull loose too easily.) I climbed back out of the car, leaving Colby inside with Dave, who by now had stopped screaming, but was still moaning piteously and cursing under his breath.

The fire department had the door off, and had a ram set up to push the dash off his legs. I was concerned that when we got the dash off him, he'd crash. As the ram started pushing the dash back, Dave started screaming again. "Stop! You're hurting my fucking legs! For Christ's sake, stop!"

"Whoa, hold up, guys!" I hollered at the extrication crew. "Let me check something out." I stood beside the car and worked my hand between the dash and Springfield's legs. There seemed to be a little room, so I signaled the crew to start up again. Immediately, the metal started buckling around my hand and his legs. Now there were two of us screaming for the fire department to stop, which, mercifully, they did. I mentally counted my fingers.

*Okay, that was a dumb idea. Let's try Plan B.*

"Hey, look, guys. This isn't going to work. We either have to cut some more or figure out another way."

The fire department guys put their heads together while I talked to Dave. Understandably, he was somewhat less than confident in our extrication abilities. It wasn't the fault of the crew; it was just that we'd never seen a car folded up this way. Finally the crew chained off the front end of the car, hooked a wrecker to the back axle, and started pulling. Amazingly enough, the dash started slowly creeping back off Dave's legs. His color changed from red-faced to pasty gray before my eyes. He was still conscious, though, as we wedged a board under his seat.

"Hey, Dave? We're almost there, man. I've got to straighten your legs as we pull you out, okay? I ain't gonna lie, man. This will hurt like hell."

"Just fucking do it, Kelly. Don't warn me, just do it," he muttered through clenched teeth. He had his eyes closed tight, and I nodded to the firefighters as we slid him up the board. He yelped as I straightened out his mangled legs, then passed out.

We quickly got him packaged and hustled him up the bank to the rig. The road was cleared, but there was still no helicopter, and we'd been on scene for almost forty-five minutes. As we were loading Dave, two girls climbed into the back, sobbing. They were Kathy Barton, our dispatcher, and her sister Gail. Both of them were friends of Dave Springfield.

"Uh, Kathy, not for nothing, but what the fuck are you doing here? Shouldn't you be answering the radios?" She didn't reply, just sobbed hysterically. Impatiently, I pushed her out the back doors and hollered for Colby to drive.

*Jesus Christ! What does she think she's doing there? She could be fired for this!*

As Colby turned the rig around, he yelled back to me, "Priority Air is still ten minutes out. What do we do?"

"Tell them to divert to Fort Sperry. We'll meet them there. Call in a quick report."

*Who was answering the radio?*

As we drove, I dropped another 16-gauge in Dave's left arm and did a quick secondary survey. As expected, both legs were crushed—multiple fractures in both femurs and tibias. His pelvis didn't feel too bad, no crepitus I could detect, but he moaned when I palpated it. I couldn't feel a distal pulse in either leg, but his BP was only 80/52 now.

I opened up the lines, and by the time we got into Fort Sperry, his BP was up to 96/64. His lungs sounded good, and he regained consciousness as we pulled into the hospital.

Priority Air's bird was already on the pad, with the crew waiting outside with their stretcher. The nurse was Robin Miller, a gorgeous blonde in a form-fitting jumpsuit. I had no idea who the medic was, and really didn't care. It was kind of hard to divert my attention away from Robin.

"Hey, Dave! Looks like the bird's here! You'll be at LSU Medical Center in thirty minutes. And wait till you see what your nurse looks like. *Muy caliente*, my friend. Very hot."

He grinned weakly and grabbed my hand. "I'll get her number for you, man. Hey, thanks for everything."

"No problem, Deputy Springfield." I grinned back. "I always enjoy working on my fellow public safety professionals. You just raised the limit on my misdemeanor credit card."

He chuckled as we unloaded him, and Robin leaned over him, talking to him, listening to his chest, generally looking him over. Her boobs were right in Dave's face. He managed to tear his eyes away from heaven and looked over at me. I winked at him. "See what I mean?"

I gave Robin a brief handoff report as we loaded him into the bird. Dave gave me a thumbs-up as they shut the doors.

Later, I watched as the emergency physician at Fort Sperry ordered Jeff Norman discharged, despite the fact that Jeff remembered nothing about the accident and was convinced he'd wrecked his truck on the way to work. Bobby Grisham told me that the doc met the truck in the ambulance bay and started stripping off the collar and head blocks until Bobby stopped him. The only reason he X-rayed anything was because Bobby threatened to get nasty about it and make a scene.

After a discreet word with his dad, Jeff's parents drove him to West Oneida Regional Medical Center in Oneida Parish for evaluation. He wound up in the intensive care unit for two days with a severe concussion.

# DWPA (Dead with Paramedic Assistance)

His name was Frankie Maryland, and he was twenty-five years old. He came around to visit me occasionally, usually when I was feeling pretty cocky. He reminded me that I was fallible, that I made mistakes.

Frankie was black, well over six feet tall and 250 pounds, and was a pretty good linebacker during his high school days. His friends would tell you he was a funny guy, the kind who was quick to lend money to a friend and then forget about the debt. His friends weren't the most reputable people around, but Frankie was extremely protective of his younger brother and sister. He didn't bring his friends around the house, and he was pretty strict about who his brother and sister ran around with.

Frankie and his siblings lived with their aunt, a single woman with no kids of her own. Carlotta had raised Frankie and his little brother and sister since Frankie was eight years old, when their mother abandoned them and ran off to Detroit with her dealer.

I first met Frankie on his twenty-fifth birthday. He wasn't having much fun, the festivities having been interrupted by gunfire from persons unknown. Frankie took a round in the belly.

I was called to Fort Sperry at three-thirty that morning to transfer Frankie to West Oneida Regional Medical Center for exploratory surgery. I was tired, groggy, and in a foul mood. They called me from Mason Ferry to make this transfer while the Fort Sperry crews slept comfortably less than a mile from the hospital.

I only half-listened as the nurse gave me report.

*Blah, blah, blah...BP 100/52...blah, blah...two IVs, good for you... blah, blah, blah...oxygen at two liters, yeah, you people think oxygen is a poisonous gas...blah, blah...combative, huh? Well, can't blame him. I wouldn't be happy about being in this fucking Band-Aid station, either...blah, blah, blah...restrained on a long board...blah, blah...yeah, you, too. Thank you for calling the big white taxi.*

Fifteen minutes into the trip, I was taking vital signs and I couldn't get a blood pressure reading. No big deal. It was hard to hear in the rig. I'd just palpate one. While I was trying unsuccessfully to palpate a blood pressure, Frankie moaned and said, "I'm gonna puke."

"Just hold on," I told him, scrambling for an emesis basin. "Take deep breaths."

He did just that as I found an emesis basin and set it beside me on the seat.

We were evaluating a new vital signs monitor, so I figured now was as good a time as any to try it out, and I wrapped the cuff around his arm. As the cuff was inflating, Frankie moaned again and vomited before I could get the emesis basin under his chin. It was pure, bright red blood, and there was a lot of it. Frankie heaved again, and more blood fountained out.

*Holy shit! Where was all this blood coming from?*

I scrambled to loosen the straps and tilt him on his side with one hand, while reaching for the suction with the other. He was too big to tilt with one hand, so I yanked at the suction tubing to untangle it, then dropped the suction tip on the seat. I grabbed him with both hands and rolled him onto his side, and the blood drained out of his mouth and puddled on the floor. His eyes were rolled back, and he was making horrible gurgling sounds.

*God, he's aspirating this stuff right here in front of me!*

I jammed the rigid suction tip into his mouth and flipped the switch, but nothing happened. In my haste, I'd pulled the tubing loose from the suction canister. I hurriedly reattached it as Frankie vomited again. I was having trouble tilting him and working the suction unit at the same time. I applied suction, and watched the blood creep up into the suction canister at an agonizingly slow rate. Frustrated, I yanked the catheter tip off and stuck the hose in his mouth, and I breathed a sigh of relief as the blood cleared. But he still had a nasty rattle when he breathed.

I looked up at the vital signs monitor, and the blood pressure was only 72/40. The cardiac monitor showed a sinus tachycardia at 130. I pulled my knee from under the board where I'd been attempting to prop him on his side, and put a non-rebreather mask over his face. I opened up both the IVs wide, but they seem to be running pretty slow. I looked carefully at the lines and at both sites. Both of them were 22-gauge catheters—in the antecubital veins, no less.

"Goddamnit!" I blurted in frustration.

Who was the idiot nurse who put 22-gauge catheters in a trauma patient?

"Everything all right back there?" asked my partner, Terry Mitchell.

Aunt Carlotta was riding in the front passenger seat, and she had turned around and was watching through the small window between the box and the cab.

"No, everything is not all right!" I shouted back. "Step it up! And call West Oneida and tell 'em he's crashing!"

"That all you want me to say?" he asked as he hit the lights and siren.

"No, but I'm too busy to talk right now. Just drive!"

I managed to see a little stretch of vein above the IV site in Frankie's left arm. I delicately inserted a 14-gauge and switched the IV line over, and it flowed quickly with no swelling. So far, so good. I was taping down my second line when Frankie vomited again. It was more blood, and it kept on coming.

*Oh, no, not that again! Please, please, stop this. Where in the fuck was all this blood coming from?*

I stuck the suction tubing back into his mouth and reached with one hand for the airway kit. I grabbed a tube and stylet and assembled my laryngoscope, and without warning the suction unit stopped working. It was still making noise, but it wasn't clearing his airway anymore. I looked disbelievingly at the full canister. "Goddamnit!" I shouted. "Don't do this to me!"

That was what, more than a liter of blood in just a couple of minutes? And his heart rate was only forty-four beats a minute! What was I supposed to do now?

I'm not sure if I was screaming at Frankie or at fate, but I kept shouting as I hurriedly tried to intubate. "Frankie! Frankie! Can you hear me? Stay with me, man. Hang in there!"

I couldn't see the airway through all the blood. I tried to scoop out as much as I could with my fingers, but it only welled back up as soon as I scooped it out. I tried to empty the suction unit and dump the entire canister into the biohazard bag, but when I reassembled the unit, it didn't work. Apparently I'd put it back together incorrectly in my haste, and I snarled, "Fuck me!" as I gave up on using the suction unit. Frankie still had a pulse, but it was a faint one. He wasn't breathing anymore.

"Frankie, stay with me!" I shouted at him, my voice rising. Even I could hear the fear and desperation in my voice. Aunt Carlotta was sitting in the front seat, watching, but I couldn't shut up. "Don't you give up! Hang on! You sonofabitch, you will not die on me!"

I tried again to intubate, and still could see nothing.

I was blindly inserting the tube. If it went into his trachea, I'd have an airway. If it went into his esophagus, at least the blood would go out the tube and onto the floor.

Sure enough, the tube wound up in his esophagus. The blood wasn't coming as quickly as it had before, just slowly oozing up out of the tube, but then I can't imagine there was too much blood left.

I felt for a pulse as I reached for another tube. He had one, I thought. The cardiac monitor showed a rate of 36 in an ugly idioventricular rhythm.

I was just getting ready to try another intubation attempt when the back doors flew open. We'd already backed into the ambulance bay, and I hadn't even noticed. Terry looked scared. I couldn't even imagine what I looked like at that moment. Carlotta was standing off to one side, sobbing uncontrollably. I tossed the tube, bag valve mask, and laryngoscope onto Frankie's chest as Terry got the IV bags. They were both nearly empty.

The doctor met us right inside the door. I didn't recognize him, but he didn't look pleased with me. At the time, I couldn't have cared less. The doctor looked at me, at Frankie, and at the tube and started yelling, "What the hell is going on here? What happened?" He hooked up the BVM and squeezed it once, auscultating Frankie's stomach as he did. "This tube is in the stomach!" he said angrily.

"Wait, don't pull the—" I start to say as he snatched the tube out, but I was too late. "Well, that's just great! Now try to get an airway! Fucking idiot!" I screamed at him, spittle flying as Terry wrestled me away.

The doctor and several nurses wheeled Frankie hurriedly into a room. I calmed down enough to see that everyone had stopped what they were doing and were staring at me uneasily. I look down at myself to see that I had great smears of blood all over my uniform shirt and pants. There was blood all over my forearms. Aunt Carlotta acted as if she hadn't heard a thing, standing behind us sobbing quietly.

"Come on, Kelly. I'll buy you a Coke," Terry said quietly as he steered me into the nurses' lounge. He said nothing to me as I cleaned up at the bathroom sink. A nurse walked in a bit later. She handed me a scrub top.

"Here. It's about the only thing we have in your size." I nodded gratefully and ducked into the bathroom to change. My eyes were red, as if I'd been crying. I couldn't remember. When I came back out, the nurse was still there. "You okay?" she asked me, concerned.

"Yeah, I guess so." I sighed shakily. "Is he gonna file a complaint?"

"Nah, I doubt it. He's not really a bad guy. You just took him by surprise. I think he thought you were gonna flip out and whip his ass. We all tried to convince him you weren't really unstable." She grinned at me and winked. It worked—I felt a little better.

"Thanks. How's my patient?" I asked her, dreading the answer.

"We called it about five minutes ago," she said softly. "Never did get an airway," she added, as if this would make me feel better.

"Yeah, I figured that. Well, thanks for the scrubs. I appreciate it," I told her as I turned to leave. She shrugged as if to say, "Don't mention it."

Outside, Carlotta was leaning against the wall, smoking. She had stopped crying, but I couldn't face the look I'd see in her eyes. I tried to slip by her as if I hadn't seen her, but I felt her hand on my arm as I walked past, and she gently turned me to face her. I just stood there, afraid to say anything.

She reached up and pulled my head down to her shoulder, and put her hand on the back of my head. "It's okay," she whispered in my ear. "You did all you could. I know you did your best." She held me there for a few seconds longer and then grasped both of my arms, forcing me to meet her gaze. "Really," she said seriously. "Thank you." I nodded dumbly and walked away.

Terry and I didn't talk on the ride back to Mason Ferry. The sun was coming up as we pulled into the station. I walked alone into my bathroom and turned on the shower. I sat down under the spray, arms wrapped around my knees, rocking and crying uncontrollably. I rocked and shook and wept for I don't know how long, then quietly dried off and climbed into bed.

Frankie Maryland died on his twenty-fifth birthday, fifteen years ago. It was my fourth call as a paramedic.

# That Biohazard Bag Is Moving...

BOBBY GRISHAM AND I were fishing at Hawg Creek. Technically, we were supposed to be on duty, but we never let a little thing like work get in the way of recreational opportunities.

Our Mason Ferry station had been open for only a couple of months, and we were supposed to be meeting and greeting people in our coverage area, kind of a "Hi, we're the people who will be barging into your homes in your time of need, so we figured it would be nice to know ya."

Our assignment was to drive around the Hayle community, talking to folks and being as visible as possible. Every morning for the past three days, dispatch had paged us out with the same instructions: "Unit Two, Dispatch. Go to Hayle." (Given the strong Southern drawl around here, I wasn't sure if they were pronouncing it right or wrong—on purpose.)

Hayle is the southern corner of a triangle made up of the communities of Mason Ferry, Liddieville, and Hayle. It is an area the locals quaintly refer to as "Ignorant Thicket." Judging from our encounters with the residents so far, I was beginning to understand why. The family trees up there do not fork.

One fringe benefit of our community relations efforts was that Bobby and I had gotten the straight dope on where the best fishing was. On this day we were taking advantage of that information, with our unit parked on the boat ramp at Hawg Creek, sitting on the back bumper with an ice chest of Cokes and sandwiches between us.

We had got a respectable stringer going, with maybe thirty or so big "titty bream" caught so far. They call them titty bream because they're so big you have to hold them under one arm, up against your titty, to get the hooks out. We'd called in a radio and cell phone check, and informed dispatch that we'd be "ten-eight in our unit, in and around the Hayle area." Technically, we were in our unit, and Hawg Creek was in Hayle.

"Unit Two, Dispatch."

Yes, Satan?

"Unit Two, go ahead," Bobby answered, groaning.

"Respond to Crossroads on a Priority One. Back up Unit One on a motor vehicle accident." Well, we'd figured it was too good to last. Sigh!

I quickly collapsed the poles and stowed them under the bench seat as Bobby stowed the cooler. I gathered up the stringer of fish and, not knowing what else to do with them, dropped them in a biohazard bag and put them under the seat with the fishing poles.

Bobby took it all in stride. He cut through to Highway 808, taking Hayle Fire Tower Road. It was desolate out there, far enough in the sticks that they have to pipe in sunlight, but Bobby knew where he was going.

Next to Mickey Sanders, Bobby was the Emergency Medical Technician I trusted the most. He wasn't the smartest guy I knew, but he possessed an abundance of common sense and his hands could do things his brain couldn't. I first met him in an EMT class where I was serving as assistant instructor.

The instructor coordinator subscribed to the softer, gentler school of EMT education in which all of the students make excellent grades, the staff spends time building their self-esteem, and they all get a warm, fuzzy view of Emergency Medical Services, while learning precisely zero useful skills. Knowing this, I kind of laid it on thick on the first day of class. I paced back and forth in front of the class, making eye contact with everyone I could, and I let them know exactly what they could expect from me:

"I am not here to coddle you. I am not here to hold your hand. I am here to identify those of you who can become good EMTs, and to quickly weed the rest of you from this class. Those who remain I will teach to the best of my ability. I do not believe EMT class should be easy. Our profession is not easy. You need to know that now, before you even start this class. On my tests, a good score is a seventy-five. If you can pass my tests and my practical exams, the National Registry exam will be easy. I believe in hard work. If you work hard and give me one hundred percent in class, I will do my very best to see that you finish. If you do not work hard, good test grades will not save you. I will make it my mission in life to run you out of this course. If you can't handle the pressure, leave now."

While I was giving my spiel, I noticed a cowboy sitting in the front row. He had longish hair and a bushy mustache, a western shirt, and Wrangler jeans. He had a nose like a soggy strawberry perched crookedly on his face, a visible reminder of his total facial reconstruction, courtesy of a bull that wasn't happy to have a cowboy on his back. His name was Bobby Grisham.

As I paced back and forth, he met my occasional glances with a defiant glare. He wound up being one of the top students in the class. After we became friends, he told me what he thought of me that first day of class. "Ever time you looked at us, trying to intimidate everbody, I figgered you were looking right at me. I figgered, All right, you big sumbitch, let's just see you run me outta this here class."

Bobby and I made it to Crossroads in good time, and in one piece. (We may have even had all four wheels on the ground a couple of times.) Unit One and Unit Four, the on-call backup unit, were already on scene, packaging five patients from a minivan that had rolled over multiple times. Our boss, Bob Graham, walked up to our unit as we parked.

"We've about got everybody packaged," he informed us. "We just need your spare Kendrick Extrication Device"

"Fine with us," Bobby said. "Do you need us to transport anybody?"

"No, but you could give Mickey and Randall a hand getting everybody loaded. Right now you're covering the world, so I need you to head to Fort Sperry as soon as you're done here."

We went to help the other crew as Bob climbed into our rig to fetch the spare KED from under the bench seat. We got busy for the next few minutes, taking vitals, assessing patients, and loading them into the rigs. Nobody was seriously injured—just bumps and bruises and minor lacerations. As we left, I noticed Bob staring at us as we drove away. He had a decidedly odd look on his face.

Later that afternoon, we got cleared back to the Mason Ferry station. Bobby and I had been there about an hour when the phone rang.

"Kelly, it's Bob. You busy?"

"Nah, we're just cooking dinner. What's up?"

"Look, I don't know what that is in the biohazard bag under the bench seat of your rig, and I don't think I want to know. But whatever it was, it was moving, and I'd appreciate it if you got it out of my ambulance immediately. Okay?"

"A moving biohazard bag?" I asked innocently. "Sure, I'll go check the rig right now. Incidentally, we're frying fish for dinner. Would you and Linda like some?"

# Hey, Kid, Where's the Cop?

I HAVE DISCOVERED that whether an address actually exists is a detail of only minor importance to dispatchers. If it isn't on their map, it isn't a part of their known universe. If it is on their map, it must exist, and if you can't find it, it's your problem.

"Uh, Dispatch? This is the third time we've been down this street. There is no number 168. The house numbers end at 160," I explained patiently for the third time. "Can you get a callback number, or maybe have someone flag us down?"

"Stand by, Unit Three," the dispatcher replied curtly.

*Boy, Kathy sounds a little pissy. Perhaps we're interrupting the day's episode of General Hospital?*

The radio crackled again, and the dispatcher spoke slowly, as if she were giving instructions to a retarded twelve-year-old. "Unit Three, the address showing on the 911 map is 168 East Mitchell. It was called in via radio by a Fort Sperry police officer. If you'll just follow the street down to its end, you'll see the pretty blue and white car with the lights on top. The patient should be somewhere nearby."

*When this call is completed, I'm coming back to the station and whipping your fat ass. That's the last time you pop off to me on the radio. I know hitting women is a no-no, but in your case, I'd need to do a chromosome check to see if you really are a woman...*

Seeing the look on my face, JoAnn Graves took the radio mike from me and answered, "Ten-four, Dispatch. I think we can find it."

Up ahead, we saw a police cruiser parked in front of a house on a side street.

*Dumb bitch. That house isn't even on East Mitchell, it's on Hartley. Either the cop is retarded, or you are. I'd bet on you.*

The house looked familiar as JoAnn and I climbed out of the rig. I grabbed my medic bag and left JoAnn behind me to bring the stretcher.

Maybe one of our frequent fliers lived there. I was pretty sure I'd been there before.

I knocked briefly on the door and announced, "Ambulance!" before I opened it. There was a little black boy sitting on the floor playing Nintendo.

"Hey, kid, somebody here call for an ambulance?" I asked him. He just stared at me, bewildered. Impatiently, I snapped, "Okay, so where's the cop?" Wordlessly, eyes wide as saucers, he pointed down the hall.

*Damned kids these days! Probably had his nose buried in that video game and doesn't have a clue. The house could burn down around him and he wouldn't notice until the power went off.*

I flung open the door at the end of the hall and asked, "Okay, so what's such an emergency that you needed—" The words froze in my throat as I realized where I was. There was a black man scrambling naked from the bed, and he was reaching for a pistol on the nightstand. I hit the floor and scooted backward into the hallway.

*Oh, fuck. No wonder this place looked familiar! This is Tony Michaels's house! I went to his housewarming party! That kid is his son!*

Tony Michaels was a Fort Sperry police sergeant who was built like an NFL linebacker, and a lot meaner. More important to me, he was a crack shot, and could run a helluva lot faster than I could. But I had momentum and the fact that he had to put on his underwear on my side. I hit the living room at a dead run, vaulting over Tony's son and bolting through the still-open door. The kid barely even looked up from his game. "Sorry about that, Tony!" I called over my shoulder. "Wrong house!"

Behind me, I hear his enraged bellow of "What the fuck?" I vaulted onto the running board of the rig and hollered at JoAnn to drive before I even had the door closed. Bewildered, she complied, peeling rubber and spurting gravel as we roared up Hartley Street toward East Mitchell.

"That was the wrong house," she informed me unnecessarily as she drove. "The cop who called it in is supposed to flag us down when we get close."

I said nothing as I breathed a sigh of relief to see Tony's pursuing form dwindling in our rearview mirror. He had his service automatic in his hand, but I was wrong about one thing. He didn't pause to pull on his underwear.

# My Favorite Martin

COLONIAL SQUARE APARTMENTS was home to Martha, Clara, and Frances Martin. Despite the similarity in names, they weren't related. They all lived just a few doors apart from one another, and they were all virtually interchangeable. They all had emphysema, they all trailed fifty feet of oxygen tubing behind them twenty-four hours a day, and they were all diabetic to one degree or another. Clara took insulin, but Martha and Frances both took Diabinase. Other than that, you could probably swap their medication lists, too.

They were all warm, nurturing grandmother types like the ones that lived in your neighborhood as a kid. You know... the kind that would bake cookies for all the neighborhood kids, but be just as likely to rat you out to your mother if she noticed you misbehaving. When you speak to them, you respectfully say, "Yes, ma'am." It doesn't occur to you to do otherwise.

We got a call to Frances Martin's apartment. She had fallen and possibly broken her hip.

We were on a call rotation system with StatMedic EMS, our competitor. It worked much like a wrecker rotation in that when someone called 911 for an ambulance, if they didn't request a specific service, 911 dispatched the next ambulance on the list. It was a stupid system, guaranteed to cause friction between rival services when we inevitably both responded to the same scene.

The Chennault crews conducted themselves professionally, and for the most part, so did the StatMedic crews. Naturally, the StatMedic crews that conducted themselves professionally on scenes got their asses chewed for being chummy with the competition.

The StatMedic operations manager, Stuart Crenshaw, had been lurking around Fort Sperry in his sprint vehicle all day. The Chennault crews, and for that matter most of his own employees, considered Stuart to be the Antichrist. He was evil (and had to be destroyed). Stuart was suspicious that the rotation list wasn't being followed, and that Chennault seemed to be getting far more calls than they should.

The man might be a soulless bastard, but he wasn't dumb. Stuart radioed Grady Cochran over the Fort Sperry Police Department channel. Even though he wasn't supposed to, he used their frequency on occasion, a habit that did not endear him to Grady Cochran.

"StatMedic 101 to Fort Sperry PD 1."

"PD 1, go ahead," came the curt reply. Grady was getting old and crusty, and didn't suffer fools gladly.

Stuart needed to tread carefully here.

"What was the preference on this call?" Stuart knew damned well that StatMedic was next up in the rotation.

"Chennault is taking the call," Grady said flatly.

He sounded a little mad.

"Understand that to mean it was Chennault by patient request?"

"Listen to me, you little pissant!" Grady exploded. "Chennault Ambulance was dispatched by my request. If you don't like it, you can brush your teeth real good and I'll let you kiss a picture of my ass! Now get the hell off my frequency!"

Well, I guess that answered the ambulance preference question. Fort Sperry Police Department's radio traffic wasn't scrambled. Stuart had just had his ass spanked for everyone in Scannerland to hear.

We got to Mrs. Martin's apartment to discover that she wasn't injured and needed only a lift assist. Naturally, the other Martins were all outside their apartments and insisted on knowing what was wrong with Frances. We reassured Clara and Martha that Frances was indeed okay, and didn't need either of them to sit with her overnight. (Patient confidentiality didn't mean a thing to them, and besides, they'd all know the whole story down to the last detail inside of an hour. The entire complex was like one big sewing circle.)

Of the three, Clara was the most nervous and required the most reassurance. She called us no fewer than four times a week, complaining of difficulty breathing. She was nothing but lonely, an old lady who had outlived her children, and her grandchildren all lived out of state. Most times when she called, she just wanted company.

"Miss Clara," the dispatcher would ask, "just how bad is your breathing? Do you need an ambulance right away?"

"Oh, if you're busy I suppose I could wait awhile," she'd answer, "as long as someone can come check on me when you get a chance." When she truly was sick, you could tell, and an ambulance would respond right away. Otherwise, one of the rigs would ease out to Miss Clara's as soon as the opportunity presented itself.

She usually had freshly baked cookies or Rice Krispies Treats, even though she didn't eat them herself. We'd often stop at Brookshire's and buy some sugar-free ice cream, and spend an hour or so at Miss Clara's, eating cookies and ice cream and visiting. We'd program the speed dial on her phone, or program her VCR to tape her soaps while she watched Jerry Springer. She'd as soon take up hang gliding or bungee jumping as she would let a four-letter word escape her lips, but Jerry Springer was her guilty little pleasure. She never missed a show.

Over the past few months, Clara's health had deteriorated. She'd spent just about as much time in the hospital lately as she had at home. Her diabetes had finally wrecked her kidneys, and now we picked her up for dialysis transfers three days a week. Normally either Randall Murphy or I got the honors, but one week Linda Graham took Miss Clara to Boothville for dialysis.

"I hear you run a home for destitute paramedics," she told Linda.

"Excuse me?" Linda answered, puzzled.

"Randall and Kelly told me they live in your Mason Ferry station because they can't afford to live anywhere else. So I figured you must be pretty nice people to run a home for destitute paramedics," Miss Clara told her teasingly. "Do you just take the room and board out of their pay?"

"No," Linda chuckled, "they stay there for free. Actually, we don't pay them much, and right now we can't even pay them that often. So Randall and Kelly stay at the station to save money."

"You can't pay them very often? What do you mean by that?"

"Well, we kind of started on a shoestring budget, and it's taking us awhile to get our billing straightened out. So we have problems making payroll occasionally, but we're getting there."

"And they still work, even when they don't get paid?"

"Yes, ma'am," Linda confirmed. "Our people are really dedicated. Our trucks are used, our equipment is all secondhand, and we don't even have much station furniture. Randall and Kelly sleep on foldout hospital chairs. But I think we have the best paramedics around."

"They must be," Miss Clara agreed. She lay back on the stretcher after that, remaining quiet for the rest of the trip. After the call, Linda said she didn't act like her old self. I didn't think she looked good those days, either.

A week later, I got a call to Miss Clara's apartment. She was having respiratory distress, and she'd asked for an ambulance right away. With Miss Clara, that meant she was really having a problem. Bobby and I arrived to find her in severe respiratory distress. She had that ominous, one-word dyspnea.

"I—can't—breathe!" she panted desperately, pausing for breath after each word.

Bobby hooked up a non-rebreather immediately and gently placed it over her face. He looked worried, as was I. I'd never seen her look this bad. Her lungs were nasty, with scattered wheezes and crackles, and severely diminished sounds in the bases. We didn't have a pulse oximeter, but I didn't need one to guess what her saturation is. Whatever the number was, it wasn't good. I motioned for her not to talk.

"Miss Clara, we're going to step up your oxygen, and in a little bit we're going to give you a nebulizer to help open you up some. We'll take good care of you." I smiled reassuringly at her. She nodded in understanding.

Bobby and I quickly loaded her and boogied toward Boothville General Hospital, in Lakewood Parish. Miss Clara's legs were swollen up to her knees with pitting edema. Her EKG was sinus tach at 140, with the tall, peaked T waves you see in hyperkalemia. I quickly mixed up a nebulizer cocktail of Proventil, Atrovent, and four milligrams of Decadron. I pulled the oxygen mask from her face and squirted a shot of nitroglycerin under her tongue.

She looked worse than I'd ever seen her. This was either CHF (congestive heart failure) due to her kidney failure, or pneumonia and her COPD (chronic obstructive pulmonary disease) acting up. It was probably both. And her kidneys didn't work, so giving Lasix would be useless. Well, we could always drive real fast, give her nebulizer treatments, and vasodilate her with nitro.

I detached the reservoir bag from the non-rebreather and hooked the nebulizer chamber to it. With her crappy veins, I had to poke her three times to get an IV, finally settling for a 22-gauge in her right forearm. By the time I was done, she was crying. I felt like joining her.

"I am so sorry, Miss Clara, but I had to do that," I explained to her. She blinked back her tears, but smiled weakly and patted my hand. That made me want to cry even more.

After a few minutes, she started to look a little better. Her color had improved, and her respirations were down to 24. I listened to her lungs, and they sounded pretty much like a diesel engine at high rpms, but I thought there was far less wheezing than there had been before.

Ten minutes from Boothville, I called report. I got some doctor on the phone, but I didn't recognize the name. "Seventy-four-year-old female, severe respiratory distress," I told him. "Vitals are BP 150/100, heart rate 140, sinus tach, respirations 24. Lungs have scattered wheezes and rales bilaterally. We've given her—"

"What's her oxygen saturation?" the doctor interrupted impatiently.

"Don't have one," I explained. "We don't have a pulse oximeter. We've given her a neb treatment and sublingual nitroglycerin, and she seems to be doing a little better. She has a history of insulin-dependent diabetes, renal failure, and emphysema…"

"How much oxygen are you giving her?" the doctor interrupted again.

This guy was about to get on my nerves.

"Fifteen liters," I answered, "But she's—"

"Back the oxygen down to two liters by nasal cannula," he ordered. "Never give a COPD'er more than two liters of oxygen."

"But she uses oxygen all the—" I stopped when I realized I was talking to dead air. The doctor, having pronounced his royal decree, apparently considered the conversation finished, and hung up.

Asshole. This lady wore two liters of oxygen twenty-four hours a day. If two liters were doing the job, she wouldn't have called us.

I briefly considered ignoring his order, but the cardiac monitor made the point moot. Something caught my eye, and I noticed that the rhythm had changed to ventricular tachycardia. I checked Miss Clara, and her eyes were rolled back and she was barely breathing. There was no pulse.

I scrambled for the defibrillator paddles and hastily put the gel pads in place. I charged the paddles and yelled, "Clear!" before I shocked her. It then occurred to me that clearing the patient wasn't necessary if I was the only person working the code. Her rhythm changed to ventricular fibrillation after the first shock, so I hit her again at 300 joules. With that, she converted to a sinus bradycardia that rapidly sped up and leveled out at about 130.

She still wasn't breathing, so I ripped a bag valve mask out of the cabinet, showering us both with spare endotracheal tubes, suction catheters, and oxygen masks in my hurry. I squeezed a few quick breaths into her and intubated her pretty damned expeditiously, if I do say so myself. By the time we arrived at the Emergency Department, I'd bolused her with seventy-five milligrams of lidocaine and hung a maintenance drip at one milligram a minute—or a reasonable facsimile thereof, considering the drip rate changed with every bump of the ambulance and sway of the IV bag.

(All of this, mind you, while I was continuing ventilations with one hand. Not that I'm bragging or anything.)

When we rolled into the Emergency Department, the doctor predictably exploded. "What the hell is this?" he demanded. "Is this the emphysema patient you were bringing me?"

"Yes, sir, but after you hung up, she—"

"Well, what the hell is she doing intubated?" he demanded angrily. "Why didn't you back off the oxygen like I ordered?"

"Well, I intubated her because she arrested and wasn't breathing. She was in V-fib, so I shocked her."

"You shut down her breathing, is what you did! And who gave you permission to intubate her? Didn't you even try to bag her first?"

He was in my face now, punctuating every word by shaking his finger at me. I stood there, trying not to react. There were at least three nurses and various other people nearby, watching nervously as if the thunderstorm was about to engulf them. We had a big audience—he hadn't even let us get out of the hall.

I let him finish his tirade, then beckoned him closer with my finger so I could whisper in his ear. He glared at me suspiciously, but leaned in.

"I intubated her because I'm a paramedic, and my airway of choice is an endotracheal tube," I whispered. "She coded, I shocked her, I intubated her. That's what I do. And if you don't get your finger out of my face, right now, I'm going to knock you on your old ass right here in front of your staff." I stepped back and smiled brightly at him. "Will there be anything else, sir?"

He recoiled from me as if he thought I was going to throw a punch that moment. His eyes darted around the hallway anxiously. No one had heard a thing. They were still frozen, watching both of us. I kept the insane leer on my face and bumped the stretcher slightly against his legs, and he backed out of the way to allow us to enter the room. We unloaded Miss Clara in silence. The doctor refused to make eye contact with me, and made it a point to stay on the other side of the bed.

I gave report to the first nurse I saw at the nurses' station, and winked at her as I left. I half-expected to get a call from dispatch on the way home, but it never came. Apparently, Dr. Asshole hadn't filed a complaint.

Four days later, Miss Clara died. The funeral was nice, and for the first time I got to meet the grandchildren I had heard so much about.

Martha Martin and Frances Martin were there as well, probably the only time they'd been out in years. Two days after the funeral, one of Clara's grandchildren pulled up to the Fort Sperry station towing a flatbed trailer full of furniture. He told Linda that his grandmother had left her household furniture to Chennault Ambulance, so her EMTs could sleep on good beds.

# Kismet

Randy stanton and i had been called to DeVillier Community Hospital to transfer a patient to Lake Chillicothe. The charge nurse, Mary Odom, met us outside his room.

"He's in congestive heart failure," she told us quietly. "He's had damned little urinary output for twenty-four hours, and his lungs sound like a washing machine. We've got him on fifteen liters of oxygen, and his sat is only eighty-eight percent." She looked upset. I'd dealt with Mary only a few times, but she struck me as competent. Concern for your patient is one thing; outright distress is another.

"So who is the accepting physician?" I asked her, wondering what had gotten her so flustered.

"Dr. Lehigh," she told me, noticing my expression. "Look, guys, this isn't just any patient, okay? He's Sadie's husband. I'm worried about her, too. She's not taking this well." Sadie Dawson was the licensed practical nurse on Mary's shift, a grandmotherly type in her sixties.

We entered the room to find Sadie sitting quietly at her husband's side, stroking his hair. She'd been crying; her eyes swollen and red-rimmed. Despite that, she smiled at us. Randy walked over to her and hugged her tightly. "How you doing, *ma cher*?" he asked her, lapsing into Franglish.

"Not too good," she answered, smiling tiredly. "He was doing good yesterday, but today he's just gotten so, so..." She broke off, choking back sobs.

Randy continued to hold Sadie close, crooning softly to her in French as she cried. He was good at this. He'd known these people for years, and they treated one another like family. Mary and I quietly went about transferring Mr. Dawson from their bed to our stretcher, untangling the telemetry leads, intravenous line, oxygen tubing, and Foley catheter. Soon we were ready to go.

Randy and I assured Mary we'd call and give her an update as soon as we got to Lake Chillicothe. Normally she could get this on her own from the intensive care unit staff there. I considered reminding her of this, but I didn't. I guess I'm a sucker for brunettes with doe eyes. I could see in those eyes that she didn't expect him to survive the trip. Sadie would follow us in her car.

Shortly into the trip, I tried to get another blood pressure, and could palpate a pressure of only 84 systolic. Mr. Dawson's hands and feet were an ugly purple, and cold. My pulse oximeter wouldn't even get a reading. His lungs were virtually full of fluid. Even though he was still making a decent effort to breathe, it just wasn't enough. I decided to intubate him, and slipped a tube gently into his trachea. He was so far gone he didn't even gag as I inserted the tube.

I also hung a dopamine drip, even though I was technically supposed to call for orders first. However, it was highly doubtful that Dr. Lehigh would be physically present at the ICU when I called, and I was pretty sure the DeVillier doctor, whoever that was that night, would support my decision.

Within fifteen minutes or so, Mr. Dawson's BP was up to 112/56, and his saturation was 94 percent. His lungs seemed a little clearer, too, but I couldn't be sure. The rest of the trip passed without problems, unless you counted the cramps in my right hand from squeezing a BVM for thirty-five minutes.

On the way back to DeVillier, I called Mary on the cell phone.

"Mary, this is Kelly with Stat Fleet."

"Who?" she asked, puzzled. I realized that despite the several times we'd met, I'd never told her my name.

"Kelly Grayson?" I reminded her. "I took Mr. Dawson to Lake Chillicothe?"

"Oh, Kelly. I didn't think you would call me back. So how did it go?"

"Well, I tubed him on the way. Gave him some dopamine, too. But he's got better vital signs than when we started. He looked a lot better by

the time we dropped him off. Still unconscious, though."

"I hate to hear that," Mary lamented. "They're going to have problems weaning him off the vent."

"Yeah, they will," I agreed. "But that's a bridge they can cross later. Well, we're pulling up at the station, so I'll let you go."

"Okay, thanks for calling me," she said. "Wait! Can you tell me something before you hang up?"

"That depends on the question," I answered warily.

"What kind of a name is Kelly for a guy, anyway? Your mother not like you or something?" she teased.

"Well, my first name is Steven," I shot back. "My middle name is Kelly, and I'll have you know that it is a boy's name. It means 'warrior' in Gaelic."

"If you say so, warrior," she laughed. "Thanks for calling me back. 'Bye."

I hung up and looked over at Randy. He had a big smirk on his face. "Well, it is," I insisted. "You can look it up!"

"Okay, little warrior," he said soothingly, patting my hand. "Don't get so defensive. If you ask me, though, I think you need to get more comfortable with your feminine side."

"Kiss my ass!" I retorted. Of all people, now I had Randy Stanton making cracks about my masculinity. Life is not fair.

# Crying Wolf

IT WAS NEARLY midnight, and Randy and I were feeling a bit mischievous. We'd been at the DeVillier Police Department, bullshitting with the cops and surfing the Internet on their computer. Just as we'd planned, we got there in time for the nightly chicken run.

Every night, the local Popeye's restaurant brought all their leftover chicken to the police department. We got meals at half-price during business hours, but if we could tough it out till closing, it was free all-you-can-eat chicken and biscuits every weeknight.

Engorged with spicy fried chicken and Cajun rice, Randy and I cruised over to DeVillier Community Hospital to engage in that time-honored pastime of EMS crews everywhere—flirting with nurses. The nurses, obligingly enough, flirted back. One of them, Mary Odom, had the absolutely enchanting quality of laughing at all my jokes. Her coworkers thought she was a bit *coullion*, which is Cajun for crazy. Personally, I could think of worse mental defects. Besides, she had a great smile. I found myself willing to do just about anything to see it.

Randy and I avoided the ambulance entrance and the security cameras there. Instead, we parked the rig in the north parking lot and slipped through the unlocked door that opened into the courtyard. This was the employee smoking area, and usually there was a nurse or respiratory therapist loitering out there, partaking in his or her own personal breathing treatment. This time of night, however, they would all be congregated in the break room, gossiping and eating dinner.

We sneaked down the hall, dropping to our hands and knees behind the counter at the nurses' station. We sneaked a telemetry pack out of the desk and quickly activated it.

Room number? Room 103 sounded good. There was no chart with that number, so it was probably empty. Patient name? Uben Hadd. Physician's name? Benjamin Pierce. Okay, now press "activate" and sneak down the hall to 103. Now let the fun begin!

I started to furiously tap the right arm electrode until I hear the V-tach alarm go off at the telemetry monitor in the nurses' station, immediately followed by the sound of running feet. The footsteps stopped briefly, then started again. They were getting closer, accompanied by the rumbling of the crash cart. I heard a crash just outside the door, and someone snarling, "Fuck!"

*Goodness, the mouths on some of these women!*

Three nurses burst into the room, Mary Odom in the lead. She stopped short when she saw me, and Paula Roberts and Sadie Dawson nearly knocked her over.

"How y'all doing?" I asked brightly. "Gosh, you ladies look out of breath! Whatever is the matter?"

"You bastard!" Mary exploded furiously, and then almost immediately dissolved in a fit of laughter. "You scared the hell out of us!"

Sadie and Paula were a little slower to catch on, but eventually we were all standing around, laughing hysterically. Randy was turning funny colors, rolling back and forth on the bed and holding his sides. One patient peeked out of his room, wondering if we'd all lost our minds.

"Come on," Mary gasped. "Let's get out of the hall before we wake everybody up."

Still giggling, we walked back to the nurses' station. Paula was pushing the crash cart with one hand and gingerly rubbing her knee with the other.

"Banged it on the crash cart," she explained. "Where in the hell did you guys learn that trick?"

"White lead CPR," I said with a straight face. "When you're sick and tired of doing chest compressions, just tap the white lead. It looks just like CPR compressions on your strip. Comes in handy."

Paula just stared, slack-jawed. "You mean that you—"

"Paula, I was kidding," I assured her.

Apparently, Paula is a natural blonde.

"Oh, okay," she replied uncertainly. "That's what I thought."

"You guys want some gumbo?" Mary asked. "We were just sitting down to eat."

"Actually, we already—ouch!" Randy stopped as I elbowed him in the ribs.

"Yes, Mary, we'd love some gumbo," I told her, looking pointedly at my partner. "Wouldn't we, Randy?"

"Oh, sure!" he said, finally catching on. "I'd love some gumbo!"

We sat down in the break room as Mary ladled out the gumbo. We made small talk as we ate, but I stayed mostly quiet, trying to work up the courage to ask Mary out. An hour passed, and Randy started making noises about getting to bed. We bade Mary and her coworkers good night and walked back down the hall toward the ER.

"So why didn't you ask her out, Don Juan?" Randy wanted to know.

"Damned if I know, man. Maybe I'm scared she'll shoot me down in flames."

"I'll set you up with her," Randy offered as we reached the side door leading to the courtyard. "Just call me Cupid. I know exactly what to— what the hell is that?"

Someone was pounding on the locked ER doors at the end of the hall—someone too stupid or panicked to notice the big sign that said PUSH BUTTON FOR NURSE.

We trotted down the hall to the ER, and Randy pushed open the doors. "Can we help you, ma'am?" he asked a woman, who answered by thrusting a small baby into his arms.

"Here!" she blurted, panicked. The baby was small, her cyanotic skin in stark contrast to the pink blanket wrapped around her. She wasn't breathing.

Dumbfounded, Randy looked at the woman, then down at the baby, then back at the woman. And back to the baby. Then, without a word, he gave the baby a couple of breaths and hustled into the ER, placing the baby on the nearest bed. I followed him into the ER, pausing to press the intercom button on the desk. "Code Blue in ER!" I yelled.

Randy was doing mouth-to-mouth ventilations as I searched for a pediatric BVM hanging among the oxygen delivery equipment on the wall. I finally found one in the bottom drawer of the crash cart.

"What happened?" I asked the woman as I start ventilating. Thin and haggard, she looked far too old to be this kid's mother. Randy was feeling for a brachial pulse and shaking his head. He started to attach monitor leads as I turned my attention back to the woman.

"She just stopped breathing!" the woman wailed. "She's had a cough and a runny nose for a few days, but it just got worse today and I—"

"Any fever, vomiting, diarrhea, anything like that?"

"Just fever since this morning. She was a preemie. She spent four months in the NICU. Oh, God, she's only been home for two months..." the woman trailed off, sobbing.

The baby's rhythm was sinus bradycardia, far too slow at fifty beats per minute. As I watched the monitor, her rate picked up, slowly at first, then incredibly fast. Within ten seconds her heart rate topped out at about 150. She looked as if somebody had swiped her with a pink brush, so rapidly and dramatically did her color improve.

"Look," I told the woman, prodding her with my toe and nodding toward the bed. She looked quizzically at me, then at the bed, and let out an explosive sigh of relief. The baby was moving now. She was a tiny thing to be at least six months old. She couldn't weigh nine pounds. I had to chase her face now with the BVM to ventilate her, and she was crying, getting steadily louder and more insistent.

"Okay, now this shit isn't funny anymore..." Mary said as she barged into the room. She trailed off as she looked from me and Randy to the woman to the baby and back again. She closed her mouth with an audible snap.

"The baby stopped breathing," I explained. "Her mother brought her in." Mary could see the rest for herself.

"Grandmother," the woman corrected me. "I have custody. Her mother is in drug rehab."

"Okay," Mary decided, taking charge. "We need an IV and fluids. We need a set of vitals, including pulse oximetry, and we need to see if she needs to be intubated." There was no indecision in her voice, unlike most nurses I know. She rapped out orders like she expected them to be obeyed, right the fuck now.

*Damn, this girl thinks like a medic! Good looks and brains, and calm under pressure. I have got to ask this girl out!*

Paula arrived and asked Mary if she needed any help. Mary paused for a moment, looked at the baby and the monitor, and decided. "Call in lab and radiology, respiratory, and call Dr. Alex. We need a basic chemistry panel, blood gases, and a chest X-ray. And be sure to tell Dr. Alex we have things under control." I stood back and admiringly watched her work.

*You go, girl!*

Within a matter of minutes, she had established an intravenous line and hung a bag of saline. She even drew a rainbow of blood tubes when she started the IV. The little girl, Caitlin, her grandmother told us, was breathing on her own. She had some crackles and wheezes in her large airways and upper lung fields, and she was faintly stridorous. There were little bubbles of clear, pearlescent snot coming out of her nose.

"RSV," Mary announced, reading my mind. "I'd bet on it."

"RS *what*?" the grandmother wanted to know. "What did you say?"

"Respiratory syncytial virus," Mary explained. "It's a nasty little lung infection common among babies."

Caitlin was gradually starting to slow her breathing as she tired from the effort. Her pulse oximetry value had dropped to 90 percent, and she was retracting a bit. She was beginning to look as if she couldn't keep it up on her own. I pointed this out to Mary, and she nodded.

"I was afraid of that. Can you intubate her for me?" she asked.

"You sure you don't want to wait for respiratory, or Dr. Alex?"

"Fuck respiratory," she said flatly. "I'm not going to wait." She didn't mention the doctor, not that I expected her to. I didn't really expect Dr. Alex to do much of anything other than wig out and get in our way. I'd met her only a couple of times, and I couldn't understand a word she said.

"Okay." I shrugged. "Let's do it."

Mary set up an endotracheal tube and stylet, and after I ventilated Caitlin a few times, she handed me the laryngoscope and tube. I intubated her without too much difficulty, the tube in before she got much of a chance to fuss. Her vocal cords looked red and angry as I passed the tube gently between them. Mary listened for breath sounds, nodding as I gently squeezed the bag. Caitlin's saturation rapidly rose back to 99 percent, but she felt tight. There was a bit of an air leak, which I expected with an uncuffed tube, but the pop-off valve was activating every now and then.

"Albuterol, maybe? Racemic epinephrine?" I asked Mary. She shook her head.

"Let's drop an NG tube first. She's probably got a little gastric distension." She motioned to Paula, who started looking for a nasogastric tube small enough for our purposes. By the time respiratory and lab arrived, there was nothing much for them to do. The lab tech took the blood Mary had drawn to the lab, and Kristie, the respiratory therapist, drew arterial blood gases.

"She needs an NG tube," Kristie said as she finished. "Babies get a lot of gastric distension when you—"

"We're way ahead of you," Mary interrupted her rudely. "Now, could you run those gases for us?" Paula rolled her eyes as Kristie left in a huff.

"She neeeeeds an NG tuuuube," Paula whined, doing a credible mimicry of Kristie's nasal voice. "Snotty bitch," she muttered under her breath. Mary chuckled. The nurses here couldn't stand Kristie, partly because she was snotty and condescending, and partly because she was *muy caliente*, very hot. She was the perfect girl if you liked 'em gorgeous and dumb. Kristie could refill her head from her own oxygen tanks.

"Mary, I can't find any infant feeding tubes," Paula complained. "What do you want me to do?"

"Go look in central supply," Mary replied. "They should have some in there."

"It's locked at night," Paula reminded her. Mary cursed silently.

"How about a small suction catheter?" I suggested. "Maybe an eight French, something about that size?"

"That should work," Mary agreed thoughtfully. She pulled a flexible suction catheter off the wall, lubricated it, and gently inserted it in Caitlin's mouth, through her esophagus, and into her stomach. She aspirated with a 60-milliliter syringe, pulling back a good deal of air and several milliliters of clotted baby formula. I noticed an immediate improvement in respiratory volume.

"I think that did it," I told her. "She's a lot easier to bag. The pop-off valve isn't activating anymore, either." We shared a look and a quick smile.

By the time Dr. Alex arrived, the radiology tech had taken a portable chest X-ray and gone to develop it, and the blood gases were back. They looked good. We heard Dr. Alex as she walked slowly down the hall. She had a bad knee, and walked with a noticeable limp. We could hear her rubber clogs on the tile floor long before she arrived. Squeak, thump. Squeak, thump. Squeak, thump. She looked like she was in her fifties, but was far older. Nobody was sure just how old she actually was.

"Okay, what is going on here? Who can tell me what is going on with the patient? Who is in charge?" she demanded in rapid-fire, barely intelligible English.

Christianna Alexakos, M.D., was Romanian by birth, Greek by marriage, and spoke with a thick accent. She talked like one of those fast-talking voiceover guys who read the legal disclaimers at the end of radio commercials. Medicine passed her by about twenty years ago, but her mostly elderly clientele swore by her. Dr. Alex was warm and patient with old folks, and they loved her for it. To her credit, she also knew when she was in over her head, which was pretty much whenever she stepped into the ER.

I looked at Mary, who shrugged as if to say, "You take it."

I raised my hand, like a little boy asking the teacher for permission to go to the bathroom. "Dr. Alex? The baby stopped breathing at home, and her grandmother rushed her here. Randy and I started CPR on her before the nurses arrived. She was initially apneic and extremely cyanotic, with a heart rate of fifty. She improved a good bit with ventilations and oxygen, but I intubated her because she kept tiring out. Mary got a twenty-two-gauge IV in the left AC, and we decompressed her stomach with an orogastric tube to improve ventilations. Lab is doing a basic chemistry panel, and we should have that back in a few minutes. Radiology has done a chest X-ray, and her blood gases show mild respiratory acidosis, but that's five minutes old. Right now she's in sinus tach at one-thirty, saturation is ninety-nine percent, and she has good capillary refill and distal pulses," I finished breathlessly.

Dr. Alex looked at Mary, as if for confirmation. Mary nodded. "That's about the size of it, Dr. Alex."

"Well, look at you!" she said to me, amused. "And what is your name again?"

"Kelly Grayson," I answered. She nodded, repeating my name, mangling it several times but eventually coming up with a reasonable, Romanian-flavored approximation.

"Has she had any epinephrine?" Dr. Alex wanted to know. "What is her dose?"

"No epinephrine," Mary answered. "We were just about to give her an albuterol treatment."

"She'd get about 4.5 milliliters of epinephrine 1:10,000, should she need it," I informed her as I flipped through my EMS pocket guide.

"What is this?" she demanded suspiciously, snatching the guide from my hands and riffling through it.

"Well, it's just a quick reference guide that most medics carry. It has dosing guidelines, ACLS references, that sort of..."

"This is excellent!" she proclaimed, pocketing it. "May I have it?"

"Uh, sure," I replied, afraid to say no. Her request was phrased as a question, but it was an order, no doubt about it.

I supposed fifteen bucks was a small price to pay for a little goodwill with the doctors. And if anyone needed an EMS field guide, she did.

The ER was getting a little crowded, so Randy and I walked outside for some fresh air. Well, I walked outside for fresh air; Randy seemed intent on poisoning the general vicinity with cigarette smoke. A few minutes later, Mary joined us. She smiled tiredly and leaned against the wall, sipping a Dr Pepper.

"Good job," she told us. "Both of you."

"I was going to say the same thing to you," I told her, meaning it. "You must have paid attention in pediatric advanced life support class."

"Actually, I've never taken PALS," she admitted wryly. "That was my virgin pediatric resuscitation."

"Well, you did great," I told her again. "Look, I'm a PALS instructor, so the next time I teach a class, I could call you..." Randy coughed and quickly stubbed out his cigarette, mumbling something about having left his cap in the break room.

"That's very nice of you," Mary said noncommittally as Randy made himself scarce.

"Uh, look," I stammered. "I was wondering if you would...I mean, if you wanted to...I thought it would be nice if I could take you out to dinner," I finished lamely, blushing like a tomato.

"I thought you would never ask," she replied, flashing me the most beautiful smile in the world. "Friday at seven okay with you?"

# Masculinity Lessons

I WAS FEELING pretty good. The weekend had been, to borrow a phrase from Randy, absolutely fabulous. This was turning out to be a pretty choice station assignment. We didn't run much, but when we did, it was usually pretty good.

DeVillier transferred out only its worst patients, and I didn't mind doing high-acuity interfacility transports. In the past forty-eight hours, we'd run two calls, an MI patient going to Lake Chillicothe and a suicide attempt by poisoning that was rather amusing.

Our patient had swallowed an entire refill carton of Downy fabric softener. She initially wanted to refuse care, telling us she'd simply mistaken the fabric softener for a carton of milk. When I asked her if she kept her milk in the laundry room, or her fabric softener in the refrigerator, she refused to answer. When we told her she had only two choices—restrained or unrestrained—she wisely chose to sit down on the cot and go without further argument. The Poison Control Center just laughed when we called it in. They told us all we should expect is that her poop should be April fresh for the next few days.

To further brighten my mood, I'd gotten my first decent night's sleep since I'd been there. It's not that we got that many calls at night; it was the flow of traffic right outside my bedroom window. Log trucks and four-by-four redneck-mobiles rumbled by every few minutes, but I'd learned to tune them out. What I couldn't seem to tune out, however, was the little prick on a dirt bike that passed by at two-thirty every morning.

Said prick would stop at the light right outside my window and rev his engine until I ran outside in my boxers and threatened to do him bodily harm.

DeVillier had a noise ordinance, and this guy was certainly violating it every time he goosed his little rice-burner with the chainsaw engine right outside my window. Problem was, he was crafty. He never seemed to do it when the cops were waiting for him, and I'd never been quick enough to get his license number. I had resigned myself to awakening every morning at two-thirty to the angry snarl of a 250cc Yamaha. That is, until Friday night.

I was hiding in the hedge when he stopped at the intersection, right on time. I let him have his fun waking the neighbors, and when he started to pull away I stepped out and beaned him with a full liter bottle of Coke at a range of ten feet. I hit the little bastard right in the back of the head, spilling him off his bike. Sadly for him, he was not wearing a helmet.

He lay there in the road a moment, then slowly picked himself up, got back on his bike, and rode away—quietly. The next night, I slept without interruption until Randy woke me up in time to watch the Saints game the following day.

That morning I took a shower, put on uniform pants and a T-shirt, and promptly moved my show to the couch for the remainder of the shift. Randy insisted on bustling around, doing busywork, but how many times can you vacuum a floor or wax an ambulance in seventy-two hours? I'd been trying to give him masculinity lessons, but they didn't seem to have much effect. He just couldn't seem to appreciate that men enjoy certain simple pleasures specific to their gender, and that abstaining from these pleasures upsets the natural order of things.

Men lounge around in their underwear, scratching their privates and channel surfing. Men yell at the television, in the full expectation that their team will indeed score a touchdown if the damned coach will just listen to them. Men fart and don't apologize afterward. They say manly things like "Whoa, that chili is the gift that keeps on giving!" or "Did y'all see that barking spider?" Men certainly do not call them "poots" and blush like schoolgirls.

I was once again trying, during commercial breaks from the Saints–Falcons game, to point these things out to Randy when my lesson was interrupted by the radio.

"Medic 306, Dispatch. Priority One, a motor vehicle accident on Highway 22, two miles east of Ridley."

"Medic 306 responding," Randy replied, looking thankful for the interruption. He happily bounded out of his chair and sprinted for the rig.

I just couldn't figure this guy out. I mean, the Saints were down by three points, driving on the Falcons 34-yard line, with no time-outs and less than two minutes to go, and he didn't even seem concerned! Did the man have no soul? And what kind of inconsiderate asshole wrecks his car when the Saints are playing? Whoever it was could wait for at least two more minutes.

Ten minutes out of DeVillier and maybe a little more than halfway to Ridley, the radio crackled again, "Medic 306, Dispatch."

"Go ahead," I replied.

"Be advised there are two vehicles involved, and you have three patients. We have Medic 309 en route from Lake Chillicothe."

"Ten-four."

Well that was just lovely. Our nearest backup was a BLS truck thirty minutes away, and if the dispatcher called Allemands Parish Ambulance for mutual aid, the owners would fire his ass for sure.

We arrived on the scene to find the Ridley Volunteer Fire Department already rendering care. From the looks of things, a full-size Chevy pickup had crossed the centerline and hit a Ford Taurus head-on. The firefighters were working on freeing the driver of the Taurus, who was, miraculously, still conscious.

He was lucid and alert, and from what little I could see of him, at least his color was good. His left radius and ulna were obviously broken, and the firefighters had thoughtfully propped his injured extremity on the driver's-side mirror while they work on peeling the roof. His head, shoulders, and left arm were visible, but that was about all.

His airbag has deployed, and his chest was wedged right against the steering wheel. He seemed to be breathing okay, though—at least well enough to give a running commentary on the accident to the firefighters trying to extricate him. I was trying not to focus exclusively on one patient when I already knew I had three, but I could catch snatches of the conversation as I approached the Chevy truck.

"Came right at me..." he was saying. "Didn't even have time to hit my brakes..." The driver of the truck didn't look good, even though the Chevy had sustained far less damage. He was an older man of maybe sixty years. His skin was an unhealthy gray color, and he was extremely diaphoretic.

"No, really, I'm okay. Arm hurts, though," Mr. Taurus rattled on. "How's the other guy? Jeez, I couldn't even get out of his way..."

Randy tapped me on the shoulder. "Where do you need me?" I looked back again at the Taurus, then at the driver and passenger of the Chevy. The passenger was a burly young man about my age, wearing painter's pants and a flannel shirt. He was sitting sideways on his seat, holding the tail of his shirt against a small cut on the old man's forehead. He looked okay, but was holding his right arm against his side.

"You take the guy in the car," I decided. "Call me if you need anything. Send 309 to me when they get here, and send one of the firefighters over here to me right now."

"They're all pretty busy..." he started to say.

"Randy, there's always someone standing around with his thumb up his ass. Find him and send him this way, would you please?" I turned my back to him and begin assessing the driver.

"How are you doing, sir?" I asked him, and then nodded to the passenger. "You okay, man?"

"I hurt my shoulder," he said. "My dad hit the steering wheel pretty hard."

"That true, sir? Does your chest hurt?" I asked him. He started to nod, and I stopped him quickly, stabilizing his head with both hands.

"Don't nod or shake your head, sir. Just answer yes or no, okay? Now, what hurts, exactly?" I asked as I palpated his chest and abdomen.

"Chest hurts," he told me through gritted teeth. "Knocked the wind out of me. Can't catch my breath," he said in short gasps.

No shit. His steering wheel was bent like a taco, and he'd broken just about every rib I could feel.

He didn't mention his arms, but both of them were obviously broken, just above the wrists.

"We blew a tire," the son explained. "We could see it coming, but there wasn't a thing we could do about it. Dad was on the brakes all the way..."

A pretty young woman walked up wearing a T-shirt with a Maltese cross emblazoned on it. She approached the passenger side of the truck and leaned in the window.

"Your partner sent me over here to help," she said. "What can I do?"

"Cervical collars for both of them, and get the oxygen bottle and a non-rebreather from my rig. And we need to get some of your guys to pop this driver's door."

She tried the passenger door, and it opened with a little effort.

"Okay, scratch the extrication." I grinned. "But get me rest of that stuff quick as you can." I turned my attention back to the driver, palpating what little I could reach through the window. Nothing else hurt or felt out of the ordinary, and the head laceration turned out to be small, and hardly bleeding at all.

In no time my helper was back, pushing two spine boards, the C-collar bag, and the trauma kit piled precariously on the stretcher. She had also rounded up some help; there were two equally pretty volunteer firefighters with her. All three of them made a navy-blue T-shirt look good.

"No oxygen," she informed me. "I got a mask, though."

*What do you mean, no oxygen? It's in the rack right inside the rear doors! You had to reach right over it to unlatch the cot!*

I looked over my shoulder, and Randy had the portable oxygen cylinder lying on the ground next to the Taurus. He had a blanket spread over himself and the patient while the extrication was going on. All I could see was two stubby little legs, empty plastic wrappers, and an oxygen cylinder with tubing snaking up to somewhere under the blanket.

"Get the spare from under the bench seat," I told her, then I said to her friends, "And if you two could get collars on these gentlemen..." Without further ado, they each grabbed a no-neck collar and quickly went about applying them.

Apparently, these ladies were members of the No-Neck Fits Everyone

Society. They must have chapters all over the country.

The one on my side had to squeeze in very close to me to apply the collar to the driver.

*I forgive you for not knowing how to size a cervical collar, ma'am. In fact, if you keep rubbing against me like that, I could forgive lots of things...*

The first girl arrived back at the truck carrying the spare portable oxygen cylinder. As much as hated to, I stepped back and gave her room to apply oxygen to the driver. His color had me worried.

Approaching sirens heralded the arrival of Medic 309, and I waved furiously until I got their attention. "Over here!" I yelled. Travis Deville, an EMT-B, and his partner, James Braden, an EMT-I, trotted over.

"What have we got?" Travis wanted to know.

"Randy's got a critical in the Taurus. You'll be transporting him. If one of you will go help him get that guy packaged, the other can stay here and help me and the ladies can package these two."

"Get the KED?" James asked. I bit off my reply just in time.

*Careful, Kelly. It's not his fault he has a room-temperature IQ. If you tell him how fucking stupid he is, he'll just go into a sulk and be of no use to you. And he doesn't know it yet, but today James Braden is going to have to act like an EMT-Intermediate, like it or not.*

"Good idea!" I said as convincingly as I could. "But I don't think we have the time. We need to get the driver out as quickly as possible, and to do that we have to get the passenger out first." James nodded his understanding and began assisting the ladies in extricating the passenger.

As long as one of the ladies was in charge, he'd do okay. I just hoped he didn't resent taking orders from a woman.

Fortunately, James had no such qualms. It seemed he'd much rather have someone tell him what to do than think for himself. Under the direction of my first volunteer, James and her friend got the passenger extricated and packaged, quickly and smoothly. In short order, we extricated his father as well and hustled them both to the rig. Randy and Travis were already loading the other driver into Medic 309. Travis climbed into the back with the patient as Randy trotted over to our rig.

"Well, I can hardly believe it, but the guy in the car only seems to have a broken arm. Lots of cuts and scratches, and a helluva rash from the airbag, but the arm seems to be the worst of it." He shook his head wonderingly.

"You hear that, James?" I asked. "Your patient should be pretty easy to deal with. You and Travis take that one, and Randy and I will take these two. We're bringing them all to Lake Chillicothe." James's eyes instantly got wide as saucers. He shook his head.

"No way. DeVillier is only fifteen minutes away."

I motioned for him to step out of the rig. I did not want witnesses to this discussion, so I walked him around the side of our rig and leaned forward until my face was about two inches from his nose.

"DeVillier can barely handle one of these guys, much less three at once. And they'll only wind up going to Lake Chillicothe anyway," I pointed out.

"But they're unstable, and DeVillier is closer. I think we..."

"I'm not going to debate this with you, James. They're only going to get more unstable at DeVillier, until they get transferred to someplace that can perform surgery. That place is Lake Chillicothe Regional Medical Center."

"But I don't really feel comfortable—"

"Oxygen. IV access. Fluids. Secondary survey. Rapid transport to Lake Chillicothe. Right the fuck now, James. You got me?"

He nodded nervously and returned to his rig, climbing into the back. Hopefully, Travis had gotten a decent secondary survey and some vital signs by now, and there would be fewer things for James to fuck up.

In the back of my own rig, the first volunteer was kneeling between our two patients, taking a blood pressure on the passenger. I waited until she was finished, then motioned for her to hand me the cuff and scope.

"This one's vitals are stable," she said, writing the blood pressure on the back of her glove. "He's got a broken clavicle, I think, maybe from the shoulder belt." She nodded toward his father on the stretcher. "I can't hear a pressure on him, but he's got a faint radial pulse. Pretty tachy, too," she added.

"Thanks for the help," I told her as I listened to the driver's chest. "We'd have been up a creek without you guys." His lung sounds were absent on the right side. The left side wasn't much to brag about, either. I couldn't hear a blood pressure. When we tried to rouse him, he opened his eyes only briefly.

"Want me to ride in with you?" she offered. "I'm a registered nurse when I'm not playing hose monkey."

"The more the merrier," I told her, then yelled up front, "Randy! Light it up!" I motioned for the nurse to switch places with me so I could sit in the jump seat. She kneeled between the cot and the bench seat as I called Lake Chillicothe.

"Chillicothe Regional ER," a bored, disinterested voice answered.

"This is Kelly with Stat Fleet Medic 306. I need to speak with the physician for orders, please."

"What have you got?" she asked.

"Wreck victims from Ridley. I need to speak to the doctor ASAP, please," I repeated.

"From Ridley? Why are you bringing them here?"

*Because the fucking zoo is closed and there's nothing good at the movies, that's why.*

"Look," I snapped at her, "I need the doctor on the phone right now! I can satisfy your curiosity later!"

"Hold on!" she snarled back. I covered the phone with my hand.

"Can you get me a line?" I asked my volunteer. "A big one, or maybe even two?" She nodded yes and started rummaging through the cabinets for IV fluids. I waited patiently for perhaps thirty seconds, and still got no doctor on the line. Finally, I gave up and dropped the handset to the floor without breaking the connection. If the doctor ever got on the line, he could eavesdrop on what I was about to do.

"Can you hand me a ten-milliliter syringe, a prep, and one of those big honking fourteen-gauge catheters while you're in that cabinet?" I asked politely.

"What are you going to do?" she asked me, handing me the syringe and catheter.

"I'm going to decompress his chest," I said matter-of-factly. "He's got a tension pneumothorax." Of course, I didn't tell her that this would be my very first, and that you couldn't drive a knitting needle into my anus with a sledgehammer right now. That wouldn't be very paramediclike.

"Without orders?" she asked, pausing from spiking a bag of saline. "Better you than me, buddy." She shook her head. "Well, you're lucky. Dr. Hennesey is on duty in the Emergency Department today. He's pretty cool."

*Not as lucky as you might think, sister. He's also our medical director. I'm going to have to justify this to him.*

I attached the syringe to the flash chamber of the IV catheter and drew up about three milliliters of saline into the syringe. I found and cleansed my landmark, one intercostal space below the Angle of Louis in the midclavicular line, just like I was taught in PHTLS (prehospital trauma life support) class. The nurse was watching me in rapt fascination.

Now, if this worked as advertised, I should see bubbles in the saline when I entered the pleural space. Then I withdrew the—

Pop! The plunger popped out of the syringe like a champagne cork and landed on the floor, showering us with a fine mist of saline. There was a prolonged rush of air, as if someone had deflated a tire.

"Shit!" the nurse exclaimed. "Is it supposed to do that?"

"It happens occasionally," I said, as if I'd done a hundred of them. "Nothing to worry about, though." I then went about fashioning a flutter valve from the finger of a latex glove, just like the illustration in my *Paramedic Emergency Care* second-edition textbook, by Bledsoe, Porter, and Shade.

It immediately became apparent that taping the finger of a latex glove to a catheter hub in the back of an ambulance at eighty miles an hour was easier said than done. A couple of times I succeeded, but in both cases it happened to be a finger of the glove I was wearing. I came to the realization that I looked like a monkey fucking a football, and that I was destroying my newfound credibility with the hot little nurse in turnout pants and well-filled T-shirt, so I just gave up on the flutter valve.

The patient seemed to be doing fine without it, however. His color was vastly improved, and his lungs sounded better. At least, I thought they sounded better. The engine sounds on the left side were much louder, with a hint of breath sounds underneath. There might even have been some sounds on the right side now, if my imagination wasn't running away with me.

*Note to self: The latex glove trick does not work. File that little tidbit right next to the one marked "Tape does not stick to Vaselined gauze." Maybe Dr. Bledsoe needs to know about this. Maybe he should fire his illustrator.*

By the time we made it to Lake Chillicothe, our patient had had close to a liter of saline, and his pressure could be easily heard at 104/62. He was awake but groggy, and the nurse and I even found time to splint his broken arms.

James was unloading his patient as we pulled into the ambulance bay. He was proudly holding an IV bag as Travis towed the cot behind him. James had cut the patient's clothes off, and his arm was even splinted.

*Damn! You go, James!*

I looked a little closer as they walked past. The IV fluid was 5 percent dextrose, on a microdrip infusion set. The IV catheter was a 22-gauge, neatly held in place with pretty little chevrons of tape.

*Try as hard as you want, you just can't polish a turd.*

I sighed to myself as I trudged dejectedly into the ER. I still had to explain myself to Dr. Hennesey.

And the weekend had started so well! I wondered who'd won the game.

# Two Saves in Two Days

GREEN ACRES NURSING Home wasn't too bad, as nursing homes go. The prevailing stench there was of Clorox and baby powder, but without the faint essences of shit and stale urine common in so many other nursing homes.

The trend around here is to build large, sprawling "geriatric care centers" with pastoral-sounding names like "Oak Lawn Manor," or "Shady Lane Care Center," but the only thing that really distinguishes them from the older nursing homes is that there are urine stains on carpet instead of linoleum. Other than that, it's a wash.

I have a major problem with an industry that warehouses old people, and considers fifty-to-one an acceptable patient-to-nurse ratio. So families will know what they're doing to their parents and grandparents, I think they ought to give them names that describe the actual living conditions, like maybe "Our Lady of the Clogged Feeding Tubes," or "Aspiration Manor," or my personal favorite, "Chateau of Methicillin-Resistant Staphylococcus Aureus."

Some of these places are really grim. There is one in Lake Chillicothe where you see people shuffling around in a drug-induced fog, with dried food on their faces and feces and urine stains on their clothes—and that's the nursing staff I'm describing. The patients are *really* bad.

There is a love–hate relationship between paramedics and nursing home nurses. We hate them because of the ignorance and apathy we see in them, yet we probably couldn't get paid without the patients they ask us to transport. They hate us because we're often arrogant and condescending, with no concept of how tough and emotionally draining their jobs are, yet love us because we're trained to handle emergencies, which is not the forte of the average nursing home nurse.

I was reflecting on this relationship when Randy and I were called for a cardiac arrest at Green Acres. Our relief crew, Lance Bidwell and

Mike Treme, had managed to alienate most of the staff at the local nursing homes, which reflected poorly on Stat Fleet EMS in particular, and paramedics in general.

This made my job tougher when I had to deal with these people. There was usually a distinct chill in the air when we picked up a patient from Green Acres, but not this time. This time, they were going to be damned happy to see us arrive. This time, we were the cavalry. The pros from Dover had arrived.

Randy and I were directed to a room at the far end of one wing, where we found a frail little woman in full arrest. The staff was doing effective CPR, for a change. They had even removed the head of the bed and placed it under her shoulders as a CPR board. There was an equally frail little old man in the next bed, sobbing pitifully.

"Just let her go, you bastards! Why can't you just leave her alone?" he pleaded in a quavering voice. "Please just let her go!" Everyone seemed to be ignoring him.

The nurse doing ventilations looked up at us as we entered the room.

She'd been working hard; there was sweat dripping off her nose, and her hair was in disarray.

"How long has she been down?" I asked as I did a quick look with my defibrillator paddles. The rhythm looked like ventricular tachycardia.

"Maybe five minutes," the nurse answered as I charged the paddles. "She collapsed while the aide was feeding her breakfast."

"Everybody clear!" I sang out, and then lit her up with 200 joules. The rhythm changed immediately to ventricular fibrillation, so I charged the paddles to 300 joules and popped her again. The rhythm changed to asystole. I paused to check her pulse, didn't find one, and put my paddles back in the defibrillator. I noticed that Randy was desperately scrabbling through the monitor case, opening every zippered compartment.

"No electrodes!" he said, anguished.

Well, that figured. Lance and Mike had told us the truck was stocked up and ready to go when we relieved them that morning. I should have known better.

"Well, hustle out to the truck and get some!" I snapped, and then turned back to the nurses. "Could you ladies resume CPR while I get her intubated?" I quickly opened my airway kit, grabbed my laryngoscope and a 7.5 tube, and intubated her without much trouble. An aide handed me the BVM, and I paused, looking in vain for any nurse with a stethoscope hanging around her neck. Normally, Randy checked breath sounds for me while I ventilated, but he was busy fetching electrodes.

"Uh, anybody got a stethoscope?" I asked hopefully, to which everyone replied by shaking their heads. Well, shit! Okay, then, we'd improvise. I placed my hand on the woman's stomach.

"Bag," I told the aide. She complied, and the stomach didn't rise. "Again," I told her, placing my hands on the patient's chest. Both sides of her chest rose equally. That was good enough for me.

I grabbed some tape from my thigh pocket and quickly taped the tube down, wrapping the tape all the way around her head several times for good measure. I handed off the BVM to the aide and stepped back over to my monitor. I did another quick look, and the rhythm was still asystole. I dropped the paddles next to the monitor, pulled up two milligrams of epinephrine from a multidose vial, and jammed the needle into the side of the ET tube, just above the lips. I injected the contents and ordered the nurse doing chest compressions to stop for a moment. The aide doing the ventilating took this to mean her as well and stopped bagging. I tapped her on the arm.

"Not you," I said. "Bag like hell for a few seconds." Randy reentered the room, carrying several packages of electrodes. He was red-faced and out of breath.

*You regret those cigarettes now, don't you, partner?*

He quickly attached the electrodes and switched the lead selector switch on the monitor to Lead II. The rhythm was still asystole, as flat as could be. The old man in the next bed was just crying and moaning pitifully to himself now.

"We need a line," I told Randy, who dug through the jump kit for a bag of saline and an infusion set. He cursed under his breath and straightened up.

*Shit, don't tell me. No saline, either? Lance Bidwell, you will roast in hell for this!*

I met Randy's gaze, and he looked as if he were about to cry; whether in frustration or from the prospect of sprinting to the rig again, I couldn't tell. I said nothing, just pointed at the door, and he wheeled and sprinted out of the room. I dug through my drug box and managed to find a 250-millileter bag of 5 percent dextrose and a microdrip infusion set. I handed it to a nurse, grabbed a 14-gauge catheter, and started looking for a good external jugular vein. She had a whopper, so I sank the catheter and attached the line the nurse handed to me.

I taped it off securely, opened the clamp, and watched the fluid flow. It was patent, so I closed the roller clamp, grabbed prefilled one-milligram syringes of epinephrine and atropine, and administered them both, opening the clamp briefly to flush the meds in.

"You're doing great, ladies," I told the nurses as I handed the bag off to one of them. "Just keep doing what you're doing." The pitter-patter of little feet in the hallway heralded Randy's return, and he burst into the room with a spiked bag of saline, trailing a trickle of fluid behind him. He handed me the bag without a word, and leaned over with his hands on his knees, gasping for air.

"Switch this out for me, would you, please?" I asked the IV nurse, handing her the bag of saline. As she did that, I noticed a rhythm change on the monitor. It was V-fib. Charging the paddles again, I hollered, "Clear!" and hit her with 360 joules. The rhythm changed to sinus bradycardia, then rapidly sped up to the prettiest sinus rhythm I'd seen in a long time.

Sinus rhythm at 70; I'll take that any day. And from the combination of relief and amazement on the BVM aide's face, there was good news on the airway front as well.

"She's trying to breathe through the bag," she said wonderingly.

*I'll be damned, she is! Gagging on the tube, no less!*

"Great work, ladies. She's got a pulse." I grinned at the nurses. We took a couple of minutes to get her on the stretcher, secure her arms, and bolus her with 75 milligrams of lidocaine. As we rolled her toward the door, one of the nurses stopped us as we passed the old man's bed.

"Her husband," she explained, a fact that I felt ashamed for not picking up on. He was still crying, rolled partly over in the bed, reaching feebly for the stretcher legs. Randy and I lowered the stretcher and maneuvered it as close to his bed as we could. He gently kissed his wife's cheek and stroked her hair, his hands palsied and trembling with the telltale signs of Parkinson's disease. I waited quietly, allowing him as much time as I dared, then reached down and gently pulled him away. Her cheek was wet with his tears.

"Sir," I told him softly, and a little huskily, "I promise we'll take good care of her. We'll be gentle."

He said nothing, just rolled on his side and closed his eyes. Unsure of what else to say, I nodded to Randy and we lifted the stretcher and rolled her out the door. There was no backslapping, no exchange of high fives in the hall. If this was a save, it didn't feel like one.

On the way to DeVillier Community Hospital, I took the time to hang a lidocaine drip. What the heck, I'd already got the right bag spiked.

At the emergency room, Dr. Idris took report. He listened, nodding occasionally as I talked, then looked up at me, horrified.

"You started an external jugular IV?" he asked incredulously. "Couldn't you find a vein somewhere else?"

"Uh, well, Doc," I said hesitantly, not sure of what his problem was, "I never actually looked anywhere else. Is that a problem?" He shook his head angrily.

"We cannot admit her like that!" he blurted, motioning to the nurse. "Mary, find another vein and discontinue that IV!" Mary complied, winking at me surreptitiously as Dr. Idris turned his back.

Our patient, Mrs. Couvillion, was moving now. She gagged on the tube and tossed her head, her eyes tracking Mary as she moved around the bed. I walked back into the corridor and found a middle-aged woman and her husband standing at the desk. Dr. Idris was nowhere to be found.

"Can I help you folks?" I asked.

"Edna Couvillion?" the lady asked me uncertainly. "Is she here? I'm her daughter," she explained. "The nursing home told us they sent her to the hospital."

"Oh, okay!" I said, shaking their hands. "I'm the paramedic who brought her in. The nurse or doctor should be able to let you know how she's doing in a minute."

"What happened?" the son-in-law wanted to know.

"Well, apparently she went into cardiac arrest while they were feeding her breakfast," I told him, then hurried on as I saw the shocked expressions on their faces. "It's okay, though. We managed to revive her in time, and she's awake right now. Her vital signs are good, and she's aware of what is going on around her. Keep your fingers crossed, and the doctor will be able to tell you more, but right now it looks as if she's going to be okay." I smiled reassuringly.

"But I don't understand," the woman said, confused. Her husband just looked pissed. "She didn't want any heroic measures taken. She and Dad didn't want to be resuscitated. They signed a form and everything..."

"Oh," I stammered. "I didn't know that. Well, I mean, I wasn't told... the nurses were...uh, I don't know what to say...well, the doctor will see you in a moment," I finished lamely, and beat a hasty retreat into the ER.

"Mary," I hissed as I walked back inside, "this woman has a DNR! Her family is outside, and they want to know why we did anything!"

"Green Acres," she groaned, hanging her head, "codes everybody, no exceptions."

"Even the DNR patients?" I asked disbelievingly.

"Even the DNR patients," she confirmed. "Apparently, their lawyers found something wrong with the way their Do Not Resuscitate orders were written. They said none of them were valid, so Green Acres resuscitates everybody until they get it straightened out."

*Good Lord! Well, I suppose if she codes again, we can just let her go this time.*

I say as much to Mary.

"Relax," she said, "you got a save. I'll explain things to the family."

"Well, it doesn't feel like one right now. It actually feels kind of disappointing," I confessed. "You're going to talk to the family, instead of Dr. Idris?"

"He's probably already gone home." She snorted, then grinned wickedly. "And you're not the only one who is in for disappointment today. Idris will not be happy when I send this lady to the floor."

"Why should he be disappointed?"

"Because the only vein I could find was in her foot. I've got a twenty-two gauge in it, with your fluids hooked up," she explained with a twinkle in her eye, "but I'll be damned if I'm going to discontinue a fourteen-gauge IV for a twenty-two-gauge in the foot. So I heparin-locked yours, and if Dr. Idris doesn't like it, he can kiss my ass."

Man, I liked this girl!

\* \* \* \* \* \*

After a fitful sleep on the first night of my seventy-two-hour shift, I got a call from the ER. The word was that our patient would not only live, but would be back in the nursing home within a couple of days, none the worse for wear. It was some consolation at least, knowing that even though she had a DNR, she would be going back to her husband.

A week later, there was a crawfish boil at Devillier Community Hospital to commemorate National Nurses Week. Mary, Randy, and I were sitting on a blanket on the hospital's south lawn, devouring a huge mound of crawfish piled between us. Randy and I were wearing only our T-shirts, our uniform shirts carefully removed and set aside to avoid the inevitable crawfish stains.

Dr. Idris had wandered by a few minutes earlier, looking very relaxed. He sat his drink down next to mine, and I mistakenly picked it up and drank from it. Whatever it was, it burned like fire all the way down. It was definitely not tea, and I strongly suspected it was something that a nice

Muslim fellow like Mohammed Idris should not be drinking.

Nevertheless, he seemed to be enjoying himself, and his wife could drive him home if need be. He even sampled quite a few of the crawfish with us infidels, and then wandered off mumbling something about the men's room.

"We should have warned him to wash his hands," Randy mused.

"Oh, I'm sure Dr. Idris knows to wash his hands after using the bathroom," Mary admonished.

"It's not after he takes a piss that he needs to worry about," Randy explained tolerantly. "These crawfish are spicy, and he's got cayenne all over his hands." Mary and I chuckled at the mental image.

Mary was leafing through a copy of *Brides* magazine, looking at wedding dresses. Since we'd become engaged, Randy had been dropping serious hints about being our wedding planner. Problem was, he had expensive tastes while I had an EMT pocketbook. He and Mary were constantly whispering conspiratorially over flower arrangements, photographers, bridesmaid dresses, and the like. I'd washed my hands of it, requesting only that my groomsmen and I wear black tuxedos. I hate white tuxes.

"Medic 306, Dispatch. 1158 Highway 27 North, on a cardiac arrest," the radio rudely interrupted Randy, who was extolling the virtues of a particular wedding dress. We both groaned and reached for our shirts.

"We're en route," I responded as Mary sighed. I gave her a quick peck on the cheek and sprinted for the truck.

Just north of the DeVillier city limits, an old man flagged us down. We backed into his driveway as he impatiently shouted, "Hurry up!"

As soon as I got out of the rig, he confronted me angrily. "What take you so damned long?" he demanded in a thick Cajun accent. "I call fifteen minute ago!"

"Calm down, sir," I replied, trying to placate him. "We just got the call no more than two minutes ago." I stepped around him and helped Randy unload our gear. Inside the house we found two identical burly young men wearing identical overalls and white T-shirts, kneeling beside a frail body on the floor. They had the large, callused hands of pulpwood haulers, and were delicately yet efficiently doing picture-perfect CPR on an elderly woman. The one doing compressions looked up as we entered the room.

"My grande mama," he told us breathlessly in an accent every bit as thick as his father's. "She fall out mebbe two, t'ree minutes gone."

"*Mais non*, she got a bad heart," the man's brother confirmed.

"Okay, gentlemen, step back, please," I ordered as I checked for breathing and a pulse. There was neither, and I gestured for them to resume CPR. The cardiac monitor showed coarse ventricular fibrillation, so I charged the paddles and shocked her. Her back arched violently, drawing a muttered oath from the twins. The monitor rhythm changed to sinus bradycardia and I felt for a carotid pulse, slowly breaking into a grin as I felt a strong, steady beat. She was still not breathing, however.

"Is she back?" Randy asked hopefully.

"I think so," I nodded, to the relieved sighs of everyone present. "Get some vital signs, okay?" I asked Randy as I began to prepare my intubation equipment. I asked one of the twins, "Keep breathing for her for a minute, would you?"

I'd just inserted the tube and inflated the cuff when a commotion at the door attracted my attention. Dr. Idris was standing there, brushing off the mud he got on his pants from falling on the porch steps. His wife was standing just behind him, looking concerned.

"I saw the ambulance outside," he explained. "What happened to Mrs. Pitre?"

"Ah, the doctor, he done come!" the old man exulted, throwing his hands into the air. "Everyt'ing be all right now, you watch and see," he assured his grandsons.

I was still trying to frame my reply to Dr. Idris when Mrs. Pitre arched her back again, gagged, and pulled out the endotracheal tube before I could stop her.

Ouch! That was not going to help her singing voice.

"Cardiac arrest, as best we can tell," I told him. "We shocked her once and converted her, and as you can see, she just extubated herself."

*Please don't come any closer, Dr. Idris. They'll be able to smell the liquor on your breath.*

"Okay, then give her one hundred milligrams of lidocaine and set up a drip at..." he trailed off, noting my amused expression. "Well, you know what to do," he finished. "I'll meet you at the hospital." I said nothing as he stepped into the room and helped us package and load Mrs. Pitre on the stretcher. Thankfully, her family stayed several steps away, out of sniffing distance.

"Look, we've got this under control," I said softly to him, leaning close and putting one hand on his shoulder. "Why don't you let your wife drive you home, and then call Dr. Saleh with any orders you have?" I suggested gently. He met my eyes for a long minute, then nodded and backed out the door. The Pitre family waved at him gratefully as his wife drove him away.

*"Merci beaucoup, Doc!"* they bellowed as his taillights faded into the night. "T'ank you so much!"

*Hey, folks, what about our thanks? What are we, chopped liver?*

In the truck, Mrs. Pitre was quickly regaining consciousness. She had no memory of what happened. "I felt kind of swimmy-headed, that's all," she said hoarsely. "That's all I remember."

"Well, your grandsons were doing CPR on you when we got there," I told her as I gently slipped a 20-gauge catheter into the back of her left hand. She flinched slightly, then smiled at me as I muttered, "Sorry." I bolused her with lidocaine as soon as I had the IV secured.

I had just enough time to set up the lidocaine infusion before we pulled up to the hospital. I tossed the spiked bag on her lap as we rolled her inside. Melba Guidry and Sadie Dawson met us in the ER.

"Dr. Idris already called," Melba told us. "Take her to room one-sixteen."

"Here," I replied, handing her the lidocaine bag, "I mixed this, but didn't have the time to hook it up. Dr. Idris gave me verbal orders for—"

"He called in all the orders," Melba interrupted me as we walked down the hall, "but Dr. Saleh is coming in to evaluate her. What's up with that?" she wanted to know.

"Did you see him at the crawfish boil?" I asked her pointedly. Her eyes narrowed slightly, and she nodded in understanding. She entered the room ahead of us, then shooed us away as soon as we'd transferred Mrs. Pitre to the hospital bed.

"Get out of here, you two," she told us mock-sternly. "I've got to get this lady undressed and get a gown on her."

We didn't argue as Melba ushered us firmly from the room.

Randy ducked into the men's room down the hall to relieve his bladder. I was sitting at the nurses' desk completing my report as Melba emerged from the room.

"Did they know?" she asked me quietly, meaning the Pitres.

"No, they never got close enough to smell his breath," I said, shaking my head.

"Lucky for him," she sniffed.

"He wasn't on duty, Melba. He was just at a party. He saw an ambulance at a patient's house on the way home, and he stopped to help. He had enough sense to stay out of the way, and he had enough sense to let Dr. Saleh handle things up here," I reminded her.

"I guess so," she admitted grudgingly, and then turned her head at the sound of a painful yelp coming from the men's room. Randy emerged a minute later, wincing a bit and grinning ruefully.

"Damned crawfish," he explained sheepishly. "I forgot to wash my hands first."

# Tube Me Sheila

LASSON AND I were going to pick up "Tube Me Sheila," a legendary patient from Moss Point, just north of Lake Chillicothe. This would be my first call with her, but Lasson had told me what to expect.

"Baaad asthma," Lasson said, demonstrating by bugging out his eyes and making fish faces. "She only calls us when she's about to start doing the guppy. Most times, she can only say about two words—'tube me'—between breaths."

"Do they have to sedate her?" I wanted to know.

"Not that I recall," Lasson answered, "but I might be wrong. She usually just toughs it out."

"Just takes a tube, fully awake? That's hard to believe." I shook my head in wonderment.

"Wait till you see her," Lasson said knowingly. "You'll find out. She's this huge—whoa! Now, that was a good one!" he exclaimed as the smell wafted my way. I quickly rolled down the window.

"Can she walk on her own?" I asked, trying to breathe through my mouth. This one was comparatively mild. Over the past few weeks, I'd learned to keep Lasson away from eggs, milk, and red meat.

"Not usually. She lives on the second floor, too. The elevator usually works, though," Lasson informed me. He pointed just ahead. "That building right there. Her apartment is the second one from the left, second floor."

We parked the rig and locked it, loading everything onto the stretcher for the elevator ride up to Sheila's apartment. We were thankful that the elevator worked. As an added bonus, it was even well lit and air-conditioned. If the apartments were this nice, this call might not be so bad after all.

The door to apartment 2B was slightly ajar. We knocked loudly and it swung open. We poked our heads in, and there was a large black woman sitting there on the couch, puffing on a home nebulizer. She said nothing, just waved us in.

She didn't look very good. Her color wasn't all that bad, but she was leaning forward, propping her elbows on her knees and swaying unsteadily. She had faint but audible wheezes. She took the nebulizer from her lips and addressed me.

"Can't... breathe," she gasped, pausing for breath after each word.

"Okay, ma'am, don't try to talk," I told her as I knelt down next to her and opened my jump kit.

Lasson applied a non-rebreather mask. Her pulse oximetry reading was only 80 percent, the heart rate around 140. I listened to her lungs and heard...nothing. There were faint wheezes in her upper fields, but otherwise she was as tight as a drum.

"Sheila, we're going to give you some medication to help you breathe. Have you ever taken albuterol?" I asked her as I opened my drug kit. She waved her nebulizer in front of my face and looked at me as if I were stupid.

Okay, that was a dumb question.

"Well, we're going to give you another dose, as well as some other medications." I mixed a cocktail of albuterol, Atrovent, and four milligrams of dexamethasone in her nebulizer chamber and replaced the reservoir bag from her non-rebreather mask with it.

"Sheila, have you ever had to have a breathing tube inserted? Just shake or nod your head," I told her. She nodded. "How does this attack compare—"

I stopped as she began to shake her head violently. She grabbed me by both ears, pulled my face close to hers, and heaved out, "Tube me!"

"You want us to tube you?" I asked. She nodded her head vigorously.

"Okay, we can do that," I said, looking sideways at Lasson. He had an I-told-you-so expression on his face.

We quickly lowered the stretcher and helped Sheila onto it. She leaned forward as we fastened the straps. I quickly opened my airway kit and set up a tube.

"Sheila?" I asked, tapping her on the shoulder. "We're ready to go. Are you sure you don't want me to sedate you before I put the tube in?"

She answered me by leaning back and firmly gripping the stretcher rails. She tilted her head back and opened her mouth wide. I shook my head as I picked up the scope. The tube went in easily, with only a slight gag from Sheila in protest. I bagged gently as Lasson listened, nodding approvingly.

"You're in," he said. Sheila took her hand from the stretcher rail long enough to give me a thumbs-up. I quickly secured the tube, grabbed a tee connector, and hooked up the nebulizer chamber to the endotracheal tube. I started to disconnect the bag from the tube so that I could put it down while Lasson and I raised the stretcher, but Sheila stopped me by grabbing my hand. She took the bag from me and held it as I grabbed my end of the stretcher.

"Thanks," was all I could think to say. We lifted the stretcher and I took the bag back. "I've got it now," I told her. Lasson piled our gear onto Sheila's legs and we headed for the door. In the elevator, Sheila's oxygen saturation started to creep up. It was now about 88 percent. Sheila held the bag for me again as we loaded her into the rig.

Damn, she was helpful! I wondered if she'd spike a bag for me while I ventilated, or bag herself when I started the IV?

On the way to the hospital, I gave her half a milligram of subcutaneous epinephrine. By the time we arrived at Moss Point Medical Center, her saturation was up to 90 percent, and it was considerably easier to ventilate her. A nurse stopped us as we rolled into the Emergency Department. She leaned over our stretcher and gently tapped Sheila on the shoulder.

"Hey, Sheila!" she told her. "Aren't you tired of seeing us? How are you doing?"

Sheila just opened one eye and made an "okay" sign.

"Curtain three, guys," the nurse told us, pointing. We dropped Sheila off, handing the bag to the respiratory therapist, and gave report.

"We know Sheila very well around here," he assured me. "I could probably tell you what her blood gases are from memory. Did she give you any trouble?"

"Not really," I said, shaking my head. I was still waiting for a white rabbit in a waistcoat to appear. "I've never had someone ask me to tube them before."

"Well, you're lucky. Lots of your guys have to fight her a bit to get the tube," he said, nodding at Lasson. "Your partner can tell you. Sheila tries to cooperate, but if they take too long she can't stand it." Lasson and Sheila both nodded in agreement.

Lasson and I cleaned and restocked the rig, and notified dispatch that we were available for calls.

"So that was Tube Me Sheila, huh?" I mused.

"That was Tube Me Sheila," he confirmed sleepily. "One of a kind."

"One of her kind is enough," I retorted.

"Wait till you meet some of the other regulars." Lasson yawned, closing his eyes. "If you like her, you'll love them."

I hoped I never got to meet him, then. I was really starting to miss DeVillier.

# Look, I'm an IV Pole!

THERE WAS A nasty knot of traffic on Endom Boulevard near Lake Chillicothe Regional Medical Center. Lasson hit the horn repeatedly, but the cars could move only so far. We had to park our rig more than a block from the scene. The ambulance entrance to the Emergency Department was no more than one hundred feet away.

In front of us there was a cluster of people kneeling around an elderly black woman lying partly under a medical transportation van. She was wedged just behind the passenger rear wheel, with only her upper torso and arms sticking out from under the side of the van. She was conscious and alert, talking to a kid of about fourteen. He had thug written all over him, wearing the de rigueur Starter jacket, watch cap, and sagging pants. There was a red bandanna hanging from his hip pocket. He was frantic and bordering on belligerent.

"Dispatch, Medic 304. We're on the scene of a vehicle–pedestrian accident just down Endom Boulevard from Lake Chillicothe Regional," Lasson called in on his portable. "We need fire and police here immediately." We didn't even get a call on this; we rolled up on it right after it happened, on the way to the hospital to pick up a transfer.

The woman's legs and hips were wedged somewhere near the rear differential. I lay on my stomach to get a better look, but couldn't make out much. Both of her lower legs appeared to be broken, although to what extent I couldn't tell. There was also a noticeable aroma of burned flesh under the van.

Despite her obvious pain, the woman was trying to calm the kid down before he did something rash.

"I'm gonna be okay, baby," she told him reassuringly. "Grandma goin' to the hospital pretty quick. I be all right. It was just an accident, baby." The driver of the van had thoughtfully propped her head up on a rolled-up coat.

*Trying to finish her off, buddy? Why didn't you just give her a big glass of water, too?*

"I didn't see her," the driver said, anguished. "I was just turning out of the parking lot—"

"Muthafucka just ran her down, is what he did!" the kid said hotly. He looked about one wrong word away from overt violence. "White muthafucka didn't even watch where he was goin'!"

"Now, you hush that language, boy!" the lady snapped. "I ain't raised you to talk that way!" She looked at me apologetically. "He ain't no bad boy," she explained to me. "He just worried 'bout me, is all."

The boy shut up, but glowered at all of us. Out of the corner of my eye, I saw Lasson ease a bit to his left, slightly behind the kid. A police officer was weaving through the crowd, and I heard fire engines approaching.

"Hey, kid, what's your name?" I asked him. He gave no answer, just glared at us. Lasson was inching a little closer.

"Tyree," his grandmother furnished. "His name Tyree."

"Hey, Tyree?" I asked, nodding my head toward the cop approaching us. "If you want to stay around, you gotta calm down. I need some help taking care of your grandma. I'd like you to stay here, but if I have to I'll have the man lock your ass up to get you out of the way."

His demeanor instantly softened. He looked like a scared fourteen-year-old again. "What you need me to do?" he asked.

"Well, for starters, I need you to hold her head while we put this collar on her," I told him, motioning to Lasson to get a cervical collar. Tyree kneeled down next to his grandmother, gently cradling her head where I told him to place his hands.

"Problem here?" the cop asked, looking pointedly at Tyree.

"No problem," I told him, hoping I was right.

For all I knew, the little bastard was carrying a gun.

Lasson looked pissed at me. "We just need some room so the fire department guys can get in here with their equipment. And this guy was driving the bus, if you want to interview him."

The cop took the hint and escorted the shell-shocked bus driver away from the bus, Grandma, and especially Tyree.

Lasson placed the cervical collar, and Tyree scooted over, picking up his grandma's hand. A firefighter hustled up, asking, "What have we got?"

"Her legs are hung up under there somewhere," I answered. "I can't tell where, though." Without another word, the firefighter wormed his way under the van, and almost immediately wiggled back out.

"Hips are wedged under the axle," he said matter-of-factly. "Both lower legs broken, too. One of them is wedged up against the muffler."

Well, that explained the smell of burned flesh.

The firefighter said something into his radio, and soon his cohorts were setting up high-lift airbags, cribbing, and an air compressor.

Lasson had applied a non-rebreather mask and was busy spiking a bag of saline. He glanced irritably at Tyree, who was kneeling in his way.

"Hey, Tyree," I suggested, "why don't you move over here and hold this IV bag?"

He immediately got up and walked around to his grandma's right side, holding up the bag of saline at shoulder level. Lasson quickly wrapped a tourniquet around the woman's arm.

"What you fixing to do, baby?" the woman asked, alarmed.

"Well, ma'am, I'm going to start an IV on you," Lasson explained.

"Oooh, I sho' wish you wouldn't do that." The woman shuddered, her voice muffled under the mask. "I don't deal with pain so well." Lasson and I looked at each other, dumbfounded. This woman had been under a van for ten minutes, both her legs and maybe her pelvis broken with nary a whimper, and she was afraid of an IV needle? Both of us burst out laughing before we could stop ourselves.

"What the fuck is so funny?" Tyree demanded. He didn't get the joke.

"Nothing, kid," Lasson said. "We're sorry." He shook his head and quickly inserted an 18-gauge catheter. The woman hardly noticed. Suspiciously, Tyree handed Lasson the end of the IV administration set.

*Years from now, you'll tell your grandchildren about this, Tyree.*

*You'll brag about the day you saved their great-great-grandma by being an*
*IV pole.*

In another few moments, the fire department had lifted the van several inches, and we gently slid the woman up a spine board. Her legs were slightly angulated, and she blurted out a faint "Oh!" as we quickly aligned her legs on the board. Other than that, she just lay there on the board calmly, holding her grandson's hand.

We didn't even bother going to the rig, instead choosing to roll the stretcher directly to the Emergency Department. The cops looked like they'd gotten most of the traffic cleared, but our rig was still a block away. As we rolled through the ambulance bay doors, a nurse greeted us. Her name tag said "Terri," and she was none other than my helper on the wreck scene in Ridley.

"Hey, Kelly," she said brightly. "Where did you guys come from?"

"You should look out the window more often," I told her wryly. "You can see all sorts of interesting sights." She grinned, listening as I filled in the details of what happened to Tyree's grandmother.

She consulted the patient board, and pointed down the hall. "Trauma three is open," she said. "I'll be with you in a minute."

We rolled our patient into the room and slid the board over onto the hospital bed. Lasson did not speak to me at all, and wordlessly rolled the stretcher outside. Later, we completed the transfer for which we were originally dispatched, and Lasson still didn't talk. I turned to him when we got back in the rig.

"Okay," I told him flatly, "you want to tell me what's up your ass?"

"You, goddamnit!" he exploded furiously. "You take chances with my safety when you do shit like that!"

"Like what?" I asked, puzzled.

"Like playing peacemaker with that little fucking gangbanger, that's what! For all you know, he was strapped! What if he just pulled out his piece and busted a cap in your ass?"

"Where did you learn Ebonics?" I asked, amused. "Do you really talk like that? 'Strapped'? 'Bust a cap in yo' ass'?"

"You know damned well what I mean!" he said, not backing down. "For someone who does everything else so well, you have about zero street sense, you know that?"

"Look, he didn't even set off the metal detector when we went into the hospital," I pointed out. "He wasn't carrying."

"But he could have been," Lasson insisted angrily.

"I prefer to talk, Lasson. I get better results that way."

"And most of the time that works," he agreed. "But you can't reason with everybody, Kelly. Sooner or later, you're gonna get your ass whipped, or worse."

"So what should I have done?" I asked sarcastically. "Had the cop put him in cuffs?"

"Yeah, smart ass," he said tiredly. "That's exactly what you should have done. Instead you had the cop march the van driver away, and left us with the thug. The van driver wasn't going to get violent, man. We got away with it this time, but I don't want to be with you when you're wrong."

I started to retort, but the look on his face made me stop. Lasson was no coward. I wasn't afraid to go into some pretty rough places, secure in the knowledge that he had my back, and I'd just exposed his by playing amateur psychologist. He had a point.

"All right, Lasson. I'll be more careful. If either of us gets shot, I'd never again have the singular pleasure of watching you pad around the station in those hot little boxers with the fluorescent lips painted all over them. Did I ever tell you how much that turns me on?"

"Fuck you," Lasson retorted, pulling his cap down over his eyes. But at least he was grinning.

# Back to the Promised Land

"Hey, Kelly! Come check this out!" Lasson bellowed from the bathroom.

"What?" I shouted back. I'd rather not get off the couch if I can help it. I'd settled into a comfortable nest. It was Sunday afternoon, and I was watching an episode of *Emergency!* on cable, the one where Johnny and Roy work an accident out in the sticks and find themselves pretty much running the show at the little rural hospital. It was an episode I could relate to.

My bag of Doritos was on the floor within reach, I had a bowl of salsa balanced just right on my belly, and the remote control was in my left hand. I was set.

"This turd is huge!" Lasson shouted excitedly. "It looks just like Abraham Lincoln!"

"If it's that special, take a picture!" I shouted back. "I'm busy here!"

I heard nothing else from Lasson for several minutes, then I heard the sound of the toilet flushing. After a pause, it flushed again. Then another pause, followed by a third flush.

Damn, a three-flusher! That one must have been something!

Lasson padded into the living room, zipping up his pants, and flopped down into the recliner. "Hey, cool!" he said, miming for me to turn up the volume. "I love this episode!"

The man was a true connoisseur.

"Dixie was hot for an older chick, wasn't she?" he observed.

"Yeah, she was," I agreed. "Whatever happened to these guys? You never see them on TV anymore."

"Well, Roy was the guy who owned the bar in *Road House,*" Lasson pointed out. "And I think he played some mercy-killing doctor in an episode of *Law & Order,* too."

"Really? I missed that episode. Was it the—"

"Medic 304, Dispatch," the radio rudely interrupted.

"Medic 304, go ahead." I groaned.

"Come to headquarters, please."

Uh-oh, this didn't sound good.

"Ten-four," I sighed, hoisting myself off the couch.

"It's about the Grady Forrester call," Lasson said. "I just know it."

"Well, they can't have much to say," I rationalized. "After all, it wasn't our call. We were just the backup."

The previous Friday, we'd backed up Medic 303 at Grady's house. He was a morbidly obese guy, one of our frequent fliers. Forrester weighed in excess of eight hundred pounds—just how much more than that was anybody's guess. He'd fallen at his house Wednesday afternoon, and it took him two days to wiggle on his back to the living room, where he raked the phone off the end table with his cane and called 911.

He had urinated and defecated on himself for two days, and was predictably ripe when we got there. We ended up having to carry him out on his living room carpet, and the fire department had to widen his door by a foot with a power saw. Unkind words were uttered on both sides.

"Since when does being innocent have anything to do with it?" Lasson asked sarcastically. "We work for the Weavers, remember?"

I shrugged in agreement. The man did have a point.

I was ushered to Mrs. Weaver's office as I arrived at headquarters, and Lasson was directed to a chair in the anteroom. Molly greeted me warmly, all Nurse Ratchet in her jet-black beehive, white orthopedic shoes, and starched nurse's uniform.

She was not a nurse, but she liked the uniform. In fact, all of the office staff at headquarters wore white nurse's uniforms, from the receptionists to the billing manager. Molly thought it looked professional. Old Man Weaver was sitting in a chair beside Molly's desk. He rose as I entered, pumping my hand and slapping my back.

"How ya doin', son?" he inquired. " I been hearin' good things about you, boy. Damned good things."

"That's right," Molly confirmed. "We have gotten such good feedback on your calls—your interaction with the hospital staffs, your patient rapport, everything. Nothing but positives!"

"And you finally taught Lasson how to smile," the old man added. "He's a good boy, but he needed to smile more! Does he still stink up the goddamned station all the time?" he wanted to know. Molly looked pained.

"A little, Mr. Weaver," I admitted. "He's got a sensitive stomach."

"Kelly," said Miss Molly, changing the subject. "I'm sure you're wondering why we asked you here."

"Well, now that you mention it..."

"To come straight to the point, dear," she purred, "we would like to move you back to DeVillier. Would you like that?"

"Yes, ma'am, I certainly would," I said, perking up considerably.

"That goddamned Romanian doctor up there has been bitching ever since we moved you down here," the old man informed me. "The crazy bitch told the hospital administrator that she wouldn't take ER calls until we moved you back up there."

"Now, normally we wouldn't let a hospital dictate personnel decisions to us," Miss Molly explained, "but we've been in DeVillier for a long time, and in the interest of good community relations..."

"The old goat even threatened to quit calling us for transfers!" the old man chimed in, rather indignantly. Miss Molly looked like she had swallowed a bug.

"So, would you like to go back to DeVillier, starting tomorrow?" she asked hopefully.

"You bet I—wait a minute. Starting Monday? But that's B Shift," I objected.

Mary and I would be working opposite shifts. We'd never get to see each other, at work or otherwise.

"Would that be a problem?" Miss Molly inquired sweetly. There was also a hint of menace in her voice. I started to say no, then decided against it.

*Fuck it. They seem pretty desperate. I'll ask for the sun, moon, and stars, and see what they'll agree to. The most they can do is fire me, and I was ready to quit a month ago.*

"Yes, ma'am, it would," I said sadly. "My fiancée and I would be working opposite shifts. We'd never get to see each other."

"You got engaged?" Miss Molly gushed, enchanted. "To whom?"

"A nurse I met in DeVillier," I answered. "Her name is Mary Odom."

"Well, isn't that wonderful!" she continued, patting me on the arm. "Kelly's been in our little family for just a few months, and already he's met the woman he's going to marry! Isn't that wonderful, Joe?" The old man mumbled something in the affirmative. "Well, I'm sure we can juggle the schedules a bit to keep you on A Shift. Never let it be said that Molly Weaver stood in the way of true love!"

"And there's something else, Mrs. Weaver," I added. "The drive to DeVillier was always a bit much for me, coming from Slidell and all. Gas prices are so high right now, the drive really cuts into my paycheck." The smile froze on Molly's face. The old man made a choking noise.

I plunged onward, warming to the subject. "And I've had two partners in the few months that I've worked here," I said. "Lasson and I really work well together, and I'd like him to come to DeVillier with me." The smile on Molly's face was beginning to show some cracks. The corners of her mouth were twitching a little, and there was a distinct facial tic near the corner of her right eye. I waited for maybe thirty seconds, holding my breath.

*Oh, shit, here it comes...*

"Well," she said, looking over at the old man. "I think we should be able to manage all that. Is seventy-five cents an hour acceptable?"

I nodded gratefully. The smile on her face looked more like a grimace now, but she stood up and offered me her hand. The handshake was decidedly limp. The old man did not get up, just sat there in his chair, mopping spilled coffee from his lap.

I passed Lasson in the anteroom, motioning for him to follow. Outside, he grabbed my arm.

"Okay, what happened?" he demanded. "Are they going to discipline us, or what?"

"Put your faith in me, my son," I intoned piously, "for I shall lead thee out of Egypt into the Promised Land. We're moving to DeVillier."

# Dying Alone

THE FIRST WEEK we were back in DeVillier had been good. We'd even gotten upgraded equipment. After much begging and pleading, and finally some pointed remarks like "career-ending back injury" and "workmen's compensation," the Weavers finally bought us a new stretcher, and only two short years after they'd upgraded every other stretcher in a twenty-six-vehicle fleet! I'd been promised that the next week we would even get a brand-new Lifepak 10, again only two years after everyone else got theirs.

Mary told me that the hospital administrator, bowing to pressure from Dr. Alex, finally threatened not to renew Stat Fleet's transport contract unless they moved me back to DeVillier. When I heard that, I regretted not asking for even more money.

Dr. Alex's leverage was refusing to do emergency room coverage until I was reinstated. Because the majority of the hospital's patients were admitted from the ER, and she did about half of the ER calls, it was a pretty big stick to wield. What Christianna Alexakos wanted, she got. Of course, this made her my favorite physician in the world, next to Samir Saleh. Dr. Alex would grant me permission to do anything short of opening the cranial cavity, a character asset that is hard to ignore.

Lasson was slowly adjusting to DeVillier. Transport times in Lake Chillicothe were five minutes; in DeVillier, they were often upward of twenty. He'd also never had a doctor ask him, in all seriousness, "What do you think we should do?" The doctors there trusted us implicitly, and while that kind of freedom is at first a bit intimidating, Lasson was beginning to enjoy it.

We got a call for a woman having heart problems. The house was in Longbottom, which is about five miles on the far side of that theoretical destination known as "the sticks." They pipe in sunlight to Longbottom. It's the kind of place where the men are men and the livestock are nervous.

It took us twenty-five minutes to find the place, but eventually we pulled up to a ramshackle white cabin, the kind where the porch wraps all the way around the house. There were a number of vehicles in the yard, all in varying stages of disrepair. One of them was an old Karmann Ghia convertible that looked in pretty good shape. I wondered if it was for sale.

The porch sagged under our weight as we knocked on the screen door. There was no answer, and the house was dark. I peeked inside and called, "Stat Fleet EMS! Somebody call for an ambulance?"

"In the back," a weak voice replied. We wheeled the stretcher inside, maneuvering it around head-high stacks of newspapers. There were thousands of them, some of them wrapped in bundles, stacked in the hallways and in every room. The house had no electricity and was stiflingly hot. We passed the kitchen and saw that every burner on the gas stove was turned on and the oven door was open.

We found our patient in a bedroom in the rear of the house. She was a wizened little creature, with an unhealthy grayish tint to her skin. She coughed weakly and waved us into the room. Amid the stacks of newspapers, there was a single bed with a sagging mattress and a small table, which held a flickering oil lamp and a daunting display of medication bottles. The room reeked of stale cigarette smoke and urine.

"I'm sick," the woman explained unnecessarily. "I can hardly get out of bed."

"Okay, ma'am." I smiled at her. "Sick how? What exactly is going on with you today?" Lasson squeezed into the room and started taking vital signs.

"I'm so weak I can barely move," she gasped, "and I can't get rid of this cough." As if to demonstrate, she went into a prolonged spasm of coughing. It was painful to watch.

She finally coughed up a big wad of phlegm, grimaced, and spat it into a coffee can next to her bed. I leaned over and looked in the coffee can. Amid all the cigarette butts were a number of yellowish loogies, some of them streaked with blood.

"How long have you been coughing like that, ma'am?" I asked her, concerned. I idly put a hand on her brow, finding it hot. Lasson handed me a non-rebreather mask and mouthed the word "eighty-four," pointing at the pulse oximeter.

She shrugged. "All the time, I guess. It's been worse for a couple of days, though."

"Do you normally cough up anything? What color is it usually?"

She started to reply, but was cut off by another wicked coughing fit. After it passed, she gasped for breath and said hoarsely, "White, usually. Since Wednesday it's been kind of brownish-yellow." She tilted her head back as Lasson looped a nasal cannula over her ears.

"What kind of medical conditions do you have? Any infectious diseases?"

*Tuberculosis? AIDS? Hepatitis? Legionnaires' disease? Cooties?*

She shook her head. "I've got emphysema," she said. "I smoke a little."

Judging from the stench and the nicotine stains on her fingers, I'd say it was more than a little.

"Anything else?" I prompted.

"Congestive heart failure and high blood pressure, too." I took a look at the pile of medication bottles on the table. It was the usual list of suspects, but all of the bottles were empty.

"Where are your medications, ma'am?" I asked. "All these bottles are empty."

Lasson was shaking his head and frowning, trying to take a blood pressure.

"I'm out," she explained. "I ran out of money."

Lasson stood up and massaged his lower back. Rivulets of sweat were running down his face.

"Okay, ma'am," I told her. "Let's get you on the stretcher and get you to the hospital." She was too weak to stand, so Lasson and I bodily picked her up and placed her on the stretcher. We paused to turn off the stove burners and blew out the oil lamp before we left.

As we loaded her up, Lasson told me quietly, "Her lungs sound like crap; wheezes and crackles everywhere. Heart rate is 132, pressure is 70/40."

"I figured as much. Why don't you set up a nebulizer cocktail?"

He nodded and began filling a nebulizer chamber with Proventil, Atrovent, and Decadron. "Pneumonia, do you think?" he asked me as he replaced the reservoir bag with the nebulizer chamber.

"That's my guess," I agreed. Lasson climbed out of the rig, tossing the trauma kit into the back before shutting the doors. As he pulled away from the house, I asked the woman her name.

"Ezell," she told me. "Ezell Duhon."

"Got any family, Mrs. Duhon?" I asked. "Is there somebody we can call?"

"No family," she said flatly, as if to head off further discussion. "I got a son, but we ain't talked in twenty years."

I said nothing, busying myself attaching monitor leads, starting an IV, and the like. She lived alone in that little house with no electricity or running water, with no family or friends to check on her. She belonged in a nursing home. I delicately said as much to her.

"I ain't going to no goddamned old-folks home," she said vehemently. "I'd sooner die first." I nodded meekly and let the discussion drop. I'd tell Dr. Saleh about her living conditions, in the hope that he could talk her into accepting some help.

By the time we got to DeVillier, I'd given her close to 600 milliliters of saline, and her pressure was up to 100/60. Her heart rate was down to 100, but her breathing was still ugly. She went into long, wracking coughing spasms, her face turning purple and the veins bulging on her forehead. She gasped weakly and closed her eyes, holding her arms close to her sides as if her ribs hurt.

"Does your chest hurt when you cough like that?" I asked her.

"Like knives," she said, nodding, then asked hopefully, "Can you give me something for it?"

I shook my head in regret. "There's not much we can do for the pain, other than help you breathe better. We're giving you some medication to open up your lungs a little, so maybe you won't cough as much."

She nodded in understanding. "I've had it before," she told me tiredly, leaning her head back and closing her eyes. She just looked drained, weary of life. Being a medic has taught me to appreciate life, but I've also come to understand why some people can look forward to death. Sometimes, death is a mercy.

*God, when I'm her age, let me go quickly. I don't want to be in a nursing home, and I don't want to die in a shack in the middle of nowhere, all alone.*

We dropped her off at DeVillier Community Hospital, and were called back an hour later to take her to Lake Chillicothe. She sounded and looked much better, but she just lay listlessly on the stretcher, eyes closed and saying nothing. We didn't talk during the trip. I had no idea what to say.

Two weeks later, we were called to stand by with Longbottom Volunteer Fire Department at a structure fire. The address sounded familiar, and our suspicions were confirmed as we found Mrs. Duhon's house fully involved, flames rolling out the attic vents and windows. With the wood construction and all the newspapers inside, it probably went up like a torch.

It was much too late for the firefighters to even attempt to go inside, so they just surrounded and drowned. Later, picking through the soggy wreckage, they found her in the back bedroom. We bagged her up and took her body to the morgue in Lake Chillicothe. We didn't even know the name of her son, much less how to reach him.

The morgue attendant acted bored and disinterested, directing us to place the bag on an empty table, perfunctorily copying what little information we had. She was just another piece of meat to him, but we knew her name.

# Animal Magnetism

WE GOT ANOTHER call in Cloutier the next morning. Well, it was technically morning—it was three o'clock—but in my opinion, any call that gets me up before I am ready to roll out of bed, take a shower, and eat breakfast is in the middle of the fucking night. It's not the next day regardless of the date I put on the run tickets. The old man we took to East Chillicothe earlier was admitted to the ICU, and the staff doubted he'd make it.

We were heading to a shooting. East Chillicothe Ambulance was also dispatched, but we should have arrived at the scene first. We were both about equal distance from Cloutier, but I had Lasson and a gas-burner ambulance, and straight roads all the way. Lasson took full advantage of this fact, and put the hammer down.

At this hour, I tend to sleep until we get to the scenes when I don't have to drive, rationalizing that if we do get into a fiery crash, the last thing I want to do is see it coming. I'd rather wake up in the ICU, or in some ethereal place, preparing to justify my actions to the Great Medical Director in the Sky.

Since both services ran EMS calls in Cloutier, the police called them both when they needed an ambulance. The first one to get there got the patient. If Cloutier EMS got called directly, they automatically called Stat Fleet for transport. Eddie Thibodeaux had threatened his troops with death if they ever called East Chillicothe, primarily because he knew that with Stat Fleet, his crews had to put up with condescension and rudeness only 50 percent of the time.

We arrived on scene to find Eddie Thibodeaux applying bandages to a woman sitting on the stoop of an old house that looked vaguely familiar. She was wearing an old tank top liberally spattered with blood. She was not wearing a bra, and her pendulous breasts were clearly visible through the armholes of the shirt. She was totally oblivious to the fact that her tits were hanging out, instead focusing on giving Eddie an alcohol-fogged narrative of recent events. She had abrasions all over her arms, and her neck, chest, and abdomen were peppered with hundreds of bloody little holes.

Shotgun, obviously. It looked like birdshot. She looked like she'd weigh about two hundred pounds. *Don't these people know that you're supposed to use buckshot on big game?*

"Shumbish shot me, thash what he done," the woman slurred. "I ain't done nothin', neither," she added indignantly.

*Sure, lady. You were just sitting here on your porch, drinking a wholesome glass of milk and reading the Bible, when some nearsighted bird hunter mistook you for a quail. Happens all the time. You should have been wearing your fluorescent orange tank top.*

"Hey, guys," Eddie greeted us absently, and then looked suspiciously at Lasson. "Who's this?"

"Sorry," I said, and made the introductions. "Lasson Cocodrie, meet Eddie Thibodeaux. You met his daughter and son-in-law yesterday afternoon." Lasson and Eddie nodded to each other warily.

"Recognize the place, Kelly?" Eddie asked, inclining his head toward the house.

"Wait a minute," I said, remembering. "This isn't..."

"Yeah, it is," he confirmed. "This is Ricky Gaston's mother." He turned to the woman and explained, "This is the paramedic who took care of Ricky."

"Oh, thash wunnerful," she said. "I'm sho happy to meechu. You shaved my shon's life. My name ish Donna." She offered her hand and batted her eyes at me. I smiled back at her.

"Pleased to meet you, Donna. I'm Kelly, and this is my partner, Lasson. He's going to help Eddie get you bandaged up, and then we'll get you to the hospital. We'll get these bloody clothes cut off you, and get you covered up with a warm blanket, okay?"

"Shounsh good," she agreed, her head lolling drunkenly.

She appeared to be having no difficulty breathing, and her color was good. None of the pellet holes was bleeding significantly, but with this many unnatural openings in a body, you sometimes can't tell just how bad the injuries are. I got a quick set of vital signs as Lasson and Eddie applied more bandages and tape. We weren't going to get them all, but if we could cover the worst of them quickly, I'd be happy.

Donna's heart rate and blood pressure were fine, and her breathing was unlabored. As I listened to her breath sounds, she reached up and ran her fingers through my hair. I recoiled a bit, and looked carefully at her.

"Yer cute," she said adoringly. "I like you. Yer sho gentle, an' sho kind to me...are you married?" she asked drunkenly. Lasson and Eddie were biting their lips to keep from laughing.

"Well, since you ask," I answered, feeling my cheeks blush, "I actually am..."

"Single," Lasson finished, grinning at me evilly. "He's a single man."

The bastards were enjoying this.

"Oh, thash jush wunnerful," she enthused. "I need a good man, thash gentle, an' kind...do you think I'm purty?" Lasson and Eddie were making strangled, croaking noises now.

"Well, sure, I guess so. I mean, if I was..."

"I think I'm purty," she continued as if she hadn't heard me. "I'm a purty, healthy, shekshy woman, an' I need a man who needs a purty, healthy, shekshy woman..." she trailed off, and then put her hands down the neck of her tank top, pulling out her bloody breasts and holding them up for inspection.

"I got purty titties, don't I? Purty, healthy, sheckshy titties..." Lasson and Eddie immediately fled the area, leaving me alone with Donna and her purty, healthy, shekshy titties. I could hear them around the corner, howling with laughter. I looked around nervously, wondering if anyone else was looking.

Somewhere, Alan Funt had to have a hidden camera on me...

"Uh, yeah, they look healthy to me," I told her, blushing even more as I heard Eddie and Lasson break into hysterical laughter again. "Why don't you tuck them back in, and let's get you in the truck, okay?"

"Thash fine," she agreed readily, smiling at me.

I offered her my hand and helped her stand up. She swayed unsteadily and linked her arm in mine. She leaned against me as I walked her to the truck, rubbing her breasts against my arm and smiling naughtily. I sat her on the stretcher, told her to stay put, and slammed the doors. She crossed her arms across her chest and pouted.

I found Lasson and Eddie leaning against the side of the house, breathing heavily. When they saw me, they broke into renewed peals of laughter.

"Very funny," I told Lasson sarcastically. "Do you think you could find the time to drive us to the hospital now?"

"I don't know," he said doubtfully. "Are you sure you two don't need some time alone together?"

Eddie was now on his knees, arms wrapped around his sides, laughing hysterically. I shook my head and left him there, and climbed back into the rig. Presently, Lasson got up front and started driving toward Lake Chillicothe.

Donna was lying back on the stretcher with her eyes closed, but opened them when I started putting a nasal cannula on her. She snorted and grabbed my hand, shaking her head wildly, then relaxed, clutching my hand to her bosom. I gently extricated my hand and finished looping the cannula under her ears. I got IV supplies from the cabinet and wrapped a tourniquet around her arm.

"Donna, I need to start an IV on you, okay?" I asked her. She nodded in assent, holding out her left arm. She had some good antecubital veins, so I grabbed a 16-gauge catheter. I looked around for the alcohol prep but couldn't find it, so I rested her arm on my knee as I twisted around on the bench seat to look behind me. Immediately, she snaked her hand up my leg, grabbing my crotch. She was smiling and running her tongue across her lips. I beat a hasty retreat, backpedaling along the bench seat until I was huddled in a ball at the extreme rear of the truck.

*Find your Happy Place. Find your Happy Place...*

The truck swerved slightly, and I looked up to see Lasson's eyes in the rearview mirror. His shoulders were shaking violently. Donna just kept licking her lips seductively, patting the bench seat next to the stretcher.

I slowly, gingerly climbed off the seat without taking my eyes off her and firmly grasped her left hand. I quickly swabbed her arm, banged in the catheter, hooked up the line, secured it, and firmly placed Donna's hand on her own lap. It was quite possibly the fastest IV I had ever started. Donna just adopted a hurt expression, poking out her lower lip and batting her eyes. I carefully made my way past her and took up a position on the jump seat directly behind her.

"So, Donna, tell me what happened," I said. "Who shot you?"

"It wush my hushband," she slurred. "Or maybe hish brother."

*Some family you got there, Donna.*

"You don't know which?" I asked, less surprised than I should have been. "Why did they shoot you?"

"It wush one of them," she confirmed. "One wush holdin' the flashlight, and one wush shootin' the gun. I wush outshide in the bushes."

*Well, they do say blood is thicker than water.*

"You were hiding in the bushes? Were they chasing you?"

"Naw," she replied. "I wush slashin' their tiresh."

*Of course! Why didn't I know that?*

"Why were you slashing their tires?"

"'Caush they pushed me out on the road, after we left the bar," she explained as if I were dense. She held up one arm and pulled down the hem of her jeans with the other. "Thash how I got theesh shcrapes. Shumbishes beat me with a pool cue, too."

"Why didn't you just call the police?" I asked.

"Didn't have no phone," she explained. "Nearesht phone wush at home. I found 'em at the housh when I got there, sho I deshided to slash their tiresh."

*Well, that clears things up. I can't imagine why anyone would want to throw you out of the car. You seem like such a classy lady...*

We spent the rest of the trip in silence. Donna managed to keep her hands to herself and I was supremely grateful.

At Lake Chillicothe Regional, one of the nurses wanted to know why I hadn't started bilateral IVs. I played dumb, telling her I couldn't find a suitable vein. I was not about to tell her why I was reluctant to lean over Donna so I could start an IV in her right arm.

I asked Donna the requisite questions to fill in the blanks on the billing form, and when I asked for her phone number, she grinned wickedly.

"Are you gonna call me shumtime?" she asked coyly.

"Maybe," I allowed, extending the clipboard. "Sign here, please." She signed an illegible scrawl and handed the pen back to me.

"You better call me, shweetie," she reminded me. "What did you shay yer name wush?"

"Randy," I told her. "Randy Stanton. I'm in the book."

# Cursed

I WAS CURSED. That was the only explanation I had for why we were running our third call in Cloutier in less than twenty-four hours. Somehow, I had offended the EMS gods, and they were punishing me for my transgressions.

It was just past seven P.M., and the sun was already down. The strobes were making those weird flashbulb patterns on the pine trees. I knew an epileptic medic back in north Louisiana, and I wondered briefly how he dealt with the strobes and rotating lights. I idly leaned forward and flipped a phantom switch on the console, and a huge strobe mounted somewhere on the grill started flashing. It was incredibly bright, bathing everything in front of us in a harsh white glare. I traded a look with Lasson.

"How long has that strobe been there?" I asked.

"Ever since I started working up here with you." Lasson shrugged. "I never knew it worked."

"Neither did I. The switch wasn't labeled," I pointed out.

"You know," Lasson said, "I once had a jumpsuit like that. I wore it for six months before I found all the pockets. Seemed like every time I reached for something, I found a new one."

The call was dispatched as a generic "unknown medical emergency," which in Cloutier meant it would be a demonic possession, a toddler swallowed by an alligator, or some redneck with his penis caught in a bear trap. Whatever we found would be memorable, of that I was sure.

The address to which we were dispatched turned out to be a house trailer on stilts on the banks of the Pearl River. The stilts were tall enough that whoever lived there parked his truck and bass boat under his house. This person apparently recycled his empty beer cans, tossing the empties out of the sliding patio doors at the rear of the trailer. They'd formed quite an impressive mound, at least seven feet tall. There must have been ten years' worth of empties in that pile. Then again, this being Cloutier, it might have been a week's worth.

Lasson and I left the stretcher on the ground, hoping fervently that our patient was ambulatory. We didn't have a stair chair, and until now I really hadn't seen the need for one. We grabbed our equipment and lugged it up the steps. For once, there was an immediate answer to our knock on the door.

"Come on in!" a man called. Inside, there was a slovenly man lounging in a recliner, television remote in hand. He was wearing a T-shirt emblazoned with a silhouette of a revolver and the words "Gun control means hitting your target." He jerked his thumb toward the hallway. "Inna back," he grunted. "My momma's sick."

Lasson and I squeezed past his chair with our gear. He made no move to get out of the recliner, or even to lower the footrest to make room. In the rearmost bedroom of the trailer, there was a fat woman lying on the bed with her head propped up on so many pillows that her chin was touching her chest. There was a puddle of vomit on her flannel nightgown, and she was doing the death rattle, every breath a gurgling heave for air. The stench of alcohol on her breath was overpowering. She had a home nebulizer machine lying on the nightstand and an impressive array of pill bottles scattered around.

I jerked the pillows from under her and tilted her head, and her breathing improved only a little. Lasson cursed and sprinted for the rig to retrieve the one piece of equipment we'd left downstairs—the suction unit. I tried to rake vomit from her mouth with my fingers, but there wasn't all that much in there. While I was waiting on Lasson, I grabbed a BVM and bellowed for the man in the living room.

"Sir!" I yelled. "Could you come in here, please?"

I started ventilating the woman as best I could, considering I was wedged between her and the headboard on a full-motion waterbed. I wound up folding one leg lotus-style and propping her head across my knee, holding a mask seal with both hands and squeezing the bag under my right arm. Maybe every other ventilation went in. The man strolled into the bedroom and propped a hairy arm on the door frame.

"Yeah?" he asked. I looked at him expectantly, but he just gave me a blank stare in return, as if it was nothing unusual to see a total stranger performing artificial ventilations on his mother.

"Uh, you want to tell me what happened?" I prompted. I felt the entire trailer shudder as Lasson pounded up the steps.

"I put her to bed about five," he said, "and then I couldn't wake her up for supper, so I called y'all." Lasson burst into the room past him and handed me a suction catheter, already attached to the unit. I stopped ventilating briefly to suction, but get precious little fluids out.

"You called Stat Fleet, or you called 911?" I ask.

"Stat Fleet," he answered. "She has a membership."

Well, that explained why Cloutier EMS wasn't there. Dispatch hadn't bothered calling them.

"So she's been this way for about two hours?" I asked. "What kind of medical history does she have?"

"Naw, since five this morning," he corrected me. "We were up all night celebrating my birthday."

"Well, how was she when you put her in the bed?"

"About like now." He gestures toward the bed. "We killed about a fifth of Crown Royal between us," he added proudly.

*How touching! There's nothing that says "I love you" better than matching your grown son, drink for drink, to celebrate his birthday. Apparently she wanted to show him she could still drink him under the table, just like when he was a little sprout.*

"You were telling me about her medical history?" I prodded.

"Shit, I don't know." He shrugged. "She got lotsa problems. All her medicine is right there," he said, pointing toward the table.

Lasson handed me a laryngoscope and an endotracheal tube, and started gathering the medications from the table.

He was reading my mind. Before I could ask for something, he already had it done.

I quickly intubated her and inflated the cuff on the tube. I bagged gently as Lasson auscultated her chest and epigastrum. He nodded in affirmation.

"You're in," he told me. "Lungs sound like she's aspirated a lot, though."

"Well, let's get ready to move her," I told him.

I began pulling the fitted sheet from the bed while Lasson put her medications in a plastic bowl that, unless I missed my guess, was a Cool Whip container in a previous life.

"Bronchodilators, potassium, oral diabetic meds, something called Dyazide, and Prilosec," he told me.

Well, that told me enough. She had asthma or COPD, non-insulin-dependent diabetes, and maybe hypertension or congestive heart failure.

Lasson tossed the sealed bowl onto the bed and we bundled the woman in the bedsheet. I looked at her son.

"Sir, I need you to get one end of the sheet," I directed. "We're going to carry her to the ambulance on the sheet." He held up his hands and shook his head.

"I got a bad back," he protested. "I'm on disability."

"Look, she needs to be in a hospital right now, and my hands are full. Either get one end of the sheet, or let her die right here. Your choice," I told him flatly. I didn't trust this cretin to bag her while Lasson and I did the grunt work.

"All right, all right." He sighed heavily, grabbing the sheet bundled around his mother's head. We moved gingerly out of the trailer, bumping into walls and knocking things over, sweating and cursing, but eventually made it down to the stretcher. Miraculously, we were all in one piece, and my tube was still patent.

We deposited the lady on the stretcher, and the man straightened up and groaned, massaging his back. I had a hard time working up any sympathy.

*If there is any justice in this world, a fraud investigator just caught that on videotape.*

"Are you going to follow us to the hospital?" I wanted to know. He shook his head.

"Naw, just have 'em call me," he said, unconcerned. Without another word, he turned around and trudged back up the steps.

In the truck, Lasson checked a quick blood glucose, and the monitor read "Lo," which for our machines was less than forty. Lasson got out IV supplies while I opened the drug kit with one hand. I tossed a box of 50 percent dextrose onto the seat beside him. He got a line quicker than I could have, and administered the D50. The woman didn't come around immediately, so he backed out of the rig, slammed the doors, and drove us back down the rutted, potholed road to the main highway. When he reached the blacktop, he hit the lights and siren and put the hammer down.

In twenty minutes, we were at the hospital in East Chillicothe. Dr. Abrams, the physician who was on duty when I'd brought in the old man, greeted us at the nurses' desk. He was usually an asshole to anyone wearing a Stat Fleet uniform, which was understandable if not terribly professional. East Chillicothe Parish Hospital was the base hospital for one of our competitors. For some reason, Abrams usually cut me a break. I suspect it's because he was a good friend of Samir Saleh, and because I'd let him know quickly that I would reciprocate any nasty attitude he had.

"Every time I see you, you're bringing me an intubated patient," he greeted us gruffly. I grinned at him and gave him the story. He listened patiently, then grunted, "Didn't you just bring me this patient?"

"That's what I was thinking." I grinned. "But this one is a female," I pointed out.

"In Cloutier, how can you tell?" he replied. "Put her in room two, please."

A few minutes later, I was sitting at the nurses' desk, drinking a Coke as I wrote my report. Abrams flopped down on the chair next to me and touched me on the arm.

"The old man died about an hour ago in the ICU," he told me. "I worked the code, but he was pretty much gone anyway."

"What was wrong with him?" I asked.

"Subarachnoid hemorrhage," he told me, "plus the aspiration pneumonia, and sepsis, too. Train wreck," he concluded tiredly.

"And this woman?" I ask, nodding toward the room.

"Aspiration and alcohol toxicity, of course." He rolled his eyes. "You want a square in the blood alcohol pool?" he asked teasingly.

"No, thanks, Doc," I chuckled. "Stat Fleet doesn't pay me enough to gamble."

"Then quit and come work for us," he replied, getting up from the chair and walking away.

Later, I told Lasson about the conversation. "Abrams tried to recruit me," I told him. Lasson said nothing, just raised his eyebrows. "How much do their medics make?" I asked.

"I have no idea," Lasson answered, "but if you quit and leave me alone at this fucking place, I'll hunt you down and kill you in your sleep."

# Turn Off That Pacemaker!

GREEN ACRES NURSING Home was keeping us in business those days. We'd transferred so many people in and out of that place that the call volume from Green Acres alone could easily have paid the bills. Our last regular dialysis patient had died a month ago, and Lasson and I were enjoying a brief reprieve from thrice-weekly trips to and from Lake Chillicothe. When we got called there on a dialysis transfer, dispatch wouldn't send us home as soon as we'd unloaded the patient. Instead, we'd spend the next three hours transferring patients from St. Peter's to the MRI center just down the street until our dialysis patient was ready to go back to DeVillier.

The MRI transfers were absurdly short; it was maybe one hundred feet from one door to the other. To top off the absurdity, John Garrett had convinced the Weavers that every run ticket should include two sets of vital signs—even for transfers that lasted fifteen seconds. So, I would take one legitimate set of vitals, and I'd get the second set by using the Force. I'd wave my hand over the patient and concentrate really hard, and the numbers would just magically appear in my head.

Without dialysis transfers to do, Lasson and I had had it easy for the past month, but into each life a little rain must fall, and this week it had been raining cats and dogs. Stat Fleet had picked up three regular dialysis patients in the past week, all from Green Acres. It might have been just coincidence, but I suspect Old Man Weaver had been sneaking around, lacing cans of Ensure with antifreeze.

We arrived at Green Acres to pick up our newest dialysis patient, but there was no one at the nurses' desk—no ward clerk, no aides, no nurse. There was a commotion down the hall, however, and presently the clerk came running up. She stopped short when she saw us, and said, "Oh! I was just about to call you guys!"

"Someone already did," I answered. "We're here to pick up Mr. Richard Comeaux."

She shook her head, trying to catch her breath. "That's not who I was calling you for. We've got a lady who needs an ambulance now"—she pointed back down the hall. "Hurry." I followed her down the hall with the stretcher and sent Lasson to the rig for our gear.

The patient was an overweight sixtyish woman lying on her side in the bed, dry-heaving over a pail. She was surrounded by a nursing staff in full panic mode, tripping over one another in their haste. One of them was attempting to get a blood pressure, one was attaching a pulse oximeter probe, and an aide was holding the vomit pail, with a distasteful expression on her face. She had a pretty good sympathy retch going herself.

The charge nurse was busy trying to apply oxygen between retches, the mask hooked to an oxygen concentrator purring quietly away, generating a whopping two liters per minute. I waited until she got out of the way, and then gently reached over and removed the mask. The nurse looked at me indignantly.

"Asphyxiation," I explained politely, "is not going to help her condition."

*Granted, your method is a bit more elegant than a pillow over her face, but the effect is the same. And judging by the expression on your face, you don't know what you're doing wrong, do you?*

"Hello, ma'am," I introduced myself to the patient, smiling and sitting on the bed next to her. "I'm Kelly. They tell me you're not feeling well. Is that right?" I picked up her hand and held it, surreptitiously checking her pulse. I couldn't feel a pulse, and her hand was cold.

"So sick," the lady groaned between retches. "I'm so weak I can hardly move."

"How long has this been going on?" I asked, squeezing her hand. Her capillary refill time was close to five seconds, and her fingertips were dark blue. Her breathing was pretty shallow, too.

"Just started," she groaned, rolling over onto her back. She tossed back and forth, as if she couldn't find a comfortable position.

"It began maybe ten minutes ago," the ward clerk confirmed. Lasson burst into the room behind her, huffing and puffing under the load of oxygen case, jump kit, and cardiac monitor. I motioned him to the bedside with the cardiac monitor.

"Got a pressure yet?" I asked the BP nurse hopefully.

She shook her head, her eyes closed in concentration.

*Kind of hard to see the gauge with your eyes closed, dear.*

"Let me give it a try," Lasson suggested gently. "Maybe a different set of ears…"

She made room for Lasson as I attached monitor leads. The rhythm was third-degree block, at a rate of about 35. We traded a look, and Lasson reached for the pacing pads.

"What was her pressure?" I asked him.

"Sixty over patent-pending," he answered grimly, slapping the anterior pad in place and handing me the other one. I attached the pad to her back, just under her left scapula, and we rolled her over onto her back.

"Ma'am, we've got to do something that's not going to be pleasant," I warned her. "We've got to pace your heart to control your heart rate, and you'll probably feel some discomfort."

*Translation: Stand by for excruciating pain.*

She tossed her head back and forth, groaning, "Anything's got to be better than this!"

I turned the knob to increase the pacing current, and presently she began to grunt in synchrony with the pacemaker. As I continued to increase the current, her chest muscles started twitching violently.

"Ooh! Ooh! Ooh! Ooh!" she gasped with each jolt of current. Her color didn't seem to be improving a lot, though.

"I know that hurts, ma'am," I said sympathetically, "but we'll be able to get you something for the pain in a moment." I nodded to Lasson, who was in the process of spiking a bag of saline. "How bad is the pain, ma'am?"

"I—don't—know—I've —never—felt—like—this—before!"

I suppressed a smile and turned to one of the nurses, she of the asphyxiating oxygen mask.

"Could you hook that mask up to our oxygen tank, please? Set it at ten liters," I ordered. She hesitated and looked at me suspiciously. I smiled. "With a face mask at two liters, the patient is probably getting more carbon dioxide than oxygen. You have to run the oxygen much faster than that," I explained. Understanding dawned on her face, and she scrambled to hook up the mask. It was immediately apparent that she had never handled a portable tank and regulator before, but eventually she figured it out and placed the mask back on our patient.

The lady was looking much better now. There were too many people in the way to obtain another pressure, but she has a strong radial pulse and her color was nice and pink. Her fingertips, while not pink, were a good deal less cyanotic than before.

Lasson was still digging around on the back of her left hand with a 22-gauge catheter, apparently without much success. There was a big vein readily visible in her antecubital fossa. I grabbed an 18-gauge catheter, rolled her right arm over, swabbed the site quickly with an antiseptic prep, and sank the catheter in the vein I found there.

I tapped Lasson on the shoulder and held out my hand for the line. Embarrassed, he handed me the line and I attached it, opening up the roller clamp to see that the saline was flowing freely. I grinned triumphantly at Lasson and held out my hand like a surgeon asking for an instrument.

"Venigard!" I barked imperiously. With a sour expression, he slapped it into my hand and slowly got up. He grimaced and massaged his knees. I chuckled to myself as I secured the IV.

With the assistance of the nursing staff, we loaded the lady onto the stretcher and boogied down the hall. She still looked good, despite the rhythmic grunting at seventy beats per minute.

"What about Mr. Comeaux?" the ward clerk wanted to know.

"Call Stat Fleet back and get them to send another ambulance," I tossed over my shoulder.

"Wait!" she called out. "Don't you want to know where to bring Mrs. Harrison?"

"Nope," I answered. "She's going to the closest facility. You might want to call DeVillier Community Hospital and let them know to where she should be transferred, though."

In the ambulance, I administered five milligrams of Valium to Mrs. Harrison. It didn't have much time to kick in before we arrived at the hospital, but she did seem to be marginally less anxious as we handed her off to Dr. Saleh.

"Third-degree block," I told him, showing him the strip. "Blood pressure was sixty over nothing. As you can see, we paced her. We got capture at seventy milliamps."

"Ouch," he said, grimacing. "Madam, we will give you some medicine for the pain as soon as we can," he said to her, gently touching her shoulder.

"She's already had five of Valium." I grinned. His shoulders drooped and he sighed heavily, shaking his head. He said nothing, just held out his pen.

I stuck my clipboard under it, and he obligingly signed his name, finally breaking into a wry smile.

"Get the hell out of here," he said, pointing toward the door, "but don't get too far. She's not going to be here long."

Lasson and I took his advice and swung by The Lemon Chill for an early lunch before we got sent to transfer purgatory for the next few hours. The Lemon Chill is a little taco stand that serves huge baked potatoes stuffed with spicy crawfish étouffée. They've got everything a growing boy needs: grease, shellfish, cayenne pepper, tomato sauce, garlic, green peppers, and onions, all wrapped in a huge load of sour cream and starchy potato. An intravenous infusion of lard would be only slightly unhealthier, but far less satisfying.

"I could have gotten that IV, you know," Lasson told me.

"Maybe," I allowed. "But you didn't, did you?"

"If I had stuck the antecubital veins like you did," he said defensively, "I would have."

"You got something against sticking an AC?" I inquired.

"We were taught in medic class to start at the hands first. They said the nurses get pissed if we stick the AC."

"Right on the first one, wrong on the second," I replied. "It makes sense to start low, but the nurses only bitch if you miss an AC stick. And when the patient is circling the drain, they're usually just happy you got a line, period."

"So how do I know the difference?" he asked around a mouthful of potato. "When do you decide to stick the AC?"

"Lasson, you're a better IV sticker than I am. You just gotta miss your share and make your share before you'll be able to tell. You're about to become a medic. When you get your patch, you will stick every patient you get, for any reason you can think of. After a while, though, you'll get some sense of who needs an IV and who doesn't, and you'll recognize the ones that need an IV right then."

"Good judgment comes from experience, and experience comes from bad judgment," Lasson summarized, forking a huge mouthful of potato into his mouth.

"A good doc told me that very thing once," I agreed. "I had just—"

"Medic 306, Dispatch," the radio interrupted.

"Go ahead," Lasson answered, spewing tiny pieces of potato into the microphone. I handed him a napkin.

"Priority Three call, DeVillier Community Hospital ER. Cardiac transfer going to Lake Chillicothe Regional ICU bed five."

"That's our lady," I said, getting up.

At DeVillier, Dr. Saleh had Mrs. Harrison ready to go. She was still being paced, but he also had a heparin drip and IV nitroglycerin running. From the looks of her, he'd given her plenty of morphine, too. She opened her eyes and answered when we called her name, but quickly drifted off again.

"Who's the accepting physician?" I asked Dr. Saleh as I accepted the transfer paperwork from him.

"Dr. Spencer," he answered, frowning.

*Oh, great, the Grim Reaper.*

"Anything I need to know?" I asked.

"Well, she's pretty well sedated, but her vitals are stable. I gave her two milligrams of atropine, and it didn't raise her rate enough to put the pacer in standby. Her enzymes are starting to elevate, too."

"No twelve lead?" I asked, leafing through the paperwork.

"No," he answered. "All we would see is pacemaker rhythm, and under the circumstances I was reluctant to turn the pacer off. He did ask me to bolus her with Retavase, though." He checked his watch. "She's due for the second bolus now." I waited as Samir gave her a second bolus of thrombolytic.

"Anything else, Doc? Any orders?"

"No, you know what to do if something goes wrong. Watch the nitro and her pressure. Dr. Spencer should be waiting for you in the ICU," he told me as Lasson and I transferred her over to our stretcher.

And the hits just kept on coming. I'd be lucky if I didn't get pissed off and say something less than polite to the man.

Saleh followed us to the rig and helped us sort out the tangles as we loaded Mrs. Harrison.

The trip to Lake Chillicothe was relatively uneventful. I did have to tweak the nitro and her fluids a little to keep her pressure up, but nothing drastic. Dr. Spencer was waiting for us when we entered the ICU.

He was a dyspeptic little man with a permanently sour expression, as if someone were holding a turd under his nose all the time. He held the unshakable opinion that all paramedics were trained monkeys barely capable of thinking for themselves. He was the kind of cardiologist who heard hoofbeats and automatically thought "zebra." Not surprisingly, he was known as the Grim Reaper among the ambulance crews.

"Hold it!" he ordered imperiously, holding his hand up like a traffic cop. We stopped in the hall and waited expectantly.

"Take that damned pacer off of her." He sniffed. "I want to see what her baseline rhythm is." The nurse reluctantly started to disconnect the pacemaker pads.

"Hold it!" I announced in a fairly credible mimicry of his nasal voice.

"Before you do that, we put her on your bed and you sign my form." I handed him my clipboard and he signed my form, then waited impatiently as we transferred Mrs. Harrison to their bed.

"Thank you, Dr. Spencer," I said brightly as I took my clipboard back. "So nice to see you again!" He snorted in disgust and turned his back on me. In the hall, I grabbed Lasson by the arm.

"Just wait a second," I whispered. "This might be good." The nurse had taken off the pacemaker pads and discovered that Mrs. Harrison was still in third-degree block. Dr. Spencer reached over and grabbed her wrist.

"I can't feel a pulse!" he announced. "Start CPR!" The nurse looked wide-eyed at Dr. Spencer. Mrs. Harrison looked wide-eyed at Dr. Spencer. Lasson and I just looked at each other.

"But, Dr. Spencer, she's still—" the nurse started to protest.

"Doesn't matter," Dr. Spencer snapped. "Her pressure is too low, and that rate is too low to sustain life. Start CPR now," he insisted. Very reluctantly, the nurse stepped up and began chest compressions. Lasson and I turned and walked away. Behind us, we could hear Mrs. Harrison protesting.

"Oh—shit—that—really—hurts—please—stop—doing—that— oh God— you—bastards —are—killing—me..." she was saying. Lasson just shook his head.

"You ever think about medical school?" I asked him as we walked to the elevator.

"Never thought I was smart enough," he answered. "How about you?"

"Well, I just think about guys like that," I said, nodding back toward the ICU, "and it gives me hope."

# What Do You Mean, Dead?

Mrs. smith had altered lab values. That was why she was going to the hospital, and that was why we'd been dispatched to do the transport. The only thing I couldn't figure out was why the call for a nonemergent transfer came in after midnight. Either somewhere in Lake Chillicothe there was a twenty-four-hour laboratory that did outpatient testing for the nursing homes, or it took someone six hours to realize that Mrs. Smith should not have a blood urea nitrogen level that matches her age.

There was no one at the nurses' desk, and at first glance there was no one in Mrs. Smith's room, either. There was light under the bathroom door, however, and someone was making noise, so I knocked. The door opened just a crack and a face peeked out. Realizing that it was the boys in the Big White Taxi, she smiled in greeting and opened the door fully.

The charge nurse, a licensed practical nurse, and an aide were busy bathing Mrs. Smith. They had her propped up in the bathtub and were scrubbing, combing, and washing every wrinkled nook and cranny. Mrs. Smith just lay there quietly, not moving.

"She'll be ready in a moment, guys. We thought it would take you a little longer to get here," the charge nurse, a particularly clueless animal named Roberta, said apologetically.

I just smiled and looked a little more closely at Mrs. Smith.

"No problem," I replied. "What's up?"

"Her lab values are altered," Roberta explained as she ran a comb through Mrs. Smith's damp hair. "Her BUN and creatinine are elevated, and her potassium is a little low. We're sending her to St. Peter's for IV fluids and rehydration."

Mrs. Smith still lay there quietly, not saying anything. For a lady sitting in warm bathwater, she looked pretty pale.

"So can't they bathe her at the hospital?" I asked.

"Lord, no!" Roberta replied, mortified. "Her family is really picky, and they're supposed to meet you at the hospital. We're just trying to head off any complaints the family might have."

"They're pretty hard to please, huh?" I grunted sympathetically. Roberta nodded gravely. "Well," I told her, "imagine how pissed they're going to be when they find out she's dead."

"Well, they usually don't need a legitimate reason to—huh? What do you mean, 'dead'?"

"That lady is dead, Roberta. I've been watching you guys bathe her for maybe sixty seconds, and she hasn't even taken a breath," I pointed out. "Please tell me she has a DNR?"

They all just stared blankly at me, then down at Mrs. Smith, and as one person they jerked back their hands and backed away as if she were radioactive. Mrs. Smith slowly slid off the backrest and slipped under the water.

"Shit!" I blurted, bolting forward and catching her by the hair before she went completely under. I grabbed her under her arms, soaking my uniform shirt in the process, and struggled to pull her out of the tub. "Uh, you guys want to give me a hand here?" I asked, but they were still standing mutely, glued to the walls.

"Get the hell out of the way!" Lasson barked, shoving Roberta aside. He pushed into the room and we each took an arm, pulling Mrs. Smith unceremoniously from the tub onto the floor. The spell broken, Roberta fled the room, heading in the direction of the nurses' station.

Lasson and I started CPR, kneeling in the growing puddle of water on the floor. We needed our equipment, and all of it was in the truck.

"One of you ladies needs to get me your BVM," I order. I didn't relish the idea of doing mouth-to-mouth on this lady. They both continued to look at me with the deer-in-the-headlights stare.

"I need the BVM," I repeated. "Ambu bag? Little round thing with a mask on one end and oxygen tubing on the other?" I mimed squeezing a bag with my hand. Apparently, the CPR charades did the trick, because both of them bolted in the same direction down the hall. The aide came back holding the BVM I'd requested. She tried to hand it to Lasson, but he shook his head.

"No way," he said. "You take over. I've got to go get our equipment." He sprinted for the rig, and the aide reluctantly took his place and began bagging. After about four attempts of what could only charitably be called ventilations, I called for a switch. Gratefully, she scooted around and took up a position to do chest compressions. We got a couple of cycles completed, and Lasson came back into the room.

"Call it off," he said. "She's got a DNR." He was holding that precious piece of paper in his hand and had a relieved smile on his face. Without another word, I stood up to the accompanying music of creaking, popping knees. My pants were soaked from the knees down. Lasson and I followed the aide back down the hall to the nurses' station. Roberta was on the phone, talking to someone. She had the phone wedged to one ear as she hurriedly copied papers from Mrs. Smith's chart.

She finally got off the phone and turned to us. Her eyes were red and her lower lip was quivering. "I've almost got all the transfer paperwork ready. I just notified the hospital that you're coming."

"Coming with who?" I asked. "Mrs. Smith has a DNR, doesn't she?" She nodded in affirmation. "Then we won't be taking Mrs. Smith anywhere. Your next calls should be to the coroner and the funeral home."

"You mean you're not going to take her to the hospital?" Roberta looked heartbroken. Her lip quivered more and more, tears welled up in her eyes, and then the floodgates opened. She slumped into a chair and put her head in her hands, sobbing. Lasson and I watched her for a few moments, unsure of what to do. Finally, I wrote down the number of the Chillicothe Parish coroner on a piece of paper and handed it to the LPN.

"Here's the number for the coroner's office. Maybe you should be the one to make the call," I suggested. "And see if you can get in touch with your administrator to get some relief for Roberta." Lasson and I left her there holding the scrap of paper in her hand, with Roberta sobbing brokenly on the other side of the desk.

Six hours later, we were called back to Green Acres for a patient who had aspirated. The nursing director greeted us at the patient's room. Roberta's shift shouldn't have been over yet. Apparently, the boss nurse had

had to fill in for her.

"Mrs. Robicheaux has aspirated," she said authoritatively. "She's running a fever of 104 degrees, and she has some coarse crackles in her upper lung fields. Her blood pressure is 85/50, and her heart rate is 120."

"Okay," I said agreeably. "What makes you think she aspirated something?"

The lady looked emaciated and impossibly old, but she didn't have any type of feeding tube. Neither was there any evidence of vomiting. The old lady was awake but incoherent. Her breathing sounded pretty nasty.

"Well, she's running a fever and her lungs are junky," she explained slowly, as if to a backward child.

*Which could just as easily be a sign of pneumonia, smartass.*

"Is this her normal mental status?" I asked mildly, ignoring her condescending tone.

"Yes, it is!" she snapped. "This is the Alzheimer's unit, you know!"

*Apparently, it has permutated into a virulent airborne strain, and you and your staff have come down with an advanced case of it. Give it another couple of years, and you'll be able to hide your own Easter eggs.*

Lasson was checking another pressure, which served only to further aggravate the nurse.

"There's no need for that," she snapped at him. "I already told you her vital signs! You just need to load her up and take her to the hospital!"

Lasson said nothing, just calmly stood back up and started getting Mrs. Robicheaux ready to be moved. He pulled the cover off the bed, found the Foley catheter where it was hanging on the bed frame, and placed the catheter bag on the sheet between her legs. We quickly transferred Mrs. Robicheaux to the cot, thanked the nurse for her fine work, and left.

At the hospital, Mary greeted us at the ER desk. "Poor Mrs. Robicheaux," she said sympathetically. "Urosepsis again?"

"The director of nursing is of the opinion that it's aspiration pneumonia," Lasson said drily, holding up the Foley bag, "but I think I'll go with your diagnosis. Somehow I don't think her urine should look like beef broth with sea monkeys swimming in it."

Mary did a spit take, shooting Dr Pepper out of her nose. "Jesus Christ!" She coughed. Lasson smiled benignly, proud of his wit.

"Where do you want Mrs. Robicheaux?" I asked.

"Give me a minute to clean the bed, and you can put her in bed one," she said, shaking her head and chuckling. "You know, this poor lady comes here every couple of months with urinary tract infections. She's got cooties that Vancomycin won't touch. And of course, the nursing home does such wonderful cath care..." she concluded, her voice dripping with sarcasm.

"You mean they don't change those things regularly?" I asked in feigned disbelief. "I am shocked! Next you'll be telling me that they don't actually turn their patients every two hours!"

"Nothing you could tell me about that place would surprise me," she said. Lasson and I exchanged knowing grins.

"I bet we could," I challenged, checking my watch. "Let me tell you all about it over breakfast."

# Karma

RICKY GASTON SR. wasn't going to make it. I came to this conclusion based on Kelly's "Theory of Multiple Systems Trauma," which basically states that the more interventions I do, the more fucked you are. This isn't because I don't know what I'm doing—I do. It's because if I have time to intubate you, start two IVs, decompress your chest, bandage all your minor wounds, and splint your fractures, and you still aren't at the trauma center, you will soon be admitted to the Eternal Care Unit.

I'd done all of these things to Ricky Senior—all of them en route to the hospital—and we were still eight minutes from Lake Chillicothe. Of the successful trauma resuscitations I've had, most can be attributed more to my partners' lead feet than to my prodigious paramedic skills.

Over the years I've become a believer in karma, and that night the cosmic scales had balanced the sins of the Gaston brothers. The irony was just too rich to ignore.

On the very day they'd posted bail for shooting Donna, they'd made separate plans to celebrate their newfound, if temporary, freedom. Apparently, Ricky Senior's plan was to get tanked up on alcohol, hop in his El Camino, and drive down Greenwell Springs Road playing chicken with oncoming traffic. His brother Vincent was doing pretty much the same thing on his motorcycle, driving north on Greenwell Springs Road, and— you guessed it—both of them zigged when they should have zagged.

See what I mean about karma? What goes around comes around. Of course, I'd rather not contemplate my karma, because I must have done something pretty twisted to deserve the weird calls I got from Cloutier.

Vincent was dead on arrival, and Ricky Senior wasn't far from joining him. I intubated him in the car, managing somehow to get battery acid on the leg of my spiffy polyester pants in the process. My leg felt like it was on fire, and I idly wondered if the fabric would melt to my leg once the acid ate all the way through my pants.

I was bagging Ricky Senior and running fluids in at a wide-open rate, and Lasson was doing his part by administering the wide-open diesel infusion, but it wasn't enough. Two minutes out from Chillicothe Regional, he arrested. He was in a slow, wide pulseless electrical activity rhythm, the kind that's salvageable only in the advanced cardiac life support books. I gave him some epinephrine and atropine, and performed chest compressions on the way into the Emergency Department, but it was a futile effort. After twenty minutes of frantic activity, cracking his chest and bolusing O-negative blood along with the drugs, Dr. Hennesey finally called it.

Misreading the look on my face, he gave me a friendly pat on the shoulder as he walked past, as if to say, "You did all you could."

I knew I did. I did more than most paramedics could. What was bothering me was the thought that I couldn't shake, the one that says "no great loss" to the death of two people. A good paramedic shouldn't think that way.

On our next shift, Lance Bidwell told us that Mrs. Gaston, the matriarch of the clan, had killed herself over the weekend. With her sons dead, her grandson still relearning how to walk, talk, and feed himself, and still estranged from her daughter-in-law, she put a .410 shotgun under her chin and spattered her brains all over the ceiling.

Lance told the tale with relish. It was an entertaining gore-fest of a war story, and I laughed and said "No shit!" at all the appropriate points, but I found myself troubled by an unsettling feeling. I'd always thought that what made me a good medic wasn't so much my skills as my rapport with patients, but lately I'd been feeling that compassion was just a mask I wore to put people at ease. I didn't feel anything, even when an entire family had been wiped out, and the numbness scared me.

What the hell was wrong with me?

# Better Him than Me

SAMIR SALEH HAD become the chief of staff at DeVillier Community Hospital. With Dr. Alex's impending retirement, he was starting to build a rather successful practice. She hadn't been taking new patients for some months now, instead referring them all to Samir. He was an excellent clinician, well versed in current medical theory, and he was cool and calm under pressure. You had to earn respect from him, but once you'd earned it, he trusted you implicitly. In other words, he was my kind of guy. We'd become pretty good friends, despite our distance from each other in the medical pecking order. More than once, he'd asked me when I was going to stop doing this "paramedic thing."

"Seriously, my friend," he told me, leaning forward over his McDonald's deluxe breakfast, "when are you going back to school?"

Breakfast at McDonald's had become an end-of-shift tradition with us. He ate my hash browns, and I ate his bacon and sausage. We'd managed to corrupt Samir a good bit, even to the point of buying his own redneck-mobile—a shiny new black Chevy Z71 four-wheel drive—but he was not about to start eating pork.

"I've defaulted on my student loans, Samir," I explained. "They're keeping my income tax return this year to pay the balance. Maybe when it's paid off..."

"You need to get back to school!" he insisted. "Doing this paramedic thing is okay for now, but you are going to be married soon. You need to become a doctor, for yourself and for your family."

"Look, I enjoy 'doing this paramedic thing,' okay?" I retorted. "It's not just my job, man. It's who I am. I'm good at it."

"The best I've ever worked with," he agreed, "and I trained in Chicago and New Orleans. But medicine is medicine, my friend. It doesn't matter where you practice it. You could be so much more. You should be so much more," he concluded, frustrated. For my part, I felt embarrassed. As big as my ego is, and I'll freely admit it's huge, praise makes me uncomfortable.

"I couldn't afford medical school anyway. And I'd have a hard enough time working my way through college that I might not even get into medical school. I'm not eighteen years old anymore, and I've been out of school for so long, I'd have to take everything over again."

"Those are just excuses," he said impatiently. "You know, DeVillier would pay for your medical school, if you signed a contract to come back and practice here. They might even pay for college."

"How do you know that?" I asked, curious.

"I've been talking to Buddy about it," he informed me smugly. Buddy Goff was the mayor of DeVillier, and the man who'd recruited Samir.

"You've been talking to Buddy about me?" I asked, astonished. Samir nodded seriously. He had given this some thought, and it was becoming obvious that I should, too.

"I'd hate to just run a clinic," I said, as one last weak attempt at protest. "I love emergency medicine."

"So specialize in emergency medicine, and hang out a shingle as an internist," he retorted. "You don't have to be board-certified to practice around here. Hell, I'm the only board-certified physician of any kind in this town, and all the others have bigger practices than mine," he said with a snort. "Besides," he added, "The American College of Emergency Physicians now recognizes a pediatrics subspecialty. That would be perfect for you. You're good with kids."

"Don't remind me, you sonofabitch," I said, rolling my eyes. "I still can't believe you did that to me!"

"It was necessary!" he protested, grinning. "That lady and her child were better off with you than with me. I don't do babies."

No shit, you don't do babies, you big chicken. You just pawn 'em off on me.

The night before, Samir had called us for an obstetrical transfer to Moss Point. He and Mary were both busy charting when we arrived, but waved us into the room ahead of them.

"Go ahead and load her," Samir ordered. "I'll be with you in a second."

Lasson and I rolled the stretcher into the ER and introduced ourselves to our patient, a twenty-four-year-old girl named Tameka. With just a few questions, I learned that Tameka was thirty-eight weeks pregnant with her fourth child, she had had no complications with her pregnancy, and she was expecting a little girl. Her second child was born at thirty weeks, but was otherwise healthy. Her other two children were carried to term and delivered vaginally without any complications.

Tameka was uncomfortable, but didn't feel the urge to push or move her bowels. Her water had broken about thirty minutes earlier, which was why her mother had driven her to the hospital. By the time Samir was ready to give us a report, we had Tameka loaded and ready to go.

"Well, I see they have you all squared away," Samir greeted her warmly when he walked into the ER. Turning to me, he said, "She is thirty-eight weeks, no complications so far. Her water broke about forty-five minutes ago, with no meconium present as far as I could tell. She is gravida four, para three, with three surviving children. Fetal heart tones are normal, at a rate of about 140. Her contractions are six minutes apart, and about thirty seconds in duration. She is, oh, maybe three or four centimeters dilated, I think," he said judiciously. He seemed a little rushed, but I didn't think too much of it at the time, attributing it to his natural squeamishness with kids and newborn babies.

"Where are we taking her?" I asked.

"She's going to Moss Point, in the Labor and Delivery Unit. I've already notified them, and I have all your paperwork right here," he said, thrusting the packet into my hands. "Now go."

"Okay," I said, curious about what had him in such a hurry.

He walked ahead of the stretcher, opening the doors for us and then helping us load Tameka into the ambulance. He slammed the rear doors on the ambulance, slapped them twice, and walked back into the hospital without another word.

What had his panties in a bunch?

I didn't have to wonder long. Lasson was driving at his usual speedy clip, but we weren't running hot. Maybe twenty minutes into the trip, I was sorting paperwork, taking vital signs, and untangling the oxygen and IV tubing when Tameka cried out.

"Ooooooohhh!" she said, gritting her teeth. "Shit, I gotta push!"

"You have to what?" I asked, moving over onto the bench seat to sit beside her. I placed my hand on her abdomen. "Are you having a contraction?"

"Just started," she said, nodding. "This is a hard one." I checked my watch and kept my hand on her abdomen, feeling her gravid uterus bunch up.

"Tell me when it stops, okay?" I reached into the cabinet and got out the obstetrical kit. Tameka just nodded, squeezing her eyes shut. She groaned for an alarmingly long time, then finally opened her eyes. I checked my watch to find that two minutes had passed.

I opened her IV wide open and replaced her nasal cannula with a mask, turning the oxygen flow up to eight liters. I opened the obstetrical kit and had Tameka lift her hips so I could slide a sterile drape beneath her. She lifted her hips slightly, then plunked them back down on the stretcher and screamed.

"Aaaahhhh, here it comes again!" she bellowed. "Shiiit, I gotta puuuush!" I peeked under the sheet to find her crowning. I checked my watch again to find that less than two minutes had passed since the last contraction.

*Goddamn you, Samir Saleh. Six minutes apart, my ass!*

"Do NOT push!" I told her. "Whatever you do, DO NOT PUSH!"

"Eight minutes out," Lasson called out. "You need to call report."

"Fuck report!" I blurted. "Light it up! You can call report for me!"

I rocked backward with the truck's acceleration as Lasson stuck his foot in the carburetor. He hit the lights and siren and started weaving through traffic. Hanging on to the ceiling bar, I struggled to keep my balance in the swaying truck.

"I've got Moss Point on the phone," Lasson called out. "What do you want me to say?"

"Tell them we'll be lucky if she doesn't deliver before we get there!" I hollered. "Tell them our ETA, and make sure they're ready!" Lasson dutifully relayed the information.

"They want to know how far apart the contractions are, how long they last, and what the baby's heart rate is," Lasson called out.

"What? She's crowning, for God's sake! What else do they need to know?"

"Okay," he called. "They'll be waiting for us in the L and D Unit."

"I've got news for you, Lasson," I replied. "We're not going to make it to the unit."

"Do you need me to pull over?" he called back, concerned.

I peeked under the sheet again, and saw baby hair. Lots of baby hair. Meanwhile, Tameka just kept grunting and pushing for all she was worth, despite my frantic pleas to the contrary.

"Just drive!" I hollered.

*By the time you get pulled over and get into the back, I'll have delivered this little girl.*

I proceeded to do precisely that. With one Herculean push from Tameka, the baby's head popped out. I grabbed the bulb syringe and suctioned thoroughly as I felt the truck brake hard, turn, and then shift into reverse. Before Lasson could fling open the rear doors, I had a wrinkled, bluish little infant lying on the stretcher between Tameka's legs.

"Almost made it!" Lasson cried happily. "Congratulations, Tameka!"

*When this is over, I'm going to strangle Samir Saleh, and then I'm coming after you, Lasson. Just for that, you get to clean the truck by yourself.*

I wrapped the little girl in a towel and scrubbed her vigorously, and presently her color improved and she began crying lustily. I hadn't even clamped or cut the cord when we rolled the stretcher into the ambulance entrance. The resident on duty unsuccessfully tried to block our way when we rolled into the Emergency Department, saying something about taking them both straight upstairs. I wordlessly handed him the cord clamps and scissors, then held out my arms, still holding the squirming little girl. He gave me a dumbfounded look, but proceeded to clamp and cut the cord.

"Tameka, can you scoot over to the other bed, please?" I asked her politely. After she had moved over, I handed her daughter to her. "Personally, I think 'Kelly' is a great name for a girl, if you haven't already got one picked out. Just a suggestion, of course." I grinned. She gave me an exhausted smile in return. I turned to the resident.

"They're all yours, Doc," I said to him, extending my clipboard. "Sign here, please." I took my signed form and my bloody stretcher and left him there, wondering what to do next.

When we got back to DeVillier, Samir had already gone home for the afternoon. Mary asked me, "Did you make it okay?"

"Nope," I replied, shaking my head. "I delivered right there in the ambulance bay at Moss Point."

"Oh, no!" she gasped. "Are the mother and the baby okay?"

"Just fine," I assured her. "I just can't figure it out, though. We should have had plenty of time to make it there before she delivered. Everything just went so fast, even considering it was her fourth delivery." Mary gave me a guilty look.

"About five minutes after you left, Dr. Saleh was charting. He looked up from his chart and asked me, 'Mary, about how much is four centimeters of dilation?' I held up my hands to show him"—she demonstrated, spreading her index and middle fingers about an inch apart—"and he just nodded and went back to charting. A minute or so later, he looked up and said, 'Mary, how much dilation is this?' He was holding his hand like this"—she demonstrated again, holding her hand cupped, like a blooming flower. "I said, 'Dr. Saleh, please tell me she wasn't that far along! That's fully dilated!' He just shook his head and stuck his nose back in the chart, and said, 'Better him than me. He's more comfortable with babies than I am, anyway.' I wanted to call you, but by then you were more than halfway there," she concluded sympathetically, then asked, "Are you sure you're okay?"

"I'm fine, babe," I assured her. "But when you see that sonofabitch later tonight, you tell him he's paying for breakfast in the morning."

# Uh, Who's Running the Hospital?

FIRST AMONG KELLY Grayson's "Great Observations About EMS" is the strange fact that although many of our fellow medical professionals deem us unworthy of respect, those same people will never hesitate to play paramedic when the opportunity presents itself. The first corollary to this rule is that whenever a doctor, nurse, or respiratory therapist feels the need to play paramedic, he or she will invariably fuck up, panic, or generally get in the way of the actual medics responding to the call.

I was reminded of this unfortunate fact as Lasson and I arrived at the scene of a motor vehicle accident right in front of DeVillier Community Hospital. A Chillicothe Parish sheriff's deputy had struck a gasoline tanker at high speed, and the entire staff of DeVillier Community Hospital was attending the poor deputy. A sea of green scrubs and white lab coats surrounded him, and Lasson and I had to part this sea to get to the patient.

The wreck itself wasn't too terribly bad. The tanker was essentially undamaged, but the deputy's patrol cruiser was firmly wedged beneath the undercarriage of the big rig. The cruiser's airbags had not deployed, which isn't that unusual, and there was minimal damage to the interior of the vehicle. From the looks of things, the tanker turned right in front of him as the deputy was leaving the parking lot of the DeVillier Police Department.

Dr. Idris had the driver's door open, and was yelling for everyone else to be quiet as he auscultated breath sounds. The deputy was grimacing and shaking his head, his arms wrapped around his chest. No one had stabilized his cervical spine. Julie Elton was standing on the passenger side of the cruiser, hands fluttering nervously. Apparently, her role was to run in place, beckon frantically, and shout "Hurry up!" when the ambulance arrived. It was a role tailor-made for her, one she'd played so often that she had become typecast as the prototypical hysterical nurse.

As we approached the car, Paula Roberts skidded up pushing

a wheelchair. "I got a wheelchair!" she said breathlessly to no one in particular.

"Good!" Lasson replied. "Why don't you put Julie in it and wheel her back to the ER?" he suggested.

"Everybody quiet!" Dr. Idris bellowed. "I cannot hear anything!" I butted Julie out of the way and leaned into the passenger window.

"What's up, Doc?" I inquired. "Need some help?"

"Yes." He nodded vigorously. "He struck the steering wheel with his chest, and the windshield with his head, and he is complaining of headache and neck—"

"Then why don't we immobilize his neck and get him out of the car?" I cut him off.

"Yes, of course!" Idris agreed. "If you will hand me a cervical collar, I will... "

"Dr. Idris," I said, "if you don't mind me asking, how many patients are in the hospital?"

"Eight," he replied automatically. "Why do you ask?"

"Well, from what I can see," I told him, looking significantly around me, "the entire medical staff of the hospital is out here. Who is taking care of the hospital patients?"

A horrified expression spread across his face and he backed hurriedly out of the car, bumping into Lasson, who was standing patiently behind him with a spine board, cervical collars, and head immobilizer.

"We'll take care of this one, Doc," Lasson assured him. "We'll have him in the ER in just a few minutes." Idris nodded gratefully, a nervous smile hovering around his lips.

"Everyone back to the hospital!" he barked, herding the nurses back across the street. Paula looked disappointed, pushing her wheelchair reluctantly back to the hospital.

Inside the car, I took the cervical collar from Lasson and applied it to the neck of the injured deputy, holding his head firmly in both hands. "You hurt anywhere, Mark?" I asked him. He unsuccessfully tried to nod his head. "My chest hurts a little," he admitted.

"Were you wearing your seatbelt?" Lasson asked, mockingly stern. Mark just looked embarrassed.

"Uh, actually I wasn't," he admitted sheepishly. "I was responding as backup on a traffic stop when this asshole turned right in front of me. I had just pulled out of the parking lot—didn't even have my seatbelt on."

"So you weren't going very fast?" Lasson inquired as he palpated Mark's chest.

"Maybe forty—ouch, that hurts!—miles an hour," Mark answered, flinching in pain. "I gassed it pretty hard as I was pulling out."

"Well, bud, looks like you busted some ribs," Lasson told him matter-of-factly, "but we'll know more when we get you to the hospital."

"Not this hospital, huh?" Mark asked fearfully. "Those people are fucking crazy!"

"Big tough guy like you shouldn't be afraid of a few petite little nurses," Lasson observed as we pivoted Mark onto the board. "Besides, we'll be there to hold your hand the whole time," he added, grinning wickedly. Mark just closed his eyes and groaned.

Inside the ER, Dr. Idris had things well in hand. Respiratory, lab, and radiology were all waiting patiently for us to arrive. We quickly slid Mark over to the hospital bed and got out of the way.

"Okay, I need a CBC, type and match, blood gases, chest and cervical spine films," Dr. Idris ordered. "Right now, everyone!" Julie moved around to the left side of the bed and wrapped an IV tourniquet around Mark's left arm.

"You want an IV, Doc?" I asked. "How about oxygen?"

*What the hell, if we're going to push the panic button, let's overtreat in spades, right?*

"Two IVs," he corrected, "and oxygen wouldn't be a bad idea. Lasson, why don't you give him a couple of liters per minute?"

*That's right, Doc. Get aggressive!*

I quickly spiked a bag of Ringer's solution and slipped a 14-gauge catheter in Mark's right arm. As I hooked up the IV tubing, I noticed Julie was kneeling at the other side of the bed, cursing under her breath.

She had Mark's arm dangling off the bed, hoping that gravity would help her find a suitable vein.

Lasson finished applying the nasal cannula and looked over Julie's shoulder at what she was doing. She had a 20-gauge catheter in Mark's left hand, and was methodically digging around, trying to puncture the big, engorged vein that ran across the back of his hand. Meanwhile, Mark was whimpering pitifully and sucking the bedsheet up his ass. Lasson shook his head in disgust. He picked up another IV catheter and looked over at me, eyebrows raised.

"Go ahead," I told him, "if you think you can get it." Rolling his eyes, Lasson leaned over Julie's shoulder and, with one hand, inserted a 16-gauge catheter in Mark's left arm.

"Hook that up for me, would you, Julie?" he asked politely. She slowly looked up at him in fury, attached the IV tubing to the catheter, and stomped from the room without another word.

A few minutes later, Mark's chest films showed two rib fractures on the left side, but no pneumothorax. Otherwise, there was nothing else we could find wrong with him. Within an hour, he was discharged home with a chest wrap and a prescription for analgesics. On the way home, Lasson wanted to know Julie's story.

"What's up her ass, anyway?" he asked.

"She doesn't like Stat Fleet in general, and me specifically," I replied. "She was the one who got me transferred to Medic 304. Now that I'm back, she can't stand it."

"Well, she might hate you, but she doesn't have any reason to dislike me," Lasson pointed out. "I haven't done anything to her."

"You're my partner," I replied, "so you're guilty by association. Plus, you made her look stupid, which admittedly isn't hard to do. I wouldn't let it bother you, though. If you're disliked by Julie Elton, and dislike her in return, you're in pretty good company."

# Pissing Contest

I SEEMED TO be developing a prodigious talent for pissing people off. I'm a nice guy. I was courteous and compassionate with my patients. Well, most of my patients. My coworkers liked me. The volunteer EMS agencies in the area worshipped graven images of me. But for some reason, I occasionally gave the wrong people a serious case of the red ass.

A cynic might say it's because I have a difficult time concealing my disdain for people I consider stupid. A cynic might say that I'm occasionally, unintentionally arrogant and condescending. But cynicism doesn't jibe with my overall sunny worldview, so I am forced to conclude that some people just search for reasons to get their panties in a bunch, and that I just tend to be their most convenient target. I'm sure that's what it is.

I mean, it sounds plausible, doesn't it?

The latest inductee to the "Kelly Grayson Hate Society" was Elaine Milner, the director of nursing at DeVillier Community Hospital. Elaine was a starchy old battle-ax who had fond memories of white nurse's caps, support stockings, and orthopedic shoes. She knew the original recipe for blood, was close personal friends with Florence Nightingale herself, and thought the rest of her staff could learn a lot from Julie Elton. Naturally, we cordially detested each other. The only thing that kept us on fairly amicable terms was the great relationship Lasson and I had with the doctors and her nursing staff, Julie excepted.

Our latest clash involved a patient suffering a myocardial infarction Lasson and I had just brought in to DeVillier. Since we didn't have a twenty-four-hour cath lab nearby, a lot of our chest-pain patients went to the local hospitals first. Lasson, Mary, and I had found our own little groove in treating ischemic chest pain. Quite often, the patient received a thrombolytic within fifteen minutes of arriving at the ER.

That wasn't the case this morning, however, primarily because Elaine

Milner seemed intent on getting in the way of everything we were trying to do. She had some very definite opinions about the role of paramedics, all of which can be summed up in three short sentences: She calls. We haul. That's all.

She probably had some vague idea that we did oxygen therapy and CPR, but not much more than that. So, being the nursing director, she was naturally curious as to why a paramedic was mixing an Activase infusion in her Emergency Department while his EMT-Basic partner was starting a heparin drip. Activase infusions were a Big Deal around here. A lot of the nurses treated the stuff like kryptonite, to be handled only in the direst of emergencies, and only when a physician had insisted upon it.

A lot of the help we gave the ER staff blurred the line between pre-hospital and Emergency Department. Hell, let's be realistic—it erased the line. Most of the nurses and doctors didn't have a problem with that, when it was necessary, but Elaine Milner and Julie Elton tended to get all pissy about it. Elaine blustered and protested everything Lasson and I did, asking inane questions and generally getting in the way. Mary seemed unfazed by her chicken-with-its-head-cut-off routine, but my tact and diplomacy were being sorely tested.

Finally, I looked at Dr. Alex with a plea in my eyes. "Elaine, don't you have something better to do?" asked Dr. Alex, taking the hint.

Mrs. Milner, who had just spiked a bottle of nitroglycerin with the wrong tubing, stopped what she was doing and just stared blankly at Dr. Alex, who simply stared back. "I think Mary and the paramedics have this under control," Dr. Alex said firmly.

"But they're not supposed to—"

"Elaine, let these people do their jobs," she said evenly. "They know what they are doing."

"But Mary needs the help!" Elaine protested. Mary said nothing, just quietly took the nitroglycerin setup from Elaine and changed the tubing.

"They have it under control," Dr. Alex repeated. "Why don't you get on the phone with the house supervisor at St. Peter's and arrange for an ICU bed for this man?"

"Mary can do that later," Elaine blustered. "I really think we need to—"

"Leave, Elaine," Dr. Alex ordered bluntly, pointing to the door. "You are getting in the way."

Ouch, that stung! But the good doctor had a point. At least Dr. Alex knew when to step aside.

Mrs. Milner just glowered furiously, the color rising in her face, then stomped out of the room. Lasson and I breathed a sigh of relief. The patient just looked from one face to the other, bewildered by the exchange.

"She'll make you pay for that," Mary informed us grimly.

"But we didn't do anything!" Lasson objected. "Dr. Alex asked her to leave."

"You made her look stupid," Mary pointed out. "She's not going to do anything to me, and she can't do anything to Dr. Alex, but she can do something to you. It's just a matter of when."

"Let her," I retorted. "I didn't say a word to her. I wasn't rude, and I wasn't condescending. She has nothing to complain about."

"You can be condescending without saying a word," Mary said ruefully, shaking her head. "As far as she's concerned, you overstepped your bounds, and then you saw her ordered out of her own ER. She won't let it pass," she concluded simply.

I was afraid she was right.

Later that evening, Lasson and I stopped by the hospital to return the IV pumps we'd used. Thankfully, Mrs. Milner had long since left for the day, and Mary's shift ended in ten minutes.

"Brought back your stuff," I told her, depositing the pumps on the desk at the nurses' station. "Got your Activase replaced, too," I added, handing her the vial I'd picked up from the pharmacy at St. Peter's.

"Thanks." She smiled tiredly. "Any problems with the trip?"

"Nah, he did fine," I told her. "Want to get some dinner when your shift ends?"

"Sounds good," she answered, checking her watch, "but I have one condition. Lay off my boss. Mrs. Milner may be a little behind the times, but she's a good nurse."

"Bullshit," I said flatly. "She's useless, and she panics. You're twice the nurse she is."

"She is a good nurse," Mary insisted doggedly. "Not every nurse is comfortable with emergencies. Mrs. Milner has thirty years of experience, and she looks after us. She's a good boss," she concluded.

"Okay, fine, she's a good boss," I relented, "but she has a serious attitude problem where paramedics are concerned."

"And I suppose you don't have a problem with nurses?" she asked, amused. "Did it ever occur to you that she just mirrors your attitude? You intimidate the hell out of every nurse here."

"I do not intimidate people," I protested. "I make it a point to be courteous and professional. Sometimes I joke around and tease people, but that's just to lighten everybody up."

"Yes, you do intimidate people," Lasson interjected, "even the other medics. You never get flustered, and you know the answer to everything. That can be very intimidating," he concluded simply.

*Damn, do I really do that? If they only knew...*

"Even to you guys?" I asked them both. "Do I intimidate you?"

"Nah, we know how full of shit you really are," Lasson said, grinning evilly.

"And I've seen you naked," Mary pointed out playfully. "Nothing intimidating there!"

*Well, fuck you both very much.*

# Deep in the Arms of Prince Valium

THERE WAS AN eight-year-old girl seizing somewhere just ahead. It was two in the morning, and we had no idea where we were going. The girl's aunt had notified us of the emergency by pounding frantically on our station door until we woke up. Apparently they had no phone at this little girl's house, or they did have a phone but had not grasped the concept of 911. Why the woman didn't just throw her niece in the car and drive her to the ambulance station, I'll never know.

I had given up trying to figure out some of the things people do when they're panicked. The woman was lucky she woke us up at all. Lasson couldn't hear anything from his bedroom, and I had trained my ears to register only two noises when I am sleeping—my pager tones, and anyone calling my unit number on the radio.

Lasson and I tried to keep the taillights of her green Chevy Nova in sight as she weaved through the back roads of southern Choctaw Parish as if she were auditioning for a role in *The Dukes of Hazzard*. Frankly, I wasn't that concerned. Provided we could avoid dying in a fiery crash before we got there, we would no doubt find a postictal kid and a room full of hysterical family.

I've learned over the years that most seizure patients are best treated with "Tincture of Time" and "Benign Neglect." By the time we arrive on scene, they're usually postictal. On the odd occasion when they are still seizing, they usually stop before I even draw up the Valium. After the mother of all seizures we'd experienced with little Ricky Gaston, nothing else held much fear for me.

We cautiously pulled into the driveway behind Auntie Whatsername, who stopped in a boiling cloud of dust, skidding into the yard in a sideways bootlegger slide. She scrambled out of the car and hit the front porch at a dead run, taking the steps two at a time. The scene wasn't unusual for these parts: a dusty yard, a tire swing, a house that is mobile, and five cars that aren't.

Inside, there was the expected crowd of panicky family, and, to my surprise, a still-seizing child. She was a delicate little thing, pale and freckled, with flaming red hair. She was lying cradled in her daddy's frightened arms, in the throes of a violent grand mal seizure. She was burning up with fever and had lost control of her bladder, and was urinating all over herself and her daddy's legs.

"How long has she been seizing?" I asked as I knelt down next to them, careful to avoid the wet spot on the carpet. Lasson quickly applied a non-rebreather mask and went about assessing vital signs.

"*Mais non*, she done had a fit!" the father sobbed in a thick Cajun accent. "She been fittin' for a long, long time."

"Does she have a history of seizures?" I asked, to the blank stares of everyone present. "Fits?" I clarified. "She ever had a fit before? Does she take medicine for it?" The aunt nodded nervously, handing me a bottle of Dilantin.

"Does she take her Dilantin regularly?" I asked as I opened my narcotics pouch, only to be answered by more blank stares.

*Shit. Sooner or later, I have got to learn Cajun French.*

"Her fit medicine? Does she take it all the time?" The aunt nodded again.

I grabbed a syringe and needle while Lasson searched for a decent IV site. I pierced the vial of Valium with the needle and injected a little air, and the rubber stopper blew out of the vial, squirting ten milligrams of Valium directly into my eyes.

Okay, THAT was not supposed to happen. The Valium was supposed to have drawn quickly and freely into my syringe when I pressurized the vial. The vial was not supposed to explode and squirt a double dose of Valium into my eyes. This qualified as a Big Problem. Shit, that stuff burned!

I blinked my eyes rapidly to clear them, but there was still an oily haze of Valium clouding my vision. I could dimly make out Lasson's figure as he shook me by the shoulder.

"Kelly, are you okay?" he asked, alarmed.

"I'm fine." I nodded uncertainly as I wiped at my eyes and blinked furiously. "I just can't see very well. You're going to have to give the Valium."

"I can't get an IV!" he blurted. "How am I supposed to give it?"

"Rectal," I answered. "Give it to her rectally." Try as I might, I could not clear my eyes, although they were no longer burning.

"How much?" Lasson wanted to know. "I have no idea how much to give a kid!"

"Just hold on a minute," I told him calmly, trying to remember the dose. "Give her five milligrams—no, wait—make that ten milligrams."

"The whole thing?" Lasson asked dubiously. I nodded as reassuringly as I could.

"The whole thing," I confirmed. "The rectal dose is double the IV dose, and her IV dose ought to be around five milligrams. Just draw it up, take the needle off the syringe, lube up the syringe, and squirt it in her rectum."

I turned to the family members clustered behind me and asked, "Can someone point me to a sink where I can wash this stuff out of my eyes?" One of them took my arm and guided me to the bathroom.

After flushing my eyes thoroughly, my vision cleared somewhat, although I'd managed to soak the front of my uniform shirt in the process. I could see fairly well, although the edges of things still seemed a little blurry. My vision was not what concerns me, however. I was starting to feel a little, well, weird. It's kind of hard to describe, but suddenly the situation didn't seem so bad after all. In fact, things were just rosy. I was Supermedic, and there was nothing I couldn't handle.

I sauntered back into the living room to find that Lasson had finished packing up our gear. He was daintily holding a syringe stained with feces, looking for someplace to put it. He finally just took off his gloves, turning them inside out around the syringe and dropping them on the stretcher. Our patient was still seizing, her daddy rocking her back and forth and crooning softly to her.

"Are you all right?" Lasson asked warily.

"Fine and dandy," I answered, smiling benignly. "Shall we go to the hospital now?"

Shaking his head and muttering, Lasson helped me lower the stretcher, and the girl's father gently deposited her on it. As we strapped her carefully in place, I had some trouble making the buckle ends mate properly. They just wouldn't fit, no matter how hard I tried. I stared at them stupidly until Lasson snatched them away and fastened them correctly.

*Oh, that's right. A male buckle won't mate with another male buckle. You need one male buckle and one female buckle, unless of course you have two homosexual buckles...*

After we loaded the stretcher, Lasson grabbed me by the arm and hissed in my ear. "Are you sure you're okay to ride in with her?" he demanded.

"Whatever you want." I smiled agreeably. "I can do it all. I can drive, or I can tech—"

Cursing under his breath, Lasson spun me around, pushed me into the back of the rig, and slammed the doors behind me. I took up a position on the bench seat beside my patient, who had finally stopped seizing. Groovy. She looked so peaceful, lying there and snoring like that. She could almost be asleep. *...Why is the reservoir bag on her mask collapsed like that? Maybe I should switch her over to the main oxygen tank. Yeah, that should work. Wait a minute—why isn't this damned flow meter working? I've turned it all the way open, and there's still no—Hey! I'll bet it would work better if I opened the valve on the oxygen tank! Yup, that did the trick. It's all good now. She's definitely postictal. I wonder how they came up with that word? It must mean "after-ictal," which means that she must have been "ictal" before. Does "ictal" mean the same as seizure, and if so, why don't they just call it "postseizure"? I wonder what the doc would say if I said that the patient was in grand mal "ictal." I bet he wouldn't know what I was—Hey! We're at the hospital already! Boy, that was a quick trip...*

Lasson jerked open the rear doors and motioned me out of the rig.

He carefully positioned me out of the way and ordered, "Stand here. Don't move." He unloaded the stretcher and motioned for me to take the foot end, which I did. "Just walk," he directed, pointing to the ER doors. "Don't talk, don't do anything, just walk."

*Gosh, he's a bit pushy! Buy 'em books, send 'em to school, and before you know it they think they know everything...*

Inside, Dr. Saleh took a long look at me, turned his back, and spoke directly to Lasson.

"What is wrong with him?" he asked, jerking his head toward me.

"He is deep in the arms of Prince Valium," Lasson answered wryly, handing Samir the ruined vial as Julie Elkins entered the ER. "He got a full vial squirted right in his eyes."

*"Deep in the arms of Prince Valium." I like that. Who knew Lasson was so witty? And I am either high as a kite or Julie Elton is looking muy caliente this evening. Nope, I must be high, because Julie normally looks like six pounds of soft shit in a four-pound sack.*

"In his eyes?" Dr. Saleh asked incredulously. "How?"

"Directly in the eyes," I confirmed with a sleepy smile.

"It's a long story, Doc." Lasson sighed. "Let's unload her and I'll tell you all about it."

# Dead Bodies and Burnout

I HAVE DISCOVERED that within any organizational hierarchy, you will invariably find a certain percentage of assholes. In EMS, they are usually found near the top of the organizational chart, having risen to their particular level of incompetence through management's misguided attempts to get them off the streets and into the office, where they can't kill anyone. Stat Fleet had an overabundance of assholes, however, assuring that as soon as one arrogant, incompetent jerk got promoted, another would take his place. Lance Bidwell was just such an asshole.

The only reason I was working this particular day was because Lance insisted on swapping shifts rather than just coming in to relieve me on the night I got the Valium squirted in my eyes. Hank Williams Jr., David Allan Coe, and Lynyrd Skynyrd were playing a show in Lake Chillicothe that night. Mary and I had tickets, and now I had to miss redneck nirvana because my relief had not learned to work and play well with others.

To top things off, I had to work with Mike Treme, a man with the personality of a cinder block. He seemed to think that his job on scene was to stand around with his thumb in his ass until I told him to do something, and his primary topic of conversation around the station was his sexual conquests among the local Stat Fleet groupies. Tonight, Mike seemed intent on entertaining yet another groupie in the privacy of his bedroom.

She was a real catch, too—about 170 pounds, all acne and bad teeth, with an annoying habit of snorting like a pig when she laughed. Fortunately, before I was subjected to the trumpeting of mating elephants in the next room, the scanner crackled with the urgent voice of a DeVillier police officer.

"DeVillier, this is PD 12! Send fire department and an ambulance right away!" Tom Tate radioed breathlessly. "MVA north of town on Highway 26, just past the skating rink! Pickup truck in the trees and on fire!" The wreck was less than a mile away. I immediately jumped up and pounded on Mike's door until he answered.

"Get your clothes on and say good-bye to the lady," I told him curtly when he opened the door. "We've got a bad wreck just north of town."

I turned around and walked away before he could frame a reply. It took him three and a half minutes by my watch to emerge from the station. The groupie followed him out the door and waddled across the street to where she'd parked her car.

"So where is this damned call?" he snapped irritably, slamming the driver's door of the rig and snatching at his seatbelt. "I didn't hear our pager tones."

*My, aren't we testy! You should thank me for interrupting you when I did. Otherwise, right now you'd be screwing Acne Girl.*

"The pagers didn't go off," I explained patiently, "because we haven't gotten the call yet. I heard it over the scanner. Now, let's go," I ordered, pointing to my left. "It's just north of town." Grumbling, Mike turned north on Highway 26 as I called dispatch with the particulars.

"Holy shit!" Mike blurted not thirty seconds later. Tom Tate was desperately hosing down a blue Dodge Dakota pickup that had left the road and struck several trees. The fire was creeping out from under the ruined hood and growing steadily larger. Standing too close to the fire for safety's sake, Tom was doggedly trying to extinguish the flames. Mike and I bailed out, each grabbing one of the two extinguishers we carried on our rigs.

"Thank God," Tom gasped as we drew nearer. "My extinguisher just ran out." He dropped the empty canister on the ground and bent over, coughing and trying to catch his breath. Between Mike and me, we managed to beat the flames down enough to get close to the wreck, and Mike finally put the fire out for good by dumping the full load of his extinguisher on the source of the flames, a ruptured fuel line near the rear of the engine compartment.

"Mike, check the passenger side." I coughed as I moved to the driver's door. "And be careful!" I added. The driver's door was sprung open, and the driver's left leg was hanging out, clad in a yellow paisley pair of stirrup pants. Her shoe was missing. As I reached in to check a pulse, I noticed that she had been decapitated, with the top of her skull and most of her brains lying in the bed of the truck behind her. "The driver is DOA!" I called out to Mike.

"So is the passenger," he answered, walking around the back of the truck, grimacing in distaste and wiping his hands on his pants. "He's hanging out of the window over there. I ran right into him." Mike put his hand to his mouth and retched.

"You okay?" I asked, concerned. He nodded, swallowed hard, and spat on the ground.

"Yeah," he said shakily. "I couldn't see anything through the smoke and extinguisher chemical, so I bent down to see better, and wound up face-to-face with him. He's pretty torn up."

"Dispatch, be advised we have two fatalities at this scene," I radioed. "Please notify the state police and the coroner's office."

"Ten-four, Medic 306. We'll notify LSP and the coroner," dispatch replied. I walked over to check on Tom, who had finally managed to catch his breath. He was walking the ditch bank, shining the beam of his flashlight over the broken ground.

"They passed me hauling ass, all over the road," Tom said, shaking his head. "I got them on radar at ninety-four. By the time I got turned around, they had wiped out. Looks like they left the road here"—he indicated a set of tire marks with his flashlight beam—"went airborne here when they hit this culvert"—pointing the beam at the spot where the tracks ended—"and then hit the tree sideways." It was nearly a hundred feet from the point of impact to the spot where they left the road. "Are they dead?" Tom asked, already knowing the answer.

"Yep, both of 'em," I answered as we walked back up to the truck.

From the rear of the truck, it looked as if one of the red bucket seats had broken loose from its mount and split wide open from the impact.

There was pale yellow padding visible through the split fabric. As we got closer and the smoke and fire extinguisher chemical dissipated, we were horrified to see that it was not a bucket seat at all, but the back of yet a third victim. She was pushed upward by the impact, erupting through the roof of the truck.

What we thought was the seat back was actually her torso showing through her red sweatshirt. She was split in half from pubis to sternum. Her left arm was amputated and was lying on the roof of the truck. The woman's torso had burst just to the left of her spine, spilling all of her chest and abdominal organs onto the floor beneath her. I could literally look right through her at Mike Treme walking around on the other side of the wreck.

*Whoa, cool!* You don't see that every day.

"Oh, my Lord," Tom breathed, playing his light over her body. "Is that what I think it is?" he asked fearfully.

"Yup, that's what you think it is," I confirmed, then keyed my radio microphone once more. "Dispatch, Medic 306. Uh, be advised that's three fatalities at this scene."

"You advised 'three fatalities,' Medic 306?" our dispatcher inquired sweetly, in a voice that communicated quite clearly that I should learn to count.

"Yes, three fatalities," I confirmed.

Beside me, Tom whispered a prayer and crossed himself. "Hey, Mike!" I yelled. "Found another one!" He came trotting over, looking all around the truck. "Check it out." I grinned, handing him the flashlight. Mike pointed the flashlight beam at the truck, squinted, and did a double take. His reaction was pretty much the same as Tom's—shock and horror.

By the time the DeVillier Fire Department arrived, there was no fire to suppress, no living victims to extricate. The smoke had cleared enough to show every gory detail, starkly lit by the halogen lights the firefighters had set up. Their men and their extrication equipment sat idle, waiting for the moment when they would be asked to pull the bodies from the wreckage.

The curious and the bold had all long since satisfied their morbid curiosity, and the only ones poking around the wreckage now were the state trooper and the parish coroner. They were shooting photographs, documenting the scene from every conceivable angle. The state trooper straightened from where he had been kneeling near the passenger side of the truck and beckoned me over.

"Thanks for the film," he said, handing me my camera. "I thought I had enough."

"No problem." I grinned. "Just make a set of prints for me, too. I'll blur the faces when I use them in class." The trooper nodded in understanding.

"Check that out, would you?" he said, pointing to the body of the passenger.

Unlike the other two, his body was remarkably intact, especially considering the fact that he was closest to the point of impact. He was hanging from the waist up from the passenger window, partially wedged against the tree. I bent down to get a closer look, and saw that this guy was still holding an empty Miller pony bottle clenched in his left hand. I grunted and straightened up, shaking my head in amazement.

"Pretty damned weird, huh?" the trooper asked rhetorically. "I got a couple of good pictures of it. You see some of the damnedest—"

"Hey, Stat Fleet!" the coroner interrupted. "We're ready to get the bodies out now," he called.

The trooper and I walked over to the coroner's Ford Explorer, joining the fire captain and the coroner, who was rummaging around in the back. He finally emerged with three body bags. "Here, take these," he said, handing them to me. "I'm pretty much done here, so I suppose we need to get the bodies out and transported to Lake Chillicothe."

"Any particular way you want it done?" the fire captain asked.

"Not really." He shrugged. "Just do your best to keep from tearing them up any more than they already are."

*Easier said than done, pal. Will you settle for all the parts in the right body bag?*

The fire captain called his extrication crew over and told them, "Look, we're just gonna cut the roof off and get 'em out as best we can. You two"—he pointed at two young, fuzzy-cheeked firemen—"line up the body bags over there, where they can't be seen from the road. You can help the Stat Fleet boys pull the bodies out." These two kids didn't look very enthused with their assignment, but they obediently took the body bags from me and lined them up behind the truck.

"What's your name, man?" I asked the firefighter with me. I had to consciously resist the urge to call him "kid." He looked about fifteen, and I suddenly felt old.

"Carey," he answered nervously. "I just joined the fire department."

"Is this your first time seeing something like this?" I asked him. He bobbed his head like a schoolboy.

"Yes, sir," he said, swallowing hard and licking his lips. "I'm supposed to take your First Responder class next month."

"Well, good!" I beamed. "Look, just relax. You and I will get in the back of the truck once your guys remove the roof. We'll pull them out as best we can. There's really nothing to it." He nodded absently, only half listening.

*Jesus Christ, this kid is going to puke any minute now. How did I get saddled with this pussy?*

Presently, the extrication crew cut the roof away and gingerly manipulated it around the mangled torso of the third victim, leaving what was left of her body slumped over the guy in the passenger seat.

"Okay, Carey. That's our cue," I told him grimly, climbing into the truck. "Spread that body bag open in the back of the truck. I'll get under her shoulders, and if you can get her hips, we'll see if we can pull her out." Carey clenched his teeth and gamely took a hold.

Pulling her out required some doing. There was nothing pinning her now, but the impact has done more than split her torso in half. Both of her thighs were essentially deboned; both hips were dislocated, and the femurs had burst from the flesh all the way down to her knees. Getting her into the body bag in the bed of the truck turned out to be a messy proposition. By the time we were through, Carey was gagging. Mike and the rest of the firefighters removed the other two victims without much trouble, and Carey and I lined our body bag up next to the others.

"Hey, Stat Fleet," the coroner called out to me, "make sure everything is out of the truck. I'm calling the wrecker." I nodded my understanding and scanned the inside of the truck for personal effects, money, and meat. There was something lying in the floorboard under the jump seat.

"Carey, open that first body bag for me," I ordered. He was standing with his back to me, taking deep, shuddering breaths. Reluctantly, he turned around and knelt next to the bag, unzipping it and spreading it open. He turned his face away and closed his eyes. I grabbed a double handful of the driver's brains and dumped them unceremoniously into the bag. Carey groaned, rolls over onto his hands and knees, and vomited into the grass.

*What a pussy! If you can't handle the sight of a little blood and guts, you're not gonna last.*

An hour later, we were back at our station. Mike was asleep, but I was still keyed up, so I walked across the street for a breakfast sandwich and a soft drink. The sun was just coming up, and the parking lot was filling with early morning commuters. The wrecker driver was there with the Dakota secured to his flatbed, sipping a cup of coffee and holding court before a small crowd of gawkers. I sidled over closer to hear what he was saying.

"Musta been a bad 'un," he grunted, pointing with his coffee cup into the cab of the truck. "There's blood all in it. Cops said three people got kilt. To tell the truth, I dunno what there is to be salvaged." He shrugged, idly picking up a piece of floppy, translucent-looking plastic from the floorboard and examining it as he took another sip of coffee.

"Well, first of all," I told him as I reached over his shoulder and took the piece from him, "that isn't part of the truck. This is cartilage, probably from one of the victims." He immediately spewed most of his coffee onto the truck, followed by the rest of his breakfast.

"Second," I continued, looking at him contemptuously, "you don't need to be out here showing off the truck to every Tom, Dick, and Harry. You never know who might be in the crowd." I tossed the piece of cartilage back into the truck and walked away, to the shocked stares of the gawkers.

Back at the station, I crawled into bed and stared at the ceiling for hours.

*What in God's name is wrong with you? You thought that was funny.*

*Three people dead, and all you take from it is the opportunity to make two people toss their cookies? You used to not be that way, Kelly. You used to have compassion. You used to have empathy for people. Sure, you can't identify too closely with every patient. You can't bring it home with you, or it will just eat you up. That's what Richard and Randal taught you from day one in EMT class. But you've always said that you'd quit before you became one of those burnouts who didn't care about people. So why don't you just quit, Mr. Chickenshit? Dear God, what are you going to do if you're not a paramedic?*

When I finally drifted off to sleep, I had a nightmare about Frankie Maryland. He blamed me for killing him.

# Modified Scrotal Lead

AH, ROOKIES. GOD bless 'em. I just love those new guys with the shiny boots and Batman utility belts, just itching to go out there and save lives, help little old ladies off the floor and just generally Help People in Their Time of Need. There is no better balm for a jaded medic's soul than torturing a young, impressionable rookie. It ranks right up there with throwing imaginary spiders on your hallucinating psych patient.

Don't get the impression that I torture all rookies. I'm selective. The cocky, pretentious ones are my favorite prey.

I precepted just such a fellow last month. Kevin, barely eighteen years old, had just finished the didactic component of his EMT-Basic course in Lake Chillicothe. Kevin's instructor, Cathy Hyatt, is a friend and colleague, and she usually steers her students to whatever truck I'm working. A week before his preceptor shift with me, she called me and gave me a heads-up on Kevin.

"He's as smart as a whip," Cathy had said of him, "but he's probably the most arrogant little snot I've ever taught. He thinks he knows everything, despite the fact that he has yet to run his first call."

"Cocky and arrogant, huh?" I mused. "I know the type. Hell, I was the type. Don't worry, Cathy, I'll burst his bubble."

"Do that," she laughed. "Just don't scar him for life. He might actually become a decent EMT if we can convince him he still has a lot to learn. And for the record, you're still cocky and arrogant."

"Arrogant? *Moi?*" I protested innocently. "I am not conceited, I am convinced."

"Confused is more like it." Cathy chuckled. "Anyway, let me know how he does. 'Bye now."

Kevin and I ran a number of calls that day, most of them minor traffic accidents and transfers. It was immediately apparent that Cathy was correct; Kevin was both highly intelligent and supremely arrogant.

He quickly earned the everlasting hatred of Travis Deville, my partner for that shift. We were at "Aspiration Manor" to pick up an elderly man with a fever and difficulty breathing, and for perhaps the tenth time that day, Kevin ordered "the driver" to go fetch a piece of equipment. Travis had started giving me that "please, let me whip his ass" look about five calls before.

"Why don't we just get a pulse oximeter reading once we get him to the truck," I told Kevin, heading off a potential explosion from Travis. "We don't need it right now." Kevin looked disappointed but said nothing as Travis and I loaded the patient.

Once in the rig, I took another set of vital signs as Kevin applied the cardiac monitor. Not surprisingly, the vitals Kevin obtained on scene were right on the money. The cardiac monitor showed a crappy normal sinus rhythm, full of muscle tremor artifact. The poor elderly man had advanced Parkinson's and was shaking like a leaf.

"Is that atrial fibrillation?" Kevin asked, pointing at the monitor. I paused from preparing a saline lock to look at the screen.

"No, that's sinus rhythm with artifact," I told him.

*Pretty good guess, though. It does look a lot like atrial fib.*

"Sinus rhythm?" Kevin said dubiously. "It sure looks like atrial fibrillation."

I sighed inwardly as I flushed the saline lock and taped it down. I turned sideways on the seat and printed a strip of the rhythm.

"See these little bumps?" I said, pointing to the barely visible P waves. "Those are sinus P waves. All the rest of the stuff you're seeing is just artifact. Since when did Cathy start teaching rhythm recognition to her EMT students?"

"I didn't learn it in class," he told me proudly. "I'm reading EKG books on the side. I plan to get in a paramedic class as soon as I get my EMT."

*Just what the world needs, another paramedic with zero patient care experience but well versed in current theory. Now, if only the patients were theoretical...*

"Well, you're looking at sinus rhythm, not atrial fibrillation," I told him firmly.

"So how do I tell the difference?" he wanted to know.

*Oh, this is going to be fun. You just said the magic words, kid.*

"Well, you could pick an alternative lead placement that doesn't highlight all of this bony artifact we're seeing," I told him with a straight face. "Bones don't conduct electrical impulses all that well, so sometimes we try placing the leads to avoid any bones that might be in the way."

"So how do we do that?" he asked, intrigued.

*I thought you'd never ask, Kevin. You won't find this one in your books, kid!*

"Well, the modified scrotal lead would probably be the best for this situation. You make sure the lead selector switch is set for Lead II, and you take this black electrode here"—I pointed to the ground lead—"and place it on his testicles. On his perineum would be even better."

"And that works better than the normal placement?" Kevin wanted to know.

"Sure!" I said confidently. "See how it looks directly up from his pelvis through his thorax? That's a straight path to the heart—no bone in the way. The only reason I'm not doing it now is because I'm confident in my original interpretation." Kevin nodded sagely, filing that little tip away.

*With any luck, you will have a big audience the first time you do this. I'd give anything to be a fly on the wall when that happens.*

* * * * * *

Yesterday morning, John Garrett stopped by our station on his way to Meridian.

"Got a minute to talk?" John asked.

"Uh-oh," I said, looking around warily. "What have I done now?"

"Nothing, as far as I know." He chuckled, and then turned serious. "You precepted Kevin Barton when he was an EMT student, didn't you?"

"Yeah, he was a pretty sharp kid," I answered. "Why do you ask?"

"Well, we just hired him to work in Meridian," John answered with an odd look on his face. "He just completed his orientation shifts with me. Look, did he do anything weird when you were precepting him?"

"Not that I recall," I said, shaking my head. "But maybe you should define 'weird' for me."

"Well, we picked up this old guy from the nursing home having chest pain. The monitor showed a lot of artifact, and he just..."

*Oh, this is gonna be good!*

"....grabbed the left arm electrode and slapped it on the guy's nuts. Said it was great at reducing artifact. He called it the 'modified scrotal lead' or some such bullshit."

"That is weird," I said, struggling mightily to maintain my composure. "I've never heard of such a thing. Did it work?"

"The damnedest thing was, it did work," John said wonderingly. "The rhythm cleared up a lot."

"Well, that's a new one on me," I said, shrugging my shoulders. "Maybe you should teach that little trick to your paramedic students."

# Poor Boy CPAP

IT WAS TEN-THIRTY at night, and Mrs. Smith couldn't breathe. Her family didn't seem all that concerned when they called 911, but my partner Mickey Sanders's dad, Johnny, sounded rather spooked. Then again, Johnny Sanders would be spooked if the woman had a paper cut.

Johnny was a cop for the Fort Sperry Police Department, and he sprinted the call in his cruiser. He was six feet eight inches of solid muscle, but he didn't do blood. Or guts. Or women crying. Or kids. Come to think of it, unless he was deer hunting, or wrestling down some three-hundred-pound methamphetamine addict, Johnny was out of his element pretty much everywhere.

When Mickey and I arrived on the scene, Johnny hustled over to the ambulance with a scared look in his eyes. Mickey, sighing in exasperation, put the rig in park and opened the door.

"For God's sake, Daddy, what can be so bad that"—Mickey stopped in mid-tirade, looking over his daddy's shoulder at our patient.

Mrs. Smith was sitting on an upturned five-gallon bucket in the garage, maybe thirty feet away. We could hear her breathing over the sound of our rig's diesel engine at high idle. Mickey and I traded a look and headed for her, while Johnny breathed a sigh of relief. Had it been a three-hundred-pound rowdy meth addict, he would have had him cuffed, stuffed, and sitting penitently in his patrol car contemplating his bruises, but he was scared shitless of Mrs. Smith and her respiratory distress.

Mrs. Smith was leaning forward on her makeshift chair, hands propped on her knees, struggling for breath. She sounded like a coffee percolator, and she was coughing up pink, frothy sputum. She had that thousand-yard stare, and she was swaying ominously. Mickey fit a non-rebreather mask over her face as I applied the pulse oximeter. Her saturation was only 60 percent. I went ahead and listened to her lungs, knowing beforehand what I'd hear. She sounded full.

Mickey was checking her blood pressure as Johnny and I lowered the stretcher, and he shook his head as he pulled the stethoscope from his ears. He informed me grimly, "It's 234/130." I nodded and lifted Mrs. Smith's mask from her face. Taking her chin in my hand, I turned her head toward me and looked into her eyes. She focused on my face briefly.

"Ma'am," I told her, "I need to give you some medicine. Lift up your tongue." As directed, she lifted her tongue, and I administered a double squirt of nitro spray and placed the mask back on her face. "Let's get her on the stretcher and go," I told Mickey.

The quicker we got her loaded, the better. Mrs. Smith looked heavy. I'd have hated to have her code right there in her garage.

It took Johnny's help to get her squared away on the stretcher, a task he willingly accepted. He had got Mickey and me treating her breathing problem, but making the three-hundred-pound lady go where he wanted was his specialty.

We got her loaded into the rig, and Mickey busied himself with attaching monitor leads, switching over to the main oxygen tank, and setting up an IV access. Mrs. Smith's oxygen saturation was only up to 80 percent. I briefly considered what to do, and was struck by a novel idea.

*If this works, I'm a fucking genius. If it doesn't, Mrs. Smith won't be any worse off.*

"Get me the pocket CPR mask and the disposable ventilator," I told Mickey.

Chennault was trialing a new disposable ventilator. It wasn't a true automatic transport ventilator, but it made a pretty decent hands-free replacement for a bag-valve resuscitator. From playing with the device, I knew that it provided a pretty good amount of constant positive airway pressure. That's what I intended to try—poor man's CPAP.

Mickey, looking at me quizzically, fetched the equipment. Without being asked, he also got an endotracheal tube and the laryngoscope.

He asked, "You want a 7.5 tube and a number three curved blade, right?" I shook my head, earning an even more curious look.

"Hold off on that for right now," I replied. "I'm gonna try something.

See if you can get a line."

Looking dubious, Mickey slid down the bench seat and began looking for a suitable vein on Mrs. Smith's left arm. I quickly hooked the pocket mask to the disposable ventilator and turned on the oxygen. I strapped the mask tightly to her face and slowly turned down the rate adjustment knob on the ventilator until it began to cycle with her heaving respirations. Briefly she struggled, resisting the forceful flow of air. I grabbed her shoulders and turned her until she was looking directly at me.

"Mrs. Smith," I explained slowly and distinctly, "this may feel a bit uncomfortable at first, but it will help you breathe, okay? I want you to tell me when it gets just a little difficult to breathe out. Not easy to breathe out, okay? You should have to work at it a little."

She nodded weakly and squeezed my hand. As I slowly adjusted the ventilatory pressure, she relaxed noticeably, closed her eyes, and made an "okay" sign.

I turned to Mickey to find him still desperately hunting a vein. He was blindly fishing around inside the bend of her elbow with an 18-gauge catheter, muttering under his breath.

"Let's just go," I told him. "I'll try to get something on the way." Still muttering in frustration, he backed out of the rig and slammed the rear doors.

In seconds we were rushing to Fort Sperry Community Hospital, sirens wailing. I squirted another nitro spray under Mrs. Smith's tongue and tried to obtain an IV access on the way, with no more success than Mickey had had.

By the time we arrived at the Emergency Department ten minutes later, Mrs. Smith looked like a different patient. Her lungs were still wet, but it required a stethoscope to notice. She was awake and alert, and her oxygen saturation was nearly 95 percent. Mickey stared at her in disbelief as we wheeled her inside. Dr. Randall McMurray met us in the room.

"Acute pulmonary edema," I told him. "When we got there, her sat was only 60 percent. Breathing about forty-four times a minute, coughing up pink sputum. BP was 234/130, sinus tach at 140 on the monitor.

We gave her two double doses of nitro, and as you can see, a little jury-rigged CPAP," I finished, gesturing to my setup.

*And as you can also see, it worked like a charm, Doc.*

"CPAP?" Doc McMurray asked, cocking one eyebrow and peering at me over his glasses as he inspected the device. "I didn't realize you guys had CPAP rigs." He poked at the disposable ventilator curiously. He listened to Mrs. Smith's chest, grunted noncommittally, and straightened up. "You say she was fulminant when you picked her up? Saturation was only 60 percent?" he asked dubiously.

"Well, I got no idea what that 'CPAP' shit is, or what the heck 'fulminant' means," Mickey chimed in, "but she was CTD when we got there. She was a lot worse than this." Doc McMurray just stared at him without comprehension.

"Circling the drain," I furnished, much to his amusement. "And he's right, Doc. She turned right around."

"Okay, guys, thanks," he told us as we wheeled the stretcher outside. "Stick around!" he called over his shoulder. "You gotta tell me how this contraption works!"

I chuckled as Mickey and I walked outside.

"So that was CPAP, huh?" Mickey grunted. "Like that snorkel rig you wear at night?"

"Yep, that was CPAP," I confirmed. "That disposable ventilator provides a lot of it, if you set it properly. It wasn't ideal, but it worked."

"I figured you were fixin' to tube her." Mickey shook his head wonderingly. "That was no-shit, hands-down the damnedest thing I ever saw. I can't believe how quick she turned around. Does it always work that quick?"

*I have no fucking idea, partner. That was the first time I ever did it. But it worked, and now you think I'm a genius.*

"Sometimes it does," I allowed judiciously, "but usually it takes a bit longer. Now, if you'll excuse me, partner, I have to go teach the doctor all about CPAP..."

# That Ain't Blood

GEORGINA CHESTERFIELD WAS lying on her back in a filthy bed, totally gorked. Her blood sugar was less than twenty, a common problem for her. We pick her up for diabetic problems at least four times a month. What chapped my ass was the fact that Georgina refused to manage her blood sugar. She didn't *forget* to eat, or check her sugar, or take her insulin; Georgina would get pissed at her husband and refuse to eat or take her insulin to punish him for drinking. If I could have just woken her up with a little dose of dextrose, I'm sure she'd be bitching about Leroy and his alcoholism, and I'd be bitching at Georgina for taking risks with her health just for spite. This was a dance we'd done many times, and I knew the steps by heart.

I was sweating like a pig in her sweltering house trailer as I desperately tried to find a vein I could stick. I didn't have many options. Besides her diabetes, Georgina also suffered from chronic renal failure, hypertension, peripheral vascular disease, congestive heart failure, emphysema, and arthritis. In the parlance of our profession, she was a "Fucking Train Wreck." Those of us who regularly transported her also had tabbed her with an unofficial diagnosis of chronic low marble count.

"Son of a bitch," I whispered under my breath in frustration as I grabbed another 18-gauge catheter. Mickey chuckled as he steered Leroy to a spot on the sagging couch, leaving him sitting there in a teary-eyed alcohol fog. I'd already stuck her twice, with nothing to show for it. That's okay, though, because she had a good vein in her right arm I could usually count on when all else failed. Mickey stood over me, grinning as I made the stick.

"Don't miss, Supermedic," he teased. "You'll ruin your reputation."

"Miss? *Moi?*" I retorted in mock indignation. "Evidently, you have forgotten who you're working with," I told him as I threaded the catheter. "Maybe the mere mortals you work with will occasionally—fuck!"

The hematoma spread across Georgina's arm, a future bruise to match the many she already had. I glared up at Mickey. "You jinxed me, you bastard."

He raised his hands in protest. "Hey, I was just kidding. She doesn't have anything else to stick?" I shook my head in resignation as I straightened up.

"No, let's just haul ass with her to Fort Sperry," I told him. "Maybe I can get something on the way. Better light in the rig, anyway."

"Yeah, what's up with the lights and air-conditioning in this place?" Mickey grunted as we manhandled Georgina onto the stretcher. By the time we got her secured, we were both pouring sweat.

"Damned if I know," I answered. "She hoards money. Last time we transported her, the hospital found thirteen hundred dollars in a Crown Royal bag under her left tit. I had put the cardiac monitor on her and everything. I never had a clue."

Mickey chuckled as we gingerly carried her down the rickety steps of the house trailer. I had visions of Larry Hagman crashing through the tenement stairs in *Mother, Jugs & Speed*.

In the back of the rig, I turned on the overhead lights and began a futile search for a suitable vein as Mark slammed the doors. In desperation, I even considered doing an external jugular stick.

*Damn it, this woman had no veins! If she had a central line for her dialysis, I'd have just used that. If we had glucagon, I'd just have just given it IM. And if my aunt had a dick, she'd be my uncle. If, if, if...*

A thought occurred to me, and the more I considered it, the more plausible it seemed. I could give her rectal glucose, I mused.

*What the hell, it's a mucous membrane! It ought to absorb. And anything would be better than sitting here like an idiot for the next thirty minutes.*

Shrugging my shoulders, I reached into the cabinet and got two tubes of oral glucose. I briefly looked at the rearview mirror to see if Mickey was watching. Thankfully, he was paying close attention to the road. Quickly, I snatched down Georgina's polyester pants and squirted both tubes of glucose up her ass. From the looks of things, her ass crack hadn't seen daylight, or a washcloth, in years.

No wonder I'd missed her money stash. She'd probably forgotten where it was herself.

I quickly stripped off my gloves, turning them inside out around the empty glucose tubes and tossing them in the biohazard can. I replaced my gloves and busied myself repeating Georgina's vital signs.

By the time we arrived at the hospital, Georgina was awake and I was Supermedic once again. Her blood glucose was seventy-six. Mickey opened the rear doors and gaped at her in surprise. I smugly stepped out of the rig and helped him unload the stretcher.

"What...how did you...I mean, she was..." he spluttered as we wheeled Georgina inside. She looked just as bewildered as Mickey.

"How did I what?" I asked innocently. "Give her glucose? Wake her up?" Mickey nodded his head eagerly, and I simply smiled.

*That's for me to know and you to learn one day. One day far, far in the future, when you have begged and groveled sufficiently, I may tell you. Then again, I may not.*

The nurse looked at us quizzically as Georgina scooted over to the hospital bed under her own power. "Her blood sugar is twenty?" she asked skeptically, looking at Mickey.

"*Was* twenty," I corrected her. "That was maybe forty minutes ago. Now it's seventy-six."

"She's got a rectal bleed," the nurse pointed out, indicating a red stain on the seat of Georgina's pants. Mickey turned his back in distaste.

"That's what I thought," I told her, "but that's not blood." She looked at me curiously as I winked at her. "I tasted it to make sure, but I'm pretty sure it's cherry." She and I shared a grin as Mickey fled the room, gagging.

# Supermedic

M<small>R. MURPHY, THAT</small> evil bastard, had visited us again. Rob Daigle and I were working a code on an elderly woman in the middle of her living room floor. We were by ourselves, which was par for the course. Our backup truck was on the way from Mason Ferry, which meant they'd arrive in town just in time to smoke cigarettes and hear the war story as we cleaned our ambulance after the call. But hey, they'd had a dull day while Rob and I were running our asses off, so they could use the entertainment.

Had we known it was a cardiac arrest when we got the call, things would have been different. They could have arrived early enough to help. Who knows, they might even have arrived in time to see me do the face plant in the flower bed. They could have laughed along with Rob and held up little scorecards for my impromptu flip off the porch. At the very least, someone thinner could have balanced on the porch railing to try to look inside the living room window. Maybe then I wouldn't have been soaking wet, covered in mud, and digging geraniums out of the crack of my ass.

"Keep up the compressions," I told Rob as I intubated. White foamy sputum was trickling from the woman's nose and mouth. Muttering, I reached for the suction and cleared her mouth.

"Need some cricoid pressure?" he asked, reaching for the woman's throat. I shook my head.

*Help? Moi? Obviously, my friend, you do not realize that I am an airway artiste. Do you not recognize genius when you see it?*

I quickly intubated the woman and confirmed breath sounds. Experience had taught me to secure the tube with several wraps of tape, especially when I was working with Rob. It took a little extra effort to make the tube Daigle-proof.

"Just keep up those compressions, CPR Boy," I told him smugly. "I got it handled." I briefly looked at the woman's neck for an external jugular vein, but nothing looked promising. I slid down next to her right arm. Nothing much there, either.

"Yeah, you look like you got it under control," he replied, rolling his eyes as he continued to pump the woman's chest, sweat dripping off his nose. "Remind me why we're doing this again, would you?"

"Because we are saviors and heroes?" I asked innocently. "Because we get paid exorbitant sums of money to snatch people from the very jaws of death? Because women desire us, and men want to be like us? Because we crave the public accolades and adulation that come with the job?"

"Maybe that's why *you* do it," Rob groaned. "I signed up to resuscitate unsalvageable ninety-year-old ladies in sweltering house trailers. I signed up to do dialysis transfers. I'm living my dream. Seeing you do a half-gainer off the porch into four inches of mud is just a bonus. I'd have given you a ten if you had kept your feet together." When I don't reply, he continued, "And what's up with gettin' that IV, Supermedic? Ain't you done yet?"

*Alas, my faithful sidekick, Supermedic has found his kryptonite, in the form of an eighty-year-old dialysis patient with peripheral vascular disease. When it comes to obtaining blood from a rock, Supermedic is tragically mortal...*

"Shit, let's just give some epi and atropine down the tube and boogie," I suggested. I drew up two milligrams each of epinephrine and atropine and squirted them down the tube, knowing all the while that it would do no good.

She was in asystole when we arrived. Who knew how long she'd been down? Her grandkids hadn't heard from her since the day before, which was precisely why they'd sent us to check on her. And they'd probably sue me for kicking her door open, not to mention ruining her flower garden. All things considered, I'd rather have found her in rigor mortis and done none of this...

Rob and I rolled her onto a spine board and hustled her to the truck, no easy task considering the obstacle course of flowerpots, shrubs, birdbaths, and garden statues we had to negotiate. I motioned for Rob to climb in the back with me as we latched the stretcher.

"I'm gonna try once more for a line," I told him. "Keep doing CPR." He nodded and continued chest compressions as I resumed my futile search for a vein. *Fuck it,* I thought. *I'll just stick her dialysis shunt. One easy poke, and I'll have an IV access, and I don't care if the doctor gets pissed or not. What harm could it do, kill the dead lady?*

I tried to remember whether shunts were heparinized, and couldn't recall. I'd just stick to Kelly's "Rule of Central Venous Access"—when in doubt, aspirate and discard ten milliliters of blood.

I quickly administered another round of epi and atropine through her shunt and nodded to Rob that I was ready to transport. The woman was still in asystole as the truck started to roll, a long, unbroken stretch of flat line on the cardiac monitor. Groaning, I braced my head against the cabinetry and resumed compressions.

Rob gave me his usual rough drive as we headed, sirens screaming, to Fort Sperry Community Hospital.

*What is it with guys like this? Outta the way, everybody! Dead lady on board! We need to get to the hospital as quickly as possible so the doctor can take one look at her and call it! Can't you see that this is a death-or-death situation?*

Rob made the turn to the hospital and succeeded in tossing me to the floor, and I banged my head painfully on the cabinetry in the process. "Hard left turn!" he called out two seconds too late.

*Thanks for the fucking warning, partner. Well, at least we're here. We can call this soon. You know, maybe it wouldn't be a bad idea to check her blood sugar. She's a dialysis patient, after all. It's a good bet that she's a diabetic. Might even be hyperkalemic, too.*

I pushed another round of epi and atropine, and squirted a little blood from the syringe that I aspirated from her shunt onto a glucose test strip. Twenty seconds later, I was rewarded by a reading of "Lo" as Rob flung open the rear doors.

"Push these two syringes," I ordered, handing him a syringe each of dextrose and sodium bicarbonate. "I'm tired of doing shit with one hand." Shrugging, he administered both drugs and tossed the empty syringes onto the rig floor.

"I'll dispose of 'em later," he assured me as we removed the stretcher.

As the undercarriage of the stretcher locked into place, the cardiac monitor started beeping. Marching across the screen was the prettiest sinus tachycardia I could ever hope for. Rob and I shared an incredulous look.

"Let's hurry up and get her inside, before it changes again," I told him, pushing the stretcher with one hand and ventilating with the other. By the time we moved the lady to the bed in the ER, blood was pulsing up my IV line, spreading out into a pink cloud in the bag of saline.

"She's got a pulse," the nurse said unnecessarily, pointing at the bag. "Looks like you hit an artery." I quickly shut off the line as soon as I had a free hand.

"I stuck her shunt," I explained apologetically. "It's all I could get. I could have sworn I stuck the venous side, though."

"Sometimes it doesn't matter," she said, brushing off the apology. "Unless you're pressure-infusing it, it'll back up. So what's the story with her?"

"Found her in asystole," I began as Doc McMurray sauntered into the room. "It started out as a simple welfare check. The family hadn't heard from her, she missed a dialysis appointment this morning, and she didn't answer her phone. I was standing on the porch railing, trying to peek in her window, when it dumped me into the flower bed. But I managed to get a glimpse of her slumped in her recliner before I fell. We had to kick her door open."

"Well, that explains the garden snails in your hair and the crushed flowers on your shirt," Doc McMurray chuckled as he idly placed a hand on the woman's neck to check a pulse. "How long was she down?"

"No idea how long before we got there, Doc. But we've been working her maybe"—I checked my watch—"twenty minutes now. She was asystolic the whole time. I gave her three rounds of epi and atropine, and an amp each of bicarb and dextrose. She regained a pulse as we were unloading the stretcher."

"Why the dextrose and bicarb?" he wanted to know.

"I was playing a hunch," I told him honestly. "I was guessing maybe hyperkalemia or acidosis, or both.

She's trying to breathe now, too," I added, grinning. "Getting better every minute."

"That's a good thing," he agreed. "We have it from here, gentlemen. Good job." Rob and I traded grins as we walked out the door.

"By the way, that lady a couple of weeks ago?" Doc McMurray called over his shoulder. "The one with acute pulmonary edema?"

"Yeah, what about her?" I stopped and asked.

"She did great. We figure it was the pound of salted pistachio nuts she ate that did it. And that CPAP rig you ginned up was pretty good, but kinda hard to regulate. I talked to the department head of Respiratory Therapy, and she's ordering bilevel positive airway pressure rigs for us to use down here. You want to help me in-service the staff on it?"

"I'd be happy to," I said, beaming. "Just tell me when." I strolled jauntily out to the rig, whistling. Rob looked at me suspiciously as I climbed in.

"What's got you so happy?" he wanted to know.

"Just drive me back to the station, CPR Boy," I told him benignly. "Supermedic needs to change into a clean cape."

# TLC

THE HIGHWAY BETWEEN Fort Sperry and Mason Ferry can be a lonely stretch of road, and a dangerous one. The steep shoulders there had already claimed the life of one Chennault Ambulance EMT, and I preferred not to become number two. The road there was in a perpetual state of construction, the work progressing at a glacial pace. One day they will invent a way to make a shovel stand up by itself, and half of every Louisiana Highway Department road crew will become obsolete.

"You know those guys make eighteen dollars an hour?" Shelly Sanders asked, pointing at the flagman as we passed a long line of stalled traffic. "All they have to do is talk on a radio and turn that sign around every few minutes." She shook her head.

"Who makes eighteen dollars an hour?" Jeff Savage wanted to know, hollering from the captain's chair in the back.

"I do!" I shouted back at him. "Why do you think I come to work every day to babysit paramedic students and rookie EMTs?"

Jeff just grinned and shook his head. He had only a few shifts left to do to complete his paramedic clinical time, and he had elected to spend a week in Fort Sperry, riding with me. Mary and I had decided to move back up there, and I'd spent the last week house hunting between calls.

"Who's a rookie EMT?" Shelly asked indignantly. "I'm no rookie!"

"Okay, how many things do you have on your belt?" I asked, rolling my eyes. Shelly immediately blushed a deep shade of red. "Here, let me count them for you," I said with an evil grin, gleefully cataloging everything she was wearing. "That's quite an impressive display of doodads and paramedals you have there. I see a holster with a pair of trauma shears, a penlight, and a window punch. You have a radio, a cell phone, a glove pouch, and a pager. Here's a stork pin, one-year service pin, CPR pin, National Registry EMT pin, and a pair of wings from Priority Air. I didn't realize you were a flight medic! Let's see what else...Hey, Jeff! What other kind of sparky little accessories do rookies wear?"

"EMT pocket guide," Jeff offered helpfully. "Maybe an oxygen cylinder wrench? And don't forget the seatbelt cutter!"

"How about it, Shelly?" I teased, knowing she had exactly those items in the thigh pocket of her uniform pants. Jeff and I laughed in delight at her embarrassment.

"They gave us the wings at the ground-crew in-service," Shelly said defensively, much to her regret, as Jeff and I collapsed in peals of laughter.

"Unit Two, Dispatch," the radio interrupted.

"Go ahead," Shelly answered, still blushing furiously.

"Motor vehicle accident, just south of Mason Ferry on Highway 31. We have a report of a truck in the ditch, unknown injuries."

"Unit Two en route," Shelly confirmed as she engaged the lights and siren. "That's just up the road," she remarked to no one in particular. We passed the roadside cross that marked the spot where JoAnn died. The flowers looked faded.

Just south of the Mason Ferry city limits, we spotted the debris trail first. A pair of tire tracks crossed the road, cutting twin swaths though the roadside weeds on the opposite shoulder. Gas cans, trimmers, and assorted lawn-care tools were scattered in a narrow swath leading to a Ford Ranger pickup lying overturned in the weeds. A spool of monofilament trimmer line had unrolled, pointing a neon-yellow, gnarled path to the wreck. A teenage boy was standing outside his car on the shoulder of the road, his cellular phone pressed to his ear. He pointed frantically to the truck.

*Thank you so much, Bystander Boy. We were wondering where the wreck was.*

Jeff was the first one out of the rig, barely waiting for the truck to come to a complete stop before he hopped out carrying the medic bag. Shelly wasn't far behind. I shook my head, walking around the rig to set the parking brake before I started unloading our gear. Jeff had reached the point where he was capable of running calls without my guidance. I wanted to see if he could function independently.

I grabbed a spine board, a cervical collar, and an immobilizer and scrambled down the steep bank. Jeff met me at the bottom, looking a bit lost.

"What have we got?" I asked him. He shook his head grimly.

"The driver is pinned in the truck," he told me, "and she'd probably weigh about three hundred pounds on the hoof. Somehow she's gotten twisted around, and she's lying on her stomach with her feet pointing out the passenger window. Her face is all mashed against the roof, and her right arm is pinned between the dash and the ground."

"Can she say where she's hurt?" I asked. The roof of the truck was crushed in nearly to the top of the seats. I could see the woman's legs sticking out of the passenger window, and Shelly worming her way into the driver's window.

"She says her arm hurts, and she's having problems breathing," he answered. "So what do you want to do?"

"What do you want to do?" I shot back. He grinned.

"I already had Shelly call the Mason Ferry Fire Department for extrication. She's in there trying to assess her now—I'm too big to fit. I figure we get some oxygen and a collar on her right now, and as soon as we can, extricate her out the passenger door."

"Sounds like a plan," I agreed, "except Mason Ferry VFD can't lift the truck. Fort Sperry VFD has high-lift airbags. I'll call them."

Jeff scrambled around to the driver's side of the truck to speak to Shelly. I knelt down next to the passenger window and peered inside. I could see nothing but two thick legs leading to a mass of pale flesh protruding from under a uniform shirt of some type. Near the driver's window, I could see the top of Shelly Sanders's head as she attempted to place a cervical collar on the woman's neck.

*That ain't gonna work. This woman is built like a snowman. You'll never get a collar to fasten around her neck.*

The woman's legs and abdomen, what little I could see of them, looked reasonably intact. I reached in as far as I could and palpated as high as her knees.

"What the fuck was that?" the woman screamed. Shelly, startled by the woman's scream, banged her head against the steering wheel and cursed.

"What was what?" Shelly asked, concerned. Her flashlight beam played crazily around the cab of the truck.

"Relax, it's just me," I called reassuringly. "You need anything over there, Shelly? There's no way I can reach her."

"Some oxygen would be nice," Shelly called, "and some four-by-four gauze. She's got a nasty cut on her head."

"You got it. I'll have 'em for you in a second," I replied as another thought occurred to me. "Hey, how are you reaching her? How far in there can you get?"

"I crawled in on my stomach," she said matter-of-factly. "I can get my head and shoulders in here, but not much else. Did Jeff tell you that her arm is—"

"Yeah, he did," I answered, cutting her off. "We've got Fort Sperry VFD on the way with some high-lift airbags. You get out of there before they start lifting this truck, understand? It's not safe for you to be wedged in here. Drop whatever you're doing and get out of the way." Before she could reply, another flashlight beam appeared from the bed of the truck. Jeff, scuffed and dirty, poked his head through the rear window.

"Somebody asked for oxygen and bandages?" he asked, grinning.

"How did you fit in there?" I asked incredulously as he passed the oxygen mask across to Shelly's outstretched hand.

"There's a gap right under the side of the bed about two feet to your left. I crawled under." I shook my head in wonder and resignation.

*Both of you are a little too sparky for your own good. But I was just as foolish once.*

"Okay, do what you can," I told him, "but the same thing goes for you. When they start lifting, you get out."

"Why?" he asked reasonably, pointing his flashlight beam around the bed of the truck. "The truck can't get any lower than it is."

He was right. As long as he was in the bed and not the cab, he was not in any danger if the cab collapsed any more. There was no fuel leaking, and we were on level ground. He could stay.

"Be careful," I warned him as I scooted back out of the ruined cab. A Fort Sperry volunteer firefighter scrambled down the steep bank.

"Whatcha got?" he wanted to know.

"Big woman in an overturned Ford Ranger," I answered. "We can't tell how bad she's hurt, but she's complaining of difficulty breathing. She's lying on the roof of the truck with her feet sticking out the passenger window," I continued, pointing. "My partner says her arm is sticking through what's left of the windshield, pinned between the dash and the ground."

"Doors first, then lift the truck?" he mused.

"Yeah, that's what I figured," I agreed, "but you're the expert. If you can get the doors off, we can at least reach her a little better. But you're probably gonna need your airbags and some cribbing to lift the truck a little. Oh, and one of my guys is underneath the bed of the truck, trying to work on her. Watch out for him, would you?"

"Sure," he grunted, waving his crew down the bank. "Must be a little sumbitch to fit in there," he said, shaking his head.

*Not all that little, my man. Just totally ate up with Sparky EMT Syndrome is more like it.*

The fire captain started barking orders, pointing here and there, and his crew fired up the generator and the extrication tool and got to work. In short order, two mangled doors were on the ground, and several cribbing blocks were wedged under the hood and bed rails of the truck. These guys might have been volunteers, but they were good.

With the doors off, I could see much more of the woman. She was scraped up a bit, but she was still moving, carrying on a conversation with Shelly that I couldn't make out over the roar of the generator. Jeff crawled out of the passenger side of the truck, then reached back into the truck and dragged out the medic bag.

"She ain't breathing good," he told me grimly. "Shelly's got oxygen on her, but she's struggling. She just can't breathe lying flat like that."

"Well, they're lifting the truck now," I told him. "Shelly should be able to get her arm loose, and hopefully we'll get her out in a bit." We both walked around to the driver's side of the truck to where Shelly had wormed up to her waist into the cab. The firefighters had wedged a pair of airbags under the hood and were slowly inflating them.

"Hey Shelly," I shouted, prodding her leg with my toe, "back out of there." When she didn't respond, I grabbed her by the belt and slowly dragged her backward out of the truck. She looked up at me angrily. "I said to get out of the truck," I told her curtly.

Shelly had ground dirt and weeds into the front of her uniform shirt, and her forearms were bleeding from the bits of broken glass embedded there. I softened. "Look, get back up to the truck and clean some of that glass out of your arms. We'll be ready to move her by the time you get back."

Looking heartbroken, Shelly climbed up the bank. "She was doing a great job," Jeff said quietly. "The lady was scared, and Shelly was reassuring her. She promised the lady she wouldn't leave." I sighed and looked back up the bank. Shelly was standing outside the truck, rinsing the blood from her arms with sterile saline. Her eyes were red.

"Okay, fellas, you might be able to get to her now," the fire captain told us, nodding toward the truck. Jeff and I got on our knees and peered into the driver's side of the truck. The woman was lying with her face pressed against the roof, eyes closed and gasping painfully through the non-rebreather mask. She was wearing a cervical collar that lacked a good bit from fitting around her neck, although Shelly had attempted to secure it with several wraps of tape. The collar was more-or-less straight. Jeff and I traded a look.

"Straight out headfirst, and then logroll her onto a board," Jeff said decisively.

"And the quicker the better," I agreed. Before we could ask for one, a spine board slid into view on the ground between us. Shelly was on the other end of it, both arms wrapped with roller gauze.

"Let's go!" she said to me defiantly. She looked like she'd been crying. "What are we waiting for?"

I said nothing, just gestured for her to stabilize the woman's head as I knelt down and gently tugged the woman's arm free. From the elbow down, it had an ugly white color, but amazingly it didn't seem to be broken. The woman didn't make a sound as I moved it into line with her body.

"Okay, Shelly, on your count," I said as Jeff and I each gripped the woman's shoulders and upper arms. At Shelly's direction, we pulled the woman out of the ruined truck as gently as possible. It was not what I would call a graceful or pretty move. We quickly logrolled her onto the board and strapped her down. Several firefighters grabbed handholds on the board, and we passed her up a human chain of hands to our stretcher, sitting lowered at the rear doors of our rig.

The woman was making only occasional agonal breaths as we loaded the stretcher. Shelly was crying openly now, tears trickling down her face as she slammed the rear doors. I grabbed a bag mask resuscitator and handed it to Jeff as he positioned himself in the captain's chair at the head of the cot.

He started ventilating the woman as I cut her shirt off. There was an embroidered patch that said "Mike" on the left pocket of the uniform shirt. She didn't look like a Mike.

Her husband, maybe?

I listened to breath sounds as Jeff ventilated, and heard nothing but diesel engine and road noise. I did manage to hear a pulse, though. She was still alive.

"I can't get a seal here," Jeff said, frustrated. He was trying to keep his seat and ventilate at the same time, unsuccessfully attempting to keep a mask seal with one hand. I grabbed the mask with both hands, keeping a seal with a jaw thrust as Jeff bagged, and after a couple of minutes the woman's color was better.

"One of us is going to have to let go at some point," I told him, pointing out the obvious. "How about you try to do it solo while I set up your intubation gear?" He nodded seriously, focusing on maintaining a good seal. He'd gotten into a bit of a groove. Maybe every other ventilation was going in. I quickly set up the laryngoscope and a tube, and handed it to Jeff. He inserted the laryngoscope blade and peered around, looking for the vocal cords and finding nothing. He raised his eyes to meet mine.

"I can't see a thing," he said uncertainly. "You want to try?" I shook my head.

"Why can't you see a thing?" I asked him. "Does she need suctioning?"

"She's real anterior," he said, squinting and moving his head back and forth. The frustration was evident in his voice. "All I see is the base of her freakin' tongue!" I reached forward and pressed firmly on her cricoid cartilage.

"How about now?" I asked. Jeff's face lit up like a little boy at Christmas, and he smoothly passed the tube between the woman's vocal cords.

"Got it!" he said triumphantly as he inflated the cuff. A few squeezes of the bag later, and I could tell he was right. Her breath sounds were equal on both sides. Winking at Jeff, I handed him a tube restraint.

"Now strap it down while I get an IV, Supermedic," I told him as I wrapped a tourniquet around the lady's arm. Two minutes later, I was seriously considering asking Supermedic to switch places with me, because it was starting to look as if I wasn't going to find a vein.

*Come on, Kelly! Your reputation as the all-seeing, all-knowing Paramedic God of All You Survey is at stake. Don't miss this stick!*

Luckily, even a blind squirrel finds an acorn now and then, and somehow the 18-gauge catheter I was holding found a vein in her left forearm. I suppressed a triumphant grin as I hooked up the line.

*Yes! The blind squirrel can eat for another day!*

Fifteen minutes later, we were pulling up to the ambulance bay at West Oneida Regional. Our patient was still unconscious, and I couldn't quite figure out why. Her pressure was a bit on the low side for a big lady like her, but it was good enough at 104/64. Her heart rate was 90, but she was making only an occasional effort to breathe. Her lungs sounded good, though, and I could find no injuries more serious than the scrapes and cuts on her face and right arm. There was even a good pulse in her arm.

"Reckon she's got a head injury?" Jeff wanted to know.

"Could be"—I shrugged—"but her pupils are equal and reactive. She withdraws from pain. If she were in shock, I'd expect it to look worse than this. I just don't know," I concluded helplessly.

"Maybe she just got tired out from lying on her chest like that," Jeff mused. "She must weigh three-fifty. Kinda like a CHF patient can't breathe when they're lying flat?"

"Might be something like that," I grunted in agreement as Shelly opened the rear doors. "We might never know what it was."

Shelly's eyes were red and puffy, but she was no longer crying. I said nothing to her as we rolled the lady inside, and she immediately took the stretcher back to the rig as soon as we moved the lady to the hospital bed.

"She's still upset," Jeff observed quietly. I nodded, saying nothing as I watched her leave. Outside, I found Shelly sitting quietly on the low retaining wall bordering the ambulance bay. She was taking deep drags on a cigarette, and her hands were trembling. I sat down next to her and handed her a Coke.

"Thanks," she said shakily. "Is she gonna be okay?"

"I don't know," I answered honestly. "Her vital signs are good, and I can't find all that much wrong with her. Maybe she'll come around. My question is, are you going to be okay?" I asked gently.

"I promised I wouldn't leave her, and I left her," she said almost inaudibly, her lower lip trembling. "She was scared, and I promised I'd stay with her. But you made me leave. Was it because I'm a girl?"

Was it? Maybe a little. But I was looking out for a rookie EMT who wasn't looking out for herself. If Jeff had refused to get out of the truck, I'd have dragged his ass out of there, too.

"You made a promise you couldn't keep. But you also put oxygen on her. She might not have made it this far if it wasn't for that," I pointed out. Shelly said nothing, just took a shaky drag on her cigarette. "Look, you're a good EMT," I told her. "But you can't take chances with your safety. I know you were taught never to enter an unsafe scene, right?"

"Yes, but sometimes—"

"Sometimes you enter anyway, even when you know it isn't entirely safe," I finished. "You take a calculated risk. In this case, the risk to you wasn't worth the benefit to her. It was my call."

She still didn't respond, and I gently nudged her with my elbow. "Look, Shelly, we don't save all that many lives, even when we do everything right. We reassure people, and sometimes we ease their pain a little bit. I guarantee you one thing, though."

"What's that?" she asked, looking up at me.

"When that lady wakes up," I continued, looking pointedly at her, "she's not going to remember the man who strapped her to a board, or the one who stuck a tube down her throat. But she will remember the girl who held her hand and reassured her while she was trapped in her truck, and she'll be grateful. That's something, whether you think so or not."

Shelly nodded, taking another drag on her cigarette. A state trooper pulled up, double-parking behind a Mercedes in the doctors' parking lot. Seeing us sitting in the ambulance bay, he sauntered over just as Jeff walked outside.

"You guys bring in the wreck from Chennault Parish?" he wanted to know.

"Yeah, the lady was in pretty bad shape," I told him, "but she'll probably make it."

"Did you guys pick up her purse or identification?" he asked, flipping open a small spiral notebook. "There wasn't anything in the truck, not even an insurance card. You get her name?" Jeff and I exchanged clueless looks and shrugged our shoulders.

"The name tag on her shirt said 'Mike,' but I don't think it's her shirt," I offered. "I didn't even think to look for identification."

"Martha," Shelly furnished, sighing as she crushed out her cigarette butt. "Her name is Martha. She told me while I was in the truck with her."

# I'm a Big Girl, and I Know What I'm Doing

WELL, MA'AM, NOW we know why you were having all those fainting spells. Ventricular tachycardia will do that to you.

I had just cardioverted this woman a few seconds ago, and she was coming around, probably wondering why her bra was pushed up around her neck and where that burning smell was coming from. In my haste, I'd gotten the apex paddle just a wee bit off of the gel conduction pad. It was probably going to leave a mark.

The call started out easily enough. We'd been to this lady's house several times, and every time she had refused transport. She'd pass out, her husband would panic and call 911, and by the time we arrived, she'd be perfectly fine. She'd had CAT scans, EEGs, EKGs, and every other expensive medical acronym you can think of.

The first time this happened, the husband told us, she wore a Holter EKG monitor for the better part of two weeks. They'd found nada. One quack even had her on seizure medication for nearly two years. But despite everything they'd looked for and all the tests they'd run, Mrs. Johnson continued to pass out three or four times a year, scaring the shit out of poor Mr. Johnson.

This time, she was chatting on the Internet with her sister when she passed out. Her sister was naturally concerned when the message she was receiving ended in a long, unbroken string of "mmmmmmmmmmmmmmm," so she called the house and had the husband go into the other room and check on Mrs. Johnson. He found her out like a light, facedown on the keyboard. Of course, by the time we got there, the husband had her sitting on the couch, with the obligatory cool washcloth on her forehead. She was not happy to see us.

Quite frankly, I stalled for time. They taught me some useful things in paramedic school, one of which was the lesson that people do not just pass out repeatedly for no reason whatsoever; it simply means that no one has discovered what is causing it yet. Keeping that in mind, I had told her, "Just let us check you out, Mrs. Johnson. Let my partner put the cardiac monitor on you, let me check your vital signs, and if we don't find anything, we'll be on our way."

I was kneeling next to her, checking her blood pressure, when she suddenly slumped over onto me with a guttural moan, her eyes rolled back. If I hadn't been bright enough to figure out something was wrong with that, my partner's urgent tugging at my shirt and his cries of "Monitor...monitor...monitor...MONITOR!" would have clued me in.

A.J. Sellers may be only a First Responder, but he knows that wide, funny-looking beats on the monitor are Bad Things. When the monitor is showing nothing but Bad Things, he's smart enough to bring that to my attention. I have to admit, it surprised me a bit. I may have let my stoic paramedic face slip just a little.

Okay, let's be honest. I squealed like a little bitch.

I did have the presence of mind, however, to apply a little therapeutic electrocution, which brings us to where we were now—Mr. Johnson about to pass out himself, A.J. thinking "How cool," me about to piss my pants, and Mrs. Johnson wondering why all the men had such strange looks on their faces.

"What happened?" Mrs. Johnson asked, bewildered.

"You just had a serious cardiac event," I told her. "My guess is that's why you've been passing out."

"But I feel okay," Mrs. Johnson protested, tugging her bra into place.

"You are going to the hospital, ma'am," I told her firmly, gathering up the cardiac monitor and helping her up from the chair. "Seriously, you could die."

That got her attention, and she reluctantly allowed me to lead her into the foyer, where A.J. had positioned our stretcher. I let go of her arm just long enough to lower the cot, then firmly guide her into a sitting position on it. We quickly strapped her in and wheeled her to the rig. A.J. started to climb into the back with me as we loaded her, but I shook my head.

"Just get us to the hospital," I told him. "Don't break any speed records, but don't dawdle, either." He looked disappointed as he slammed the rear doors. On the way to Fort Sperry, Mrs. Johnson had several more short runs of ventricular tachycardia. None of them lasted for more than a dozen beats or so. I quickly started an IV in her left arm, keeping one eye on the cardiac monitor the entire time.

"How do you feel?" I asked Mrs. Johnson, after watching the latest run of V-tach march across the monitor. She shrugged her shoulders.

"Okay, I guess," she said. "The lights keep dimming every now and then." I looked up at the overhead lights, bathing us in a steady incandescent glow.

*Well, I'm damned sure not going to wait for them to totally go out again. You're about to get medicated.*

"Mrs. Johnson, I need to give you some medication to control your heart rhythm," I told her. "Are you allergic to anything?"

"Just that stuff they give you at the dentist," she told me. "Makes me sick to my stomach and I itch like crazy."

Well, that ruled out lidocaine! And I wasn't really sure I'd be safe giving procainamide, either. Bretylium it was, then.

I've never given bretylium to anyone not in cardiac arrest before, but there's a first time for everything. I recalled the words of an ER doc who told me once, "If you ever give that stuff, give it slow, son. And point their heads toward the disposable equipment, too. They'll spew like a warm beer." I mixed up a bretylium infusion and guesstimated a ten-minute infusion rate, then settled back to call Fort Sperry ER. During my phone report to the nurse, Mrs. Johnson sat up and looked out the rear window.

"You're not taking me to Fort Sperry Community Hospital, are you?" she asked accusingly.

"Well, yes, ma'am," I stammered, covering the mouthpiece of the phone with my hand. "We really need to go to the closest hospital."

"I agreed to go to a hospital, not that fucking Band-Aid station," she told me adamantly. "Once we stop at that hospital, I'm walking home!"

"Let me call you back," I told the nurse, then turned to Mrs. Johnson. "Ma'am, that hospital is much better than it used to be. They've got physicians on duty twenty-four hours a day now. They've got new equipment, more nurses, the works. It's really not all that—"

"We stop there, and I ain't going inside," she said adamantly, interrupting me. As if in punctuation, she crossed her arms across her chest and stared at her reflection in the rear windows.

"Uh, you do realize that if that rhythm happens again, you could easily die?" I asked her.

"Yup," she confirmed, still staring at her reflection.

"And that by bypassing this hospital to go to another one, you're taking you're life in your own hands?" I continued.

"I'm a big girl, sonny. I know the risks. Just take me to West Oneida."

Okay, that sounded like informed consent to me! Not that I liked it much, mind you.

I dialed the number to West Oneida Regional Medical Center and presently a voice answered. "West Oneida ER, Dr. Hamilton speaking."

"Hi, Doc," I began, "this is Kelly with Chennault Ambulance. I'm bringing you a sixty-four-year-old female who was in ventricular tachycardia. I cardioverted her successfully and—"

"Where are you coming from?" he interrupted.

"Well, northern Chennault Parish," I answered. "I'm just leaving Fort Sperry, with maybe a twenty-five-minute ETA to your—"

"Take her to the hospital in Fort Sperry. She's unstable," he interrupted again. Oh shit, here it comes...

"Well I, uh...I can't do that, Doc," I tried to explain. "She requested transport to your—"

"I don't care where she wants to go, son," he said, as if to a backward child. "If she's in V-tach, she's not stable enough to make a twenty-five-minute trip. Take her to the closest hospital."

*Yeah, Doc. That's what I told her. But she ain't buying it.*

"Tell him I ain't going anywhere but West Oneida!" Mrs. Johnson yelled out.

*You heard the lady, Doc.*

"She *was* in V-tach," I corrected him. "Now she has a sinus rhythm, she's awake and alert, and her vitals are stable. She refuses to go to the closest hospital, so I'm bringing her to—"

"Do not bring her here!" he told me curtly, his voice rising. "You're the paramedic, you know the risks better than her!"

"Doc, I've explained the risks to her. I've told her she could die. She said, and I quote, 'I'm a big girl, I know the risks.' Now what am I supposed to do?"

"You bring her here against my orders, and I'll have your ass!" he snarled into the phone.

"Well, you'll have it in about twenty minutes, because I ain't turning around!" I snarled back, slamming the phone back into its base.

"Where we going?" A.J. asked from the driver's seat, looking back at me in the rearview mirror.

"Keep going to West Oneida," I told him tiredly, "but get on the radio to dispatch, and have Linda and Bob meet us there. This is going to be one royal pissing contest."

"Just tell 'em it was my decision," Mrs. Johnson said placidly, patting me on the hand.

*Thank you, but I hardly think you're going to act as my stand-in for the ass-chewing I'm going to get. I wonder if Taco Bell is still hiring.*

When we arrived at West Oneida, Dr. Hamilton was waiting just inside the doors. He looked ready to spit nails. Linda and Bob Graham were also there, looking worried and bewildered.

"Don't go anywhere," Dr. Hamilton told me flatly as he took the stretcher and wheeled Mrs. Johnson to a room.

"What's going on?" Linda asked in a stage whisper as he closed the door. "We were at Wal-Mart when the dispatcher called us and said there was a situation here that needed our presence." I had just enough time to fill them in before Dr. Hamilton stalked back into the hall.

"You disobeyed direct orders from a physician!" he began hotly, planting a finger squarely in my chest. I pointedly looked down at his finger, and then back up at his face. Wisely, he withdrew his finger and stepped back. Bobby Hamilton wasn't a bad guy. We agreed on most things. But today, he was dead wrong.

"She was in ventricular tachycardia," I began evenly. "I cardioverted her back into a sinus rhythm. I started a bretylium infusion, because she is allergic to lidocaine. Right now, her vital signs are better than mine. She's awake and alert, and I explained the risks of bypassing a closer facility. It's an informed decision on her part, Doc. You may not like it, and neither did I. But it's her decision to make." Bob and Linda said nothing, just stood there watching.

"It's a COBRA violation, that's what it is!" Dr. Hamilton flared. "And I'll have your patch for it! You're supposed to take them to the closest facility!"

"The closest *appropriate* facility," I corrected him. "You have in-house cardiology, twenty-four-hour cardiac cath lab, thoracic and cardiac surgery..." I ticked them off on my fingers, and he rolled his eyes.

"And the standard says that the patient goes to the facility of their choice, taking hemodynamic stability and available resources into consideration," Bob broke in gently. "We try to convince them to go to the hospitals that we think would be most appropriate, but they don't always take the advice. In this case, Dr. Hamilton, she was not only stable enough to make her own decision, but our paramedic gave her all the information she needed to make an informed decision. And all due respect to you, but you don't really have the authority to take anyone's patch. If you feel he was rude or unprofessional, we will address that with him, but it sounds to me like he was simply doing his job."

"Well, I still don't like it," Dr. Hamilton insisted weakly, but sounding far less certain of his position than he'd been before. "And I'm going to look up those regulations!" he warned.

"I'll do you one better," Bob offered. "I'll provide you with courtesy copies of the applicable federal and state regulations, along with a copy of our protocols. Until then, we have a crew that needs to get back to their coverage zone." With that, Bob took my arm and steered me outside.

"Thanks for the backup," I told them gratefully. "Sorry to take you away from what you were doing."

"Don't worry about it." Bob grinned. "We're getting used to it. But you had better hope you don't transport anyone else here for the rest of this shift!"

# She Digs Me—I Can Tell

"Dispatch to unit One," the radio crackled, "Priority One call at the Lake Chennault spillway, on the Daleville side. Unconscious person." Rob Daigle sighed, stuffed his mouth with the last of his French fries, and looked at me.

"Unit One responding," I grunted in acknowledgment, extricating myself from the cramped booth at McDonald's.

"That's a twenty-minute drive!" Rob spluttered angrily, his mouth still full. "We'll have to go all the way around the lake!"

"Maybe not," I replied. I had an idea forming in my head, so I keyed the radio mike once again. "Dispatch, is the patient at the spillway itself?"

"Ten-four, Unit One. The caller advised that a fisherman had collapsed at the spillway."

"It's only six minutes to the Fort Sperry side of the spillway," I suggested to Rob. "We could push the stretcher and the gear across."

"I like it," he grinned, warming to the idea. "We'll have the guy back across the spillway to the rig before the Reagan Station volunteers even get there." With that, we took a hard left turn onto Highway 21 for the brief run to the spillway access road. In less than five minutes, we were there.

Damn, I was a genius! We'd still be fifteen minutes out if we'd gone the long way around.

Rob and I piled the medic bag, oxygen, and cardiac monitor onto the stretcher and ducked under the chain stretched across the walkway at the top of the spillway. In the summer months, the walkway is packed with fishermen, shoulder-to-shoulder with their beer coolers and bait buckets. One hundred yards down the walkway, the flaw in my brilliant plan became apparent.

The walkway was only four feet wide, and our stretcher took up two feet of it. We apologized repeatedly, pushing our way past pissed-off fishermen, knocking over bait buckets and coolers, tangling lines, and generally making asses of ourselves. I looked back and the sea had closed behind us, with most of them still directing angry looks our way as they untangled themselves.

We were going to have to bring the patient back through that gauntlet, too. We were screwed.

"Ohhhhhh, shit," Rob muttered softly, and I looked up to see what had him so spooked. There she was, about thirty yards ahead, the Immovable Object set to collide soon with our Unstoppable Force. A huge woman was perched on top of a five-gallon bucket. She was so large, she had two smaller women in a satellite orbit around her. I would say they were small, but only in comparison; each of them weighed maybe 250, but she was much bigger. The walkway at the top of the spillway was only four feet wide, and her ass easily took up three feet of that. She looked like a grotesque toadstool, perched there on her bucket. To make matters worse, she was giving us the evil eye, and she didn't show any sign of getting up to make room.

"I don't like this," Rob whispered out the side of his mouth. "You and your brilliant ideas."

"It was your idea, too!" I whispered back. "Just relax. Maybe she's friendly. Just reach out your hand and let her sniff it."

"Fuck you!" Rob retorted, edging warily closer.

This was like a scene out of a bad Western. *This walkway ain't big enough for the both of us, sister.*

"You don't still have the smell of food on your hands, do you?" I warned. "And be brave. They can smell fear." Rob turned his head and shot me a dirty look as we approached the woman.

"Uh, excuse me, ma'am..." he began hesitantly.

"What you want?" the woman demanded, a hostile gleam in her eye. Her satellites took up flanking positions, forming a virtual wall of cellulite.

"We need to squeeze past you nice ladies," Rob blurted.

*Great choice of words, partner.*

"We have an emergency on the other side of the spillway," I explained politely. "If you ladies could just step aside, we'll be on our way." At that, all three of them glared at me and turned their attention back to their fishing bobbers floating in the current thirty feet below us. If anything, their asses stuck out even farther.

Dropping our cot to its lowest position, Rob and I reluctantly prepared to run the Gauntlet of Goo. Picking our way past the acres of ass in front of us, we managed to lift our stretcher over our heads as we sidestepped through the narrow gap between them and the railing. It was a tight fit, but we weren't forced to lubricate with K-Y to slip through, and we even managed to negotiate the passage without knocking a single floppy straw hat into the water.

The walkway was mercifully clear on the other side, so we were able to set down our burden after fifteen feet or so. Apparently, their combined gravitational pull sucked in any fishermen within fifty yards. We crossed the rest of the walkway at a brisk trot, still looking for our patient, who was supposedly just on the other side.

"Awww, goddamnit!" Rob whined, pointing. He sounded like he was about to cry. I looked to see what he was pointing at, and immediately felt like crying myself. Our patient was not at the spillway. He was well downstream, at the end of a four-hundred-yard hike through pea gravel six inches deep. With big rocks. And gullies. And driftwood.

Did I mention the fucking pea gravel?

He was lying supine amid a crowd of onlookers, all of them flashing the gang sign of the International Bystanders Society—one finger pointing at the ground, the other arm waving overhead, beckoning frantically. Some of them were even shouting the IBS secret code phrase, "Hurry the fuck up!" By the time Rob and I got to the patient, I wanted to get on the stretcher myself.

Our patient was an old man of maybe seventy, lying on his back with his head propped on his soft-sided tackle box. A bystander was helpfully giving him a big sip of water. He was pale, but still sweating. From the number of empty Coors cans lying around his fishing spot, it was pretty obvious what had happened to him.

"What happened, sir?" I asked him, kneeling beside him and checking his radial pulse.

"Got plumb dizzy," he answered, "then I woke up with all these people standing over me." His pulse was rapid but strong.

"How long have you been out here?" Rob asked as he wrapped a blood pressure cuff around the man's arm.

"All morning," the man replied. "Caught a few good catfish, too. It's hotter'n hell, but I been drinking plenty of fluids." I held up one of the empty Coors cans.

"These fluids?" I asked, grinning. He grinned back.

"Hell, yeah, son! That's the real reason I fish. Gives me an excuse to drink beer!" This earned a chuckle from the crowd.

"That's as good a reason as any," I laughed, "but the problem is, alcohol dehydrates you faster. Plus, it's ninety-four degrees out, and you've been out here for five hours and drank what...a six-pack? That isn't enough to keep you hydrated, even if you were drinking water."

"I was about to go on a beer run in a few minutes," the old man explained. "I ran out, but the fishin' was too good to leave." The crowd chuckled collectively.

I was pretty certain this was a garden-variety case of heat exhaustion, but I asked him all the standard history questions anyway. He was a reasonably healthy old man, his only medical history an enlarged prostate and an allergy to, as he put it, "bitchy wimmen."

He was an entertaining old codger, but we had to get him out of the heat soon, so we cut the comedy routine short and eased him into a sitting position. Immediately, he turned a pasty white and nearly passed out. His head lolled around drunkenly, and his eyes lost focus. When he came around, he was looking into the faces of two concerned Emergency Medical Technicians, one of whom had noticed that his pulse rate jumped more than twenty points when we sat him up.

"He's orthostatic, Rob," I observed. "Let's get some fluids started and get him on the stretcher. Cardiac monitor, too." I looked back up at the spillway in dread. If anything, it was packed with even more fishermen now, and the Cellulite Sisters were still perched there on the rail like gargoyles looking for a meal.

"Hey, folks," I said to the crowd in general, "why don't y'all try to flag down a boat for us?" Immediately, they hustled en masse to the shoreline and started flashing the IBS gang sign at the boats anchored below the spillway. I'd have flagged one down myself, or had Rob do it, but neither of us had the knack. It's a lot like a tourist vainly trying to hail a taxi in New York City—only the locals really know how.

Presently, an expensive bass boat pulled up to the shore. The captain jumped to the ground and swaggered over. He was a fiftyish man in an advanced stage of midlife crisis. He had all the signs—expensive boat, hair graying at the temples, beer gut, bottle tan, mirrored sunglasses, and enough gold chains to make up a Mr. T starter kit. His first mate looked to be all of twenty-five, and she had some rather spectacular pectoral ornamentation, no doubt paid for by our new friend.

I'd just bet that if she fell out of the boat, there was no way she'd drown. But I'd have damned sure tried to help her.

"Y'all need some help?" Pimp Daddy asked brusquely.

"Yes, sir." I nodded seriously. "We have a very sick man here, and we'd like to use your boat to take him back across the spillway. Could you do that for us?"

"All three of you, plus your gear?" he asked dubiously. "I suppose I could carry that much weight. Better still, why don't I just stay ashore and let my fiancée drive you across?" The girl flashed a winning smile. I smiled. The clouds parted and a shaft of heavenly light bathed us in a comforting glow. Angels sang.

*Thank you, Lord. Your blessings never cease.*

"Would you?" I gushed. "Thank you so much!"

Without further ado, Rob and I loaded our patient onto the casting deck of the boat and piled our gear aboard, and the girl slowly backed us out into the current. I was just about to start an IV on the old man when our savior arrived, so I took the opportunity to finish my task as we bounced across the waves. The girl smiled appreciatively at my obvious skill.

*She digs me. I can tell.*

All too soon, the trip was over and the boat was beached on the opposite shore, a bare fifty feet from our rig. We unloaded our patient and our gear, and I shook the girl's hand before she left.

"Thanks for the assistance," I told her. "We're grateful."

"My pleasure," she breathed seductively, winking at me as she backed the boat off the beach. Her voice was every bit as sexy as the rest of her.

*Come back, gorgeous! I never even got your name! We'll take Pimp Daddy's money and run away together!*

On the way to the hospital, I gave our patient nearly a liter of Ringer's lactate solution. His pulse and blood pressure remained unchanged, but he was talkative and alert. He told me his name was Grady, and we chatted about the best places to fish along Bayou Chennault. He knew a few good spots I hadn't tried, and, even better, they were all easily accessible by ambulance, and within our coverage zone.

"That gal drivin' the boat sure was a looker," he observed, his eyes twinkling. "She'd be worth taking a Viagra for!"

"Yeah, she was pretty hot," I agreed. "She's too young for you, though."

"You see the way she was lookin' at me? She's partial to older men." Grady winked. "I can tell."

I chuckled and shook my head, disconnecting the cardiac monitor leads and oxygen as Rob pulled into the ambulance bay at Fort Sperry. Later, after we'd given report and handed Grady off to the ER staff, Rob looked smugly at me as we headed back to the station.

"You see the way that girl winked at me before she left?" He smirked. "She dug me. I could tell."

# Thwarting Natural Selection

"Oh shit, I can't breathe...oh God, my chest is killing me...oh man, I took too much shit...oh shit, I can't breathe..." my patient was repeating over and over.

*No shit, Sherlock! What did you expect after taking twelve ephedrine tablets? Did you think you'd just drift off to a peaceful slumber? It's the active ingredient in methamphetamine, for God's sake!*

I was trying to start an IV, a task that would be relatively easy but for the fact that my patient was slick with sweat, slippery as an eel, and thrashing around on the couch. Two volunteer firefighters were doing their best to hold him down, and right now their best was barely enough.

This guy's veins were standing out like ropes, however, and I sank a 14-gauge catheter in his forearm without much difficulty and quickly secured it with a gorilla wrap—four wraps with three-inch tape. It was ugly, but strong.

Rob was having considerably more difficulty attaching cardiac monitor leads. The guy was so diaphoretic, the electrodes wouldn't stick.

"Use the benzoin swabs," I suggested. "Wipe him off first." Rob nodded, and fumbled through the bag for the benzoin adhesive swabs.

Not as if it would be a big surprise when we finally got the monitor on him. With a blood pressure of 280/160 and a pulse like a hummingbird, I knew what I was going to see.

I was nonetheless surprised, however, when the monitor screen finally settles down to a readable rhythm. It was a figure so unlikely that I even took the time to print a strip and count the beats myself. His heart rate was 300! Yep, 300 beats a minute.

*Damn, now, that's impressive! This one goes in the scrapbook!*

Our boy was going to blow a gasket if we didn't do something quick. The local protocols don't specifically address this situation, but they do allow us to sedate combative patients. The only agent I had on hand was

Valium, which wasn't ideal, but I made a quick decision to administer five milligrams. That dose got quickly changed to ten milligrams after Ephedra Boy flailed his arm, almost causing me to stick myself with the exposed needle. I pushed the entire syringe in one fast squirt.

*Screw it! I'd rather ventilate you than fight you, buddy.*

I withdrew the needle and stepped back, half expecting him to stop breathing and collapse in a heap, but instead he simply became noticeably calmer over the next couple of minutes.

I looked at the cardiac monitor, and his rate was down to 200. He was still convinced his heart was going to explode and loudly announcing that he'd taken "waaaaaay too much shit," but at least he no longer sounded like the voice-over guy who reads the legal disclaimers at the end of radio commercials. I motioned for Rob to get another quick blood pressure.

"Okay, man, now that we're a bit calmer," I told the man, "do you care to tell me what else you took?" His pupils were so dilated that it was impossible to tell the color of his eyes. He shook his head vehemently, still squirming around.

"Nothin' dude, I swear!" he said. "I just took a bunch of speedos! I don't take illegal drugs!"

*So you just prefer to kill yourself with the legal ones, Ephedra Boy. But I ain't buying that even twelve ephedrine tablets can do this to a person.*

I already had a treatment plan in mind, but I wanted to run it by a doctor first. I thumbed the speed dial on my cell phone for Fort Sperry Community Hospital and asked for Dr. McMurray. A few seconds later, I was rewarded with a chuckle as he answered the phone.

"Well, here's a switch," he laughed. "Kelly Grayson actually calling and asking for orders!"

"Well, we're kinda off the page with this one, Doc." I grinned. "I've got a twenty-six-year-old male with an apparent sympathomimetic overdose. He swears it was just over-the-counter ephedrine tablets, but his BP was 280/160, with a heart rate of 300. He's got dilated pupils, diaphoresis, chest pain, the works."

"Any history of supraventricular tachycardia?" Dr. McMurray wanted to know.

"No medical problems at all, as far as the sister knows," I answered. "And we're not able to get much from the patient. I've already sedated him with ten milligrams of Valium, and that got his heart rate down to 200 and his BP to 190/110. I figure adenosine or cardioversion isn't going to do anything but piss him off, so I'd like to give him five milligrams of metoprolol." I was answered by a long silence.

"Tell you what," Dr. McMurray finally answered. "Hit him with some more Valium, and if you can't get his heart rate to less than 150, give him twenty milligrams of labetolol. It should also lower his pressure better than the metoprolol."

"Will do," I confirmed. "Repeat the Valium as needed, and control his rate and BP with labetolol if that doesn't get his heart rate below 150."

"Call me if anything changes," he reminded me unnecessarily before he hung up. I dropped the phone in my pocket and turned to Rob.

"Five more of Valium, and then let's get him loaded," I ordered. With another dose of sedative, Ephedra Boy got calmer, but he still wasn't what you'd call placid. He stayed on the cot when we planted him there, but he couldn't sit still, constantly turning this way and that. As we were wheeling him out the door, he turned over on the stretcher and accidentally toppled a curio cabinet standing next to the door. An entire collection of NASCAR commemorative plates crashed to the floor, accompanied by the anguished wail of his father.

"Son of a bitch! You broke Dale!" he screamed as we beat a hasty retreat to the rig.

*That will get you kicked out of the house, Ephedra Boy. You can sit on your unemployed ass and get high under his roof, but smashing his Dale Earnhardt limited-edition plate is just going too far.*

On the way to the hospital, another five milligrams of Valium got him calm enough to answer general history questions, and he told me he had no prior medical history and no allergies. He simply got in an argument with his girlfriend, went home, and took two packets of speedos "to feel better."

*Great idea, Ephedra Boy. When you're angry and upset, take a handful of stimulants to calm you down. Do you drink booze to improve your judgment and reflexes, too?*

Ephedra Boy's heart rate was still 170, so I prepared to administer twenty milligrams of labetolol.

"What's that?" he asked suspiciously, jerking his arm away and staring at the syringe.

"It's called labetolol," I answered. "It will lower your heart rate and probably help with some of those tremors you're having."

"Uh-uh," he said, shaking his head. "I learned my lesson. I took too much shit, and I don't want you giving me any more."

"Let's get something straight, buddy." I sighed tiredly, lowering the syringe. "First of all, 'shit' is what you took. What I'm giving you is medication. The medications I've given you so far are quite possibly the only reason you're still alive. So do you want to continue being a dumbass, or do you want me to give you the medication the doctor ordered?"

I held his gaze and waited patiently until he grudgingly extended his arm. Shaking my head, I slowly pushed the labetolol and disposed of the syringe. By the time we got to the hospital, Ephedra Boy's heart rate was 150 and his blood pressure was down to 160/90.

We rolled him inside, scooted him over to the ER bed, and filled Dr. McMurray in on what we'd done so far. A few minutes later, we were cleaning our rig when the nurse ran outside breathlessly, clutching a sheaf of papers.

"Did he come this way?" she asked frantically, looking around.

"Did who come this way?" Rob wanted to know. "The guy we just brought in?" The nurse nodded, out of breath.

"I haven't seen him," I answered. "Christ, we just dropped him off five minutes ago! Why would he leave?"

"He wanted to leave the hospital against medical advice, and Dr. McMurray wouldn't let him, because of the drug use and the sedatives you gave him." She groaned, anguished. "I left the room for just a second to get the involuntary commitment papers, and when I came back he was gone!" We locked our truck doors and joined in the search, but our boy was long gone.

*We should just call the cops and tell them to look for a twitchy guy in a hospital gown with his ass hanging out. He should be easy to spot.*

A week later, Rob and I were at a local convenience store when I recognized the guy in line just ahead of me. It was Ephedra Boy, and he was buying—you guessed it—speedo tablets. We just shook our heads as we watched him pay for his purchase and walk away.

"Thank God you can't cure stupidity," I observed. "As long as there are guys like that, we'll always have a job."

# When Ostriches Attack

OUR PATIENT WASN'T in good shape. She was an elderly woman dressed in overalls and a heavy flannel shirt. One of her rubber boots was lying maybe twelve feet from her body, and the flannel shirt was ripped to shreds. The flashlight beams illuminated one pendulous breast hanging through a rip in the shirt, blood still oozing from the gaping wound there. She was lying on her back with her arms folded to her chest in decorticate posturing, each breath a ragged, shuddering gasp for air. It looked as though someone has pounded her face and upper body with a potato masher, and then finished her off with a dull knife.

Her husband was already dead, lying curled on his side on the torn-up ground of the pasture, covered in loose hay and dirt, his blood seeping into the soil beneath him. His right ear had been ripped off, and the gash there went all the way down his neck and over his right clavicle. There was a gaping wound in his back that I could see ribs and spine through. Most of his clothes had been ripped away.

Their attacker was not some crazed psychopath from a slasher movie. No, the culprit was standing about thirty yards away, looking at us curiously as we worked feverishly to stabilize and package the old lady. His legs were wet all the way to his knees with their blood.

He was a rooster ostrich who stood nearly eight feet tall and weighed well over two hundred pounds. He lifted one foot and stomped it, craning his neck curiously as if what we were doing was enormously entertaining. What caused him to attack, we'll probably never know, but attack he did, and he did a number on this old man and his wife that is hard to imagine.

"According to the grandkids, the bird attacked the woman when she went into the pasture to feed him. The old man fought him off with his cane, and the bird turned on him," Danny Harmon was telling us. "It got him on the ground and just stomped and kicked him until it got tired or bored, then just walked off." I looked over at the two children in the back of his cruiser. They were no longer crying, but they both wore the vacant, hollow stares of children who have seen something too horrible to comprehend.

"Well, the damned thing probably killed her, too," I said grimly. "She just doesn't know it yet." The lady had a closed head injury and severe blood loss, and my experience told me she was simply too old to recover from a traumatic insult this severe. Frankly, I'd be happy if she just made it to the trauma center alive.

I lay on my stomach and intubated her as Mary kept her cervical spine aligned. I was securing the tube when I heard the chilling but unmistakable sound of several handgun safeties being clicked off at once. I cringed, sure that I was going to feel claws ripping into my back before the deputies could bring him down.

"Oh, my Looooorrrd..." Mary breathed, her eyes wide in fear. The ostrich was only ten feet away, head bobbing up and down, stamping his feet in agitation. At least six deputies had their guns drawn and pointed.

"Shoot the fucker!" Mickey Sanders said angrily as he taped a large trauma dressing to the woman's chest.

"I will, if he gets any closer," Danny assured him. "Just don't make any sudden moves, okay?"

"Every fucking move we make is going to be sudden!" I hissed, not taking my eyes off the bird. "Just shoot him and be done with it!" Several deputies grunted in agreement. They thought it was a fine idea, too.

"We can shoot him in self-defense," Danny said evenly, "but we can't destroy the animal without authorization. So why don't you guys just get her on the board and ease her out of here, and if the bird takes one more step this way, we'll blow him away." Grudgingly, we secured the lady onto a spine board and carried her out of the pasture, surrounded by a phalanx of armed deputies.

On the way to the South Arkansas Regional Medical Center, the woman stopped breathing altogether. She was flaccid, both pupils were fixed and dilated, and her heart rate was only 62. Her blood pressure was barely audible at 70/30. Mary got bilateral IVs and bolused her with fluid, but even after a liter of saline we still couldn't tell much of a difference.

We rolled into the ER and went straight to the trauma room with a full team awaiting our arrival. I gave report to the doctor as we moved the lady to their bed.

"Elderly female, age unknown, medical history unknown. An ostrich attacked her and her husband. He was DOA. She was decorticate on scene, both pupils blown. Estimated external blood loss of at least a liter. She has bruising and small lacerations all over her torso, plus an eight-inch laceration through the right breast that goes all the way to her rib cage. Last BP was 70/30, with a sinus rhythm at 62 beats a minute."

"And you say she was attacked by an ostrich?" the doctor asked dubiously, peering over his glasses at her chest wound. He raised one of her arms and examined her hands. "These look like defensive wounds on her arms and hands. I just don't know..."

"What don't you know?" I asked pointedly.

"Oh, I'm not criticizing you," he assured me quickly. "I'm sure you did everything you could. It's these wounds that I'm not sure about." He frowned, stroking his mustache. "They just don't look like any ostrich attack that I've ever seen."

*Huh? Well, what does the typical ostrich attack look like, Marlon Perkins?*

Dead silence followed his remark. Mary and I traded a look. Mickey and Mary traded a look. The trauma team just looked blankly at the doctor. I was the first one to dissolve into laughter, and it rapidly became contagious. Mickey was holding his sides, and he had tears in his eyes. Everyone in the room was howling with laughter. Everyone, that is, except the doctor.

"You want to tell me what you find so damned funny?" he asked hotly, a reply that resulted only in more guffaws. Mickey was the first person to catch his breath.

"Uh, Doc?" he chortled, wiping his eyes. "Not being disrespectful or anything, but just how many ostrich attacks have you seen?" Realization dawned on the doctor's face, and he blushed furiously.

"Well, actually, this is my first," the doctor chuckled. "What I meant to say was that this doesn't look like an animal attack."

"That's a relief," I said, struggling to keep a straight face. "For a minute there I thought you guys had packs of killer ostriches roaming the countryside." The doctor banished us from the ER.

"Get out!" he said, still laughing. "And if this is the kind of stuff you're going to bring us, don't come back!" We retreated to the ambulance bay as the trauma team got to work. Outside, Mickey was still amused.

"'This doesn't look like any ostrich attack I've ever seen,'" he said sonorously, in a credible mimicry of the doctor's voice. "I damned near wet myself!"

We stopped off at the scene to pick up my truck on the way back to Fort Sperry. Mary and I had been off duty when the call came in, and we'd sprinted the call in my truck. At the paddock, we found the ostrich stretched out on the ground, surrounded by six very shaken deputies. Danny Harmon looked as if he'd seen a ghost.

"Sumbitch nearly got us," he said. "We got the go-ahead to destroy him, and I went out there with my sidearm. I hit him squarely in the breast with two forty-caliber rounds, and the damned thing barely flinched. Then, he just charged. Scott had to take him out with the riot gun." Scott Barton, the shift sergeant, just shook his head.

"Two rounds of three-inch magnum, double-ought buckshot," Scott said in awe. "I hit him solidly the first time, and he still kept coming. He piled up right at our feet."

Mickey just looked back and forth from the ostrich to the deputies. "Well, there's plenty enough to go around"—he grinned—"but I've got dibs on the drumsticks."

# Ten-Dollar Words

I KEEP TELLING you, he's sick!" the mother insisted. "I told that damned home health nurse the same thing, but she refuses to listen."

The little boy I was examining was nine years old, and he weighed all of twenty-five pounds. He was lying on the bed in a frail and contracted little ball, with his head and eyes turned all the way to the left. He was whimpering pitifully and drooling. Even if he didn't have profound developmental delays and chronic medical problems, I'd think he was sick.

"So what, exactly, makes you say that?" I asked politely as I listened to the boy's lung sounds. He had some upper-respiratory crackles, but otherwise he sounded pretty good. His color was good, too, but there were some greenish secretions in his tracheostomy tube.

"Look, I know my boy!" the mother said testily. I just smiled gently and nodded, encouraging her to continue. She sighed tiredly and softened her tone. "Look, he's a happy kid. He smiles all the time, even laughs now and then. He recognizes me and his dad, and his brother. He never complains. He just acts like something is wrong!" she concluded in frustration.

"And the home health nurse didn't seem concerned when you told her all that?" I asked as I palpated a pulse. His heart rate was rapid, up around 120 or so.

"Pressure is 84/52," Mickey Sanders told me as he looped his stethoscope around his neck.

"See? That's too low!" the mother insisted. "What was his heart rate?"

"It was 120," I told her.

"Too fast," she said with certainty. "His blood pressure is usually around 90/60, and his heart rate only gets over 100 if he's sick or in pain."

I simply nodded as I picked up a frail little hand, pressing my thumb against the back of it to check his capillary refill. It was less than two seconds, but I did notice something unusual. He had six fingers on each hand and six toes on each foot.

Somebody's family tree did not fork.

"What kind of medical history does he have?" I inquired politely. The mother rolled her eyes and took a deep breath.

"He was born without a corpus callosum, and he's also hydrocephalic. He can't walk, talk, or feed himself, so he's totally bed-bound. He has a tracheostomy tube, and a PEG [percutaneous endoscopic gastrostomy] tube, and he used to have a colostomy—"

"Does he normally have those secretions around his tube?" I interrupted. She flashed me a nasty smile.

"Yes, he does. I've already suctioned him," she answered condescendingly. "He has a tube because he can't cough or swallow effectively, and he's always getting respiratory infections. This is nothing unusual for him. I've already checked his cerebral shunt and measured his head girth. It's normal. I wouldn't have called 911 if I could tell what the problem was."

*Okay, ma'am, you've used your ten-dollar word, now I get to use mine. And what in the world is a corpus callosum anyway?*

"I notice that he has polydactyly," I observed, lifting his hand. "Does he have any other genetic defects that you know of?"

"Hirschsprung's disease, and cerebral palsy," she answered.

*Okay, you win. Cerebral palsy I know about, but I've never heard of Hirschsprung's disease. You know more ten-dollar words than I do.*

I remained silent as I ran my hands over the kid's body, palpating, inspecting, and auscultating. When I palpated his abdomen around his PEG site, he flinched and moaned. I removed the dressing to discover the site inflamed, with purulent, greenish pus oozing around the tube.

He had an infected PEG site. He might even be septic.

I looked up at the mother, who was watching with growing impatience. "I think the site around his feeding tube is infected," I informed her, holding up the crusty dressing. She looked mortified.

"We change the dressing every day!" she protested. "It didn't look infected yesterday!"

I assured the mother that I believed her; her son had a number of artificial openings in his body, and he was bound to get an infection sooner or later. Mickey and I gently move him to the stretcher.

On the way to West Oneida Regional Medical Center, I accessed the kid's IV infusion port and bolused him with saline. After 200 milliliters of fluid, his heart rate was down to 100, but I couldn't tell much difference in blood pressure. The nurse at West Oneida accepted my handoff report with a been-there, done-that expression.

"We know Keyshawn pretty well around here," she assured me.

"Mom brings him in a lot, huh?" I sympathized. "She was tough to deal with."

"She can be," the nurse agreed, "but she's pretty conscientious. Keyshawn just gets sick a lot. If it's not one thing, it's another."

Back at the ambulance station, I hid in the bathroom while I looked up Hirschsprung's disease and corpus callosum in the Taber's medical dictionary.

*Oh, that explains a lot! Hirschsprung's has to do with his intestines, so that explains the colostomy he had. And the corpus callosum is that bridge of tissue between the right and left brain hemispheres! Now, why didn't I remember that?*

Satisfied, I flushed the toilet and put the medical dictionary in the magazine rack. I ran straight into Mickey as I opened the door. "Sorry about that," I apologized as I opened the door. "I didn't realize you needed the bathroom."

"It could wait," he said. "Say, what was wrong with that kid? Chronically, I mean. I didn't recognize half of that stuff the mother rattled off."

"Well, Hirschsprung's disease is a disorder where part of the colon doesn't have any nerve endings. So, no peristalsis in that section causes feces to back up there. They usually do a temporary colostomy and remove that section of colon."

"And the other thing?" he pressed. "That thing he was missing at birth?"

"You mean the corpus callosum?" I asked incredulously. "Don't tell me you've forgotten what the corpus callosum is! We covered that in anatomy and physiology not two months ago!"

"I don't remember it!" Mickey said defensively.

"If you're going to be a paramedic," I explained tolerantly, "you're going to have to retain information for longer than two months. So go look it up."

# Clueless

IT WAS MY second day at Med Star, and I was bringing in a patient complaining of leg pain. She was a nursing home patient with a list of medical problems a mile long. She got scarcely better medical care there than she'd get at home, but she fell a lot and her family didn't want to deal with her. So she spent her days wearing a shitty diaper, with a roommate five feet away who shouted every few seconds, all day long, "Hey, I need some goddamn help in here!"

Our patient had an inflamed left leg. It was swollen and painful to the touch, and when I bent her knee and flexed her foot, she experienced severe calf pain, a sure sign of a deep vein thrombosis. There was not much we could do for her, other than handle her gently and give her a safe ride, which we did.

On the way to the hospital, I asked her about her grandkids. She had seven of them, and they all lived out of state. None of them had visited her in months. I didn't know what to say to that, and she said nothing, either. We dropped her off at Sherwood General Hospital and gave the nurse a report, and I wished my patient well.

At the ER nurses' station, I sat down on a stool to complete my paperwork. It was hectic in there. Apparently there was an MI patient in the resuscitation room who was crashing. They were trying to stabilize him and get him to the cath lab as close to yesterday as possible.

Dr. Sharon Jenkins was shuttling back and forth between the desk and the room, giving orders to the nurses, talking to the cardiologist on the phone, and signing whatever was put in front of her. I could wait for her signature until things were calmer. Right now, she might as well have been juggling chainsaws. Larry, a Med Star paramedic who was also a nurse, walked up.

"Hey, check this out," he said, handing me a monitor strip. It showed a third-degree AV block, with big, ugly ventricular QRS complexes.

"Third-degree block, right?"

"Looks like it," I said as I was writing my billing ticket. "One of your patients?"

"Yeah, an asthma patient I brought into room one. He was in pretty bad shape." I stopped writing and looked back over my shoulder through the open door of the resuscitation room. They were hanging dopamine on the guy right at that moment. Now I was confused.

"Asthma patient? You just brought him in?"

"Yeah. He was having severe difficulty breathing and wheezing, so I gave him an albuterol treatment and got him here as quick as I could. He was breathing like thirty times a minute. His sat was only seventy-eight percent. Bad."

"You gave an albuterol treatment to the guy in room one? The heart attack patient?"

"No, my guy was having an asthma attack. He said he started having difficulty breathing all of a sudden, and he was wheezing real bad. When I saw the third-degree block on the monitor, I thought, Whoa, we'd better boogie with this guy, so we drove hot all the way here. I gave him the albuterol on the way."

"Well, that dude's having a heart attack now. Did you give him any nitro? What was his pressure?"

"His pressure was a little low, probably 100/60. Why would I give nitro to an asthma patient?"

I stared at him, not sure of what I was hearing.

He was dead serious. He really thought this guy was having an asthma attack, not a heart attack. And he'd given him albuterol. Clueless.

"Did the doctor say anything to you when you brought him in?"

"Well, you know Dr. Jenkins. She's always pissed about something. She didn't really say anything, just shut the door behind me as I left."

*Maybe she's always pissed at you about something...and now I know why!*

I just shrugged noncommittally. Explaining it to him would be wasted effort. You just can't polish a turd. Apparently, though, you can get a turd to memorize information long enough to earn a nursing degree and a paramedic patch. Larry walked off, eager to show someone else the evidence of his incompetence. Six months later, he got promoted to supervisor.

# Little White Crosses

IT WAS 3:17 A.M. This is our witching hour, when the weekend drunks have left the bars and headed home. Everyone else's circadian rhythms are at their lowest ebb, including mine. Around here, the cops catch the drunkest ones in town as soon as they weave out of the parking lots. The ones we see are those who've slipped the net, or those driving home from Oneida, thirty minutes away.

The strobes were hurting my eyes. I reached over and turned off the siren, earning a quizzical look from my partner. I snapped at him, "Why do you have to run that fucking thing in the middle of nowhere on an empty road?"

He said nothing, and I immediately felt like an ass. He was just following company policy, and was green enough to still worry about breaking the rules—even the ones that made no sense. But he feared my disapproval even more, so he shut his mouth and kept driving.

A.J. Sellers was a good kid, just twenty-five going on seventeen. He still acted like a carefree high school senior, despite the fact that he had two kids. He'd been a First Responder for about eight months, just long enough to be excited rather than petrified about calls like this.

We'd been slammed running transfers all day, and only got to bed just two hours earlier. My eyes were sticky, and I had a serious case of bed-head under my cap. My mouth felt like a cat shit in it. A.J., on the other hand, looked fresh.

*Fucking kid.*

We were heading to a "Signal 20-I," which is cop-speak for a motor vehicle accident with injuries. They usually turn out to be total bullshit or, at the other end of the spectrum, road pizza. Not many fall in between.

At 3:17 A.M. on the S-curves of Highway 35 South, they were always bad news. There were enough little white crosses on that stretch of road to fill a small cemetery. A.J. was not yet experienced enough to dread calls like these. I knew better. I'd cared for my share of the names on those little crosses.

A.J. slowed down as he passed the Reagan Station Volunteer Fire Department. The bay doors were open, a good sign. We didn't have direct radio contact with some of the volunteer First Responders, but I was hoping the folks from Reagan Station would be at the scene. Extra help never hurts.

As if reading my mind, the radio crackled, "Unit One, Dispatch. Be advised, Reagan Station First Responders are 10-97." Good.

A.J. slowed even more as we rounded a curve, easing over the centerline. A doe and two yearlings were standing in the ditch on my side.

"You see 'em?"

"Yep. Big buck standing just in the trees behind them."

"Well, be careful."

The moon was full, and the deer would be night feeding along the road shoulders and in the pastures. At least once a year, a doe zigs where she should have zagged, and wipes out the front end of a rig. A.J. snapped the wheel to the right, just a little jerk to get my attention. It startled me a bit and I glared at him. He was grinning at me. At least he wasn't mad at me for snapping at him earlier.

"What, you got something against eating roadkill?"

"No smartass, I just don't like wiping out at eighty miles an hour."

He snorted, unable to envision a situation where his reflexes would not be equal to the task. See what I mean about twenty-five going on seventeen?

A.J. wasn't a bad driver, just still sure of his own invincibility. I kept my mouth shut. I'd bitched at him enough, and wrecking a rig might be one of the dues he had yet to pay. A.J. slowed down anyway and started scanning the ditches. I suppressed a grin and pretended not to notice. I realized that in the past ten minutes, we hadn't met a single car coming from the opposite direction—not a good sign. My grin faded.

The scene came as a surprise as we topped a hill just south of Robichard's Grocery. The wreck had been reported as several miles farther south.

"Fuck me..." A.J. whispered.

My sentiments exactly.

On either shoulder, cars and pickup trucks were parked for a couple of hundred yards. Quite a few of the pickups had their emergency flashers on, red gumball lights on their dashes marking them as the firefighters' personal vehicles. The last few motorists started to ease over when I hit the siren in brief bursts, and the sea parted.

There were remains of a compact car sitting crossways in the middle of the road, a mass of mangled metal, like ugly origami folded in the hands of a clumsy giant. It was impossible to determine the make or model now. The front end was gone, the windshield a cloudy spiderweb of cracks.

A cluster of volunteer firefighters noticed our arrival and beckoned frantically. At least two more ignored us, leaning into the shattered windows on the driver's side.

I looked at A.J. "Spine board and trauma bag. Let's go." He nodded, threw the rig into park, and bailed out.

I was halfway to the wreck when more volunteer firefighters and Good Samaritans got my attention. A Ford pickup was in the ditch on the opposite side of the road. A girl was sitting on the ground nearby, hugging her knees and sobbing, rocking back and forth.

All the commotion centered on a spot about ten feet past the truck. I stopped, and A.J. nearly ran me over with the stretcher. I looked back at him, hesitating. In the past, I'd triaged the patients and decided which ones needed the most urgent care. A.J. had never had to manage a critical patient on his own. It looked like tonight there would be plenty for both of us, and the backup unit was just coming back into the parish, at least twenty-five minutes away.

I grabbed him by the arm and shouted over the snarling of the generator and Hurst tool the extrication crew had just fired up. "Look, holler for Unit Two, and have them start easing Unit Three this way. You take the pickup; I'll take the car. If you get anything you can't handle, come get me. Otherwise, just put the volunteers to work." He bobbed his head nervously and headed toward the pickup.

"Wait!" I called after him. I took the spine board and trauma bag off the stretcher. "Send somebody back to the rig for any equipment you need. I'll take these." He nodded dumbly, and started to turn away again. He looked scared.

"A.J.," I said softly, in my "calm voice." His eyes shifted back to me from the wreckage of the truck, and eventually locked with my own. "There's nothing I can do for 'em that you can't. Just assess and package 'em on boards, and I'll do all the paramedic stuff on the way to the hospital. You've got plenty of help. You can do this."

I turned away before he could reply. He'd have to manage on his own for the next few minutes, scared shitless or not.

The two firefighters leaning into the car were Don and Dan McNeal, identical twins and EMTs from Reagan Station. Where you saw one, you would invariably see the other. In turnout gear, I could never tell them apart. One was reaching through the driver's back window, maintaining spinal alignment while his brother was standing beside him, reaching through the front window applying a cervical collar.

The driver's face was a wreck, blood and tangled blond hair masking her features. I poked my head in between them, and Don or Dan looked at me from behind the girl's head, a grim smile on his face. "Wassup, brother?"

"You tell me, guys."

Dan or Don backed out of the car and gestured at the interior. I took his place and looked in. In addition to the front-end damage, the passenger side of the car was caved in all the way to the center console, and looked to be folded over the girl's right arm. I glanced down at her legs, and they appeared to have about four more joints than they should have had. About two inches of her right femur was protruding from her jeans. Her right ankle was folded under the accelerator pedal. Her breathing was ragged and gurgling. Amazingly, the rearview mirror was still attached to the shattered windshield. There was a graduation tassel hanging from it. Everywhere there was a fine white dust from the airbags.

"We gotta get her out now, guys. Let's see if we can pop this door first, and someone needs to get working on the passenger side to free her arm."

I backed away as the crew moved in with the Hurst tool. I got my laryngoscope and a tube from the airway kit. I heard the groan of tortured metal behind me as the spreaders popped the door open. I didn't really relish doing a seated intubation on this girl, but if we didn't get her out right this minute, that was what was going to happen.

I could reach most of her now with the door out of the way, and as I maneuvered in front of her, my arm brushed a trim piece folded over her arm. It moved easily and I tugged at it. It came away in my hand, and I noticed that her arm was not entrapped at all. The metal was just crumpled over it, but there was nothing pinning her.

Her ankle was broken, the foot folded back under and pinned beneath the accelerator. I moved her lower leg and foot gently to the left and cringed as I felt the crepitus in her ankle. But her foot popped free, and I wormed my way back out of the car and shouted for the board. I lay my laryngoscope and tube on the remains of the hood, just forward of the windshield, and my scope promptly rolled down into a crevice somewhere in the engine compartment.

*Lovely. Just fucking lovely.*

One of the McNeal twins was wedging the end of the board against the seat while his brother held spinal alignment. I grabbed the girl by her hips and torso and rotated her onto the board. It wasn't pretty and we really needed more people for the move, but there was simply no room. We managed to extricate her and strap her to the board.

I felt a hand on my shoulder and looked up. It was A.J. He had his patient packaged and on the stretcher. He looked a lot calmer now, sure of himself.

"Driver of the truck's dead," he said. "This one was ejected through the windshield. He's unconscious, but he's breathing. I'll load him and send someone back with the stretcher."

I grinned at him and gave him a thumbs-up as he moved away. Don or Dan was digging around under the car, and came up triumphantly with my laryngoscope. "Lose something, asswipe?" He grinned at me and his brother joined in.

"Boy, send a guy to paramedic school, give him cool toys to play with, and we still have to go around picking up after him..."

I rolled my eyes. "If you guys were actually any good, you would have found my tube as well. I'm not impressed." They laughed some more as we loaded the patient onto the stretcher.

Our girl was not doing well. She had agonal breathing, and we hustled her toward the truck. I got another blade from the airway kit to replace the oil-smeared one I had, and intubated her lying right there on the stretcher at the back of the rig. There was more room and light there.

A.J. was behind me in the rig, setting up IVs and cutting the clothes from his patient. The tube went in easily, with good breath sounds all around. Before I could place the tube holder, she bit down on the tube and curled her arms up to her chest in decorticate posturing.

Not good.

I had to pry her mouth open to place the bite block between her teeth. As I secured the tube, I could hear a siren approaching, and Unit Two pulled up right behind us. I loaded our patient as Roger Perkins walked up to the back of our rig.

"Need some help?"

"As usual, your timing is impeccable. You got here just in time to transport, but you managed to avoid all the hard work." I loved to give Roger a hard time.

"Yeah, we timed it just right." He grinned, then turned serious. "How many patients do we have?"

"One DOA, two critical. If you'll take the one A.J. has, I'll take this one. We're going to West Oneida."

Over my left shoulder, and twelve minutes away, was Fort Sperry Community Hospital. It was a good hospital, as small hospitals go, but they just didn't have the resources of West Oneida Regional Medical Center, twenty minutes away.

A.J. and I handed his patient out to Roger. Roger's wife, Cathy, had parked Unit Two's stretcher at the back of our rig, and they slid the spine board onto their stretcher. As I handed the head of the board to Roger, I noticed that A.J. had written vital signs on the tape securing the patient's head. The patient was moaning behind the non-rebreather mask. There were several deep lacerations on his forehead, and his upper lip was split all the way to his nose. His teeth were showing through the gap. I could smell the alcohol in his blood.

A.J. tossed Roger a spiked bag of saline. "Here. Don't say I never gave you anything." One of the McNeal twins climbed into the back of the rig as A.J. slipped out the side door.

"Found her purse in the car," Don or Dan said. "Need somebody to ride in with you?"

"I never turn down free help, man. Shut the doors and let's go."

Dan or Don took over bagging while I got an IV. I slipped in a 14-gauge and taped the line down as A.J. pulled away, forced to maneuver far onto the shoulder to get around the wrecked car.

I took the girl's vitals, and didn't like the results. Her heart rate was only 62, and her blood pressure was low at 84/40. She had stopped breathing on her own several minutes earlier. Her chest and abdomen seemed free of injuries, but her pelvis and legs felt like broken pottery. Both femurs and tibias were broken, as well as her right ankle, but I was worried mostly about her head injury.

Aside from the brief episode of posturing when I inserted the tube, she'd been completely flaccid. Both her pupils were dilated and barely reacted to light. I was still at least ten minutes away from the hospital, just passing into Oneida Parish, so I slipped another large-bore IV into her right arm and ran in some Ringer's solution. She'd had around 500 milliliters of saline, and I got Don or Dan to get another set of vitals while I contacted the ER.

Around here, all hospital contact is done via cellular phone, so I placed the call while Don or Dan struggled to hear a BP over the siren and engine noise. I recognized the nurse who answered the phone. My report was brief and to the point, nothing like the full patient report I was taught to deliver.

"Hey, Jeremy. This is Kelly with Chennault. En route to you with a female driver, frontal impact collision. Multiple lower extremity fractures, pelvis as well. Possible head injury. I've got her tubed, bilateral IVs, and about 500 cc's of fluid. GCS is 3, BP 80 palp, heart rate 60. We're seven minutes out."

I finished cutting her clothes off and assessing her. There wasn't much in the way of outward injuries to treat, and splinting her legs at this point would be wasted effort. I felt the truck lurch, and suddenly we were backing into the ambulance bay at West Oneida Regional. A.J. flung open the door and helped us unload. There was a lot of stuff to sort out—cardiac monitor, two IVs, oxygen tubing, and the shreds of her clothes hanging off the cot.

Jeremy met us just inside the door. Behind him was Dr. Donna Leary. It was late, and she was obviously tired. She looked haggard. She said nothing, just pointed to the trauma room.

As we moved the patient over on the board, I gave Dr. Leary the bullet: "Unrestrained driver, frontal impact. Airbag deployed, steering wheel deformed, windshield starred. Lots of dash intrusion. She was unconscious at the scene. Got her tubed, lines on the way, 500 cc's of saline. Pelvis and lower extremities fractured; probably a head injury, too—her pupils are dilated and unreactive."

"Any posturing?" she asked, sidestepping to the left as the radiology tech maneuvered a portable X-ray machine into the room.

"She showed some decorticate posturing when I intubated her, but other than that, nothing." I shrugged my shoulders.

It was not an expression of indifference, just helplessness. Leary smiled tiredly as she turned back to the patient. She didn't waste her breath on words like "good job" or anything so trite—she didn't have to. I knew if I had not done something to suit her, she'd have chewed my ass thoroughly.

I had a lot of respect for Donna Leary. She was a strong advocate for EMS, and always treated the crews with respect. On the other hand, she was also quick to quietly, methodically tear off a strip of hide if you fucked up. She'd taught me the basics of acid-base balance in medic school—Leary's Acid-Base for Idiots.

I collected my paperwork and walked outside. As usual, my rig was a total mess. If trashing a patient compartment were an Olympic sport, I'd be a gold medalist. A.J. was busy cleaning up behind me, but it would be at least half an hour before we were ready to go. I'd managed to get blood on the cot, the grab rails on the ceiling, and the underside of several cabinets—basically everywhere I'd put my hands. I helped him make up the stretcher and carry the biohazard bag back inside for disposal.

Everyone was filing out of the trauma room—Dr. Leary, nurses, respiratory therapist, radiology tech, everybody. Our girl coded right after we got her there, and they'd been working her for the past twenty minutes while we cleaned our rig. They'd only just now called it. Just like that, a young girl was gone.

The ER staff never even knew her name. Come to think of it, neither did I. Her purse was still outside in the rig. I went back outside to retrieve it, and I found her wallet and driver's license inside. She was eighteen years old, her birthday only a couple of weeks ago. Her name was Jennifer.

As I walked back inside with her purse, I passed a woman clutching a cell phone with a bewildered look on her face. I started to tell her that the ER waiting room entrance was around the corner, but she saw the purse in my hands and recognized it. She looked a lot like her daughter.

She stopped me and started to ask me what, where, how her daughter was, but she couldn't find the words. She just choked back tears and looked at me pleadingly. I told her that her daughter was badly injured, what I'd done for her, and what the doctor and nurses had done for her after we got to the hospital, but I was too much of a coward to tell her the rest. I wanted to be able to say something to this woman, something that would banish the horror of this night for her, but I couldn't find the words, either.

She asked anyway. "But, is she going to be okay?" My silence told her enough, and she slowly collapsed in on herself, sobbing but making no sounds.

"The doctor will be out to speak with you soon," I told her as I took her hand and led her to a chair in the waiting room. It was a lame response, and we both knew I was too much of a coward to tell her the news.

On the way out I told the ER clerk that the girl's mother was in the waiting room, and I climbed into my rig to leave. A.J. was already behind the wheel, catnapping as he waited for me. The sun was coming up.

Someday, I'm going to get better at this. Someday, I'll know what to say.

# Tank

A. J. SELLERS AND and I got a call for a seizure patient at a house on Constitution Avenue. The dispatch information was sketchy at best, so our dispatcher had asked the Fort Sperry Police Department to respond with us. The house was dark when we got there, so we hung back a bit. This wasn't the best neighborhood in town.

Kathy Shoemaker from the Fort Sperry Police Department was right behind us. She pulled up, shaking her head as she exited her cruiser. "It's Tank," she said. "This is where he's staying. Probably drinking and not taking his Dilantin again."

Tank was one of our frequent fliers. His real name was Lester. He had epilepsy, and was totally noncompliant with his medications. He drank like a fish, smoked crack, and bounced from one address to another, living with whatever friend or relative would put up with him that week. On the frequent occasions when he couldn't find a place to crash, he'd either fake a seizure or pass out drunk in someone's parking lot, knowing he'd wind up in either the hospital or the drunk tank. Either way he was assured of a bed and a warm meal.

Tank looked like his nickname, stocky and muscular at about 240 pounds, but he was a pussycat. There wasn't a mean bone in his body.

As we entered the house, we found Tank, postictal, sitting propped up in a rickety folding metal chair. He was running with sweat, shirtless, with blood all over his head and shoulders. He was holding his dick in his hand, and he stank like he hadn't bathed in a month.

It was stiflingly hot, and judging from the candles everywhere and the stench of urine and feces, I was guessing there was no electricity or running water in the house. There were some highly suspicious-looking coffee cans sitting on the floor beside a bare mattress. I didn't even want to think about what was in them.

The girl who'd called 911 told us, "He been seizing. He hit his head."

"Has he been drinking, doing crack or anything?"

*Inquiring minds want to know.*

"I don't know nothing. He just stay here," she said, turning her back on us and walking back to her bedroom.

*Gee, thanks for filling in the blanks for us, honey.*

I told A.J. to get some vital signs while I put an oxygen mask on Tank. I checked his head out to see where all the blood was coming from and found a small cut on the crown of his head. It wasn't hard to find—Tank was as bald as a cue ball. He looked a lot like a black can of roll-on deodorant. I slapped a four-by-four on the cut and quickly wrapped his head, more to keep the mess to a minimum than to control the bleeding, which wasn't all that bad.

A.J. still hadn't even laid a hand on Tank, and his face looked as if he were going to vomit. He was trying as hard as he could to avoid touching Tank. Not that I blamed him all that much, but squeamishness was a hangup I couldn't afford.

"Hey," I told him sarcastically, "he's not going to tell you his vital signs. At some point you actually have to touch the patient. Hurry up!"

This sped A.J. up a little bit, but he still went about assessing Tank with all the enthusiasm of a six-year-old boy afraid of catching cooties. Through it all, Tanks sat placidly with his dick in his left hand, swaying back and forth and snoring a bit.

A.J. was having a hard time getting the blood pressure cuff in place. He approached Tank's arm with the cuff, pulled back, then went forward again. I watched him repeat this about three times before I reached over and gently disengaged Tank's hand from his member, pulling his arm away from his body so A.J. could wrap the BP cuff around it. "Anytime soon would be nice," I told him ever so politely.

He looked up at me pleadingly but I ignored him. The kid had to learn that even the most disgusting patients get assessed and treated just like the rich folks on Lake Chennault. I was losing patience with the boy, but it was kind of funny to see him handling Tank as if he were toxic waste.

Kathy was nowhere near as kind as I was. She leaned forward with an evil grin. "Whatsa matter, sweetie? Widdle A.J. don't wanna touch the big, stinky man? Awwww, poor baby." He shot a look of pure hate in reply.

As much as I'd like to have sent him over to see what was in those coffee cans, I did have a patient to treat, and I doubted I could handle both Tank and a puking partner. So I motioned to A.J. to get one of Tank's arms so we could sleepwalk him to the stretcher.

He stood back, shaking his head. "Uh-uh, not me. He had his pecker in this hand. You come over to this side and I'll get that arm." About this time, Tank started to seize again. It started as a focal motor seizure, just his right leg twitching uncontrollably, but it would get worse. It always did.

"Look," I barked, "we don't have time for this shit. Either grab his arm right now, or about ten seconds from now you'll be bear-hugging him and carrying him to the stretcher. What's it going to be?"

A.J. said something under his breath that I couldn't hear, and grabbed Tank by the arm as we tried to stand him up. Too late. Tank bucked and arched his back, sliding off the chair and onto the ground in a full-blown grand mal seizure.

"Shit! Now what do we do?" A.J. asked plaintively.

"We do just what we were going to do. We get him on the stretcher and go. We'll work him in the truck. Now get under his arms and I'll get his legs."

I briefly pondered if A.J. hadn't gotten the better end of the deal—it was entirely possible, even likely, that Tank had pissed himself. Luckily, whatever urine might have been on his pants didn't make it past his knees, and I stayed dry. A.J., however, was not so lucky.

We quickly hustled Tank to the truck, where I popped him with an 18-gauge and give him five milligrams of Valium. The seizure continued unabated, and we boogied on our way to the hospital. I hollered at A.J. to relay a report to the hospital.

"What am I supposed to say?" he asked.

"Hell, just tell 'em what we got. It's Tank, he's seizing again, we've given him Valium, we'll be there in two minutes." I heard him relaying exactly that: "Tank...seizing...Valium...two minutes." A five-word patient report, possibly a new record.

By the time we pulled up at Fort Sperry Community Hospital, Tank had stopped seizing. My handoff report wasn't much more detailed than A.J.'s notification. These guys all knew Tank, and they'd heard it all before. Inside of twenty minutes, they had him labbed up, tucked away, and admitted to the floor. Of course, his Dilantin level was low. As a matter of fact, he had no Dilantin level, and his tox screen showed cocaine metabolites. His blood alcohol was .18, on the low side for Tank.

I checked my watch as I helped them wheel Tank to his room. It was just past six o'clock. Tank would even get a meal out of this.

# Pucker Factor: 11.0

It was Fourth of July weekend. Bobby Grisham and I had spent the previous day on the lake, ostensibly on duty as a lake patrol unit. We loaded a monitor, bag, and Dolphin board into Dr. Brothers's ski boat and cruised around, getting some sun and checking out the babes while everybody else ran their asses off. Life was hard.

Today was our turn in the barrel, though, and we got a call to the lake for a drowning. The patient was in the parking lot at the Lake Chennault Inn, near the marina. Why in hell a drowning victim was in the hotel parking lot I have no idea. I've given up trying to make sense of dispatch information. I goes where they tells me, and I don't ask no questions. (It is comforting to know, however, that if I ever suffered a traumatic brain injury on the job and could no longer function in normal society, I could still earn a living dispatching for Chennault Ambulance.)

We arrived at the scene to discover not one, but two, patients. From looking at them, I'd say the smaller of the two would go about 400, maybe 450, pounds on the hoof. Her sister made her look slim. They were both in wet T-shirts and overalls, and the bigger one was sitting on the ground, wailing at the top of her lungs.

"Lawdy, Lawdy, Lawdy, Jesus, Lawdy! Lawd, have mercy! Oh, Jesus loves me, yes, he do. Jesus done saved me in my hour of need. Lawdy, Lawdy, Lawdy, Jesus, Lawdy..." she wailed over and over.

*Tachylawdia with occasional Premature Jesus Complexes. This could be bad.*

"She just upset, thass all," the calmer sister said. "Our boat done sank. We purt near drownt. I's okay, but she done almost drownt."

"Lawdy, Jesus, Lawdy, Jesus, Lawdy, Jesus, Lawdy, Jesus, Lawdy!"

*Uh-oh, now she's got bigeminal PJCs. This is really bad.*

"Okay, ma'am, we're going to...what boat?"

"Them boats over there. We rented one. We was catfishin' under the bridge, and our boat done sank." She pointed to the boat rental stand near the landing.

*About a thousand pounds in a twelve-foot aluminum boat. No wonder it sank. I'm surprised you even made it to the bridge.*

"Lawdy, Jesus, Lawdy, Jesus, Lawdy, Jesus—Amen!—Lawdy, Jesus, Lawdy—Amen!—Jesus..." She interrupted my reverie on natural selection and our place in thwarting Darwin's theory.

*Damn! Tachylawdia with bigeminal PJCs and intermittent Amens. She's gonna faint any minute!*

"Okay, ma'am. Everything is going to be all right. My name is Kelly and this is my partner, Bobby. We're going to take you to the hospital. Don't worry, we'll take good care of you," I told her as we lowered the stretcher. I fixed a smile on my face and gave her my hand. Mercifully, she stopped wailing long enough to grasp our hands and heave herself to her feet.

*My back thanks you, ma'am.*

"Would you like your sister to ride with us?" I asked as we rolled her to the rig. She stifled a whimper and nodded her head. Bobby shot me an evil look as the little sister climbed into the passenger seat of the rig. We managed somehow to load the stretcher into the back of the rig without help, the stretcher groaning almost as loudly as Bobby.

*I take that back, ma'am. My back does NOT thank you. As a matter of fact, my back is not happy at all with you right now. And please SHUT UP!*

My prayers were answered as we rode to Fort Sperry Community Hospital. She was quiet for the most part. Her tachylawdia had mercifully degraded to an agonal rhythm with an occasional "Lawdy!" escaping whenever we hit a bump.

There was not much I could do for her; she didn't seem to be hurt, and our thigh cuff wouldn't even fit around her arm. I couldn't even find a pulse. *You are alive, aren't you?* She confirmed this with another "Lawdy!" as we pulled into the ambulance bay.

As we dropped her off and gave our report, she motioned for me to come closer. She grabbed my hand and pulled me down toward her, kissing me on the cheek and wrapping me in a ferocious hug. "Bless you, baby.

Bless both you young men. Thank you fo' bein' my angels."

"No problem, ma'am." I grinned. "That's why we're here."

*No, thank you, ma'am. And my back doesn't really hurt all that much anyway.*

Later that afternoon, we got another call to the lake. It was a drowning at Baker Beach. There was a small bandstand and concession stand there, with no lifeguards on duty. On this holiday weekend, it was crowded with drunken partygoers. Mary rode with us, doing the last of her ambulance clinical shifts to complete her paramedic course.

"Unit One, Dispatch. Be advised, your patient is out of the water and CPR is in progress." *Uh-oh, not good.*

I leaned into the back and told Mary to set everything up to run a code. She tossed the monitor, suction unit, and jump bag on the stretcher. I looked back a bit later and she was spiking a bag of saline.

As we approached the entrance to Baker Beach, the radio crackled again. "Unit One, Dispatch. Be advised, your patient is breathing."

*Well, that's welcome news. With any luck, he'll be close to the parking lot, too.*

Our luck was not that good. Our patient was farther down the shore, a hundred yards down the beach, lying motionless at the water's edge. There was a crowd of people standing around, beckoning frantically. The sand was too soft to drive the rig closer, so we all three jogged as quickly as we could to the patient. Halfway there, my ass was already dragging.

There were several scared teenagers huddled around the kid. A man wearing an Oneida Parish Fire Department T-shirt and cutoff jeans straightened up as we approached.

"They started hollering for help," he said, nodding at the kids. "We went out there and found him on the bottom. When we got him to the bank, he didn't have a pulse. We started CPR on him, me and her," he went on, gesturing to an attractive blonde in a lime-green bikini.

She nodded in affirmation. "He just started breathing right before you got here." The kid was rolled over onto his left side in the recovery position, just like it's taught in CPR class. But if this kid was breathing, it wasn't what I'd call effective. His Adam's apple was moving spasmodically, and his face and shoulders were purple. His chest wasn't rising. I turned to the kids as Mary and Bobby started to roll him over.

"Did anyone see what happened?" Everyone shook their heads. "Did he fall? Dive off something, hit his head or anything?"

"Nothing like that, mister," one of them spoke up. "He was just ducking his head underwater, seeing how long he could hold his breath." The kid, a skinny one wearing baggy shorts and the beginnings of a nasty sunburn, noticed my skeptical expression.

"Really, mister. No diving or nothing like that. He was just holding his breath when he didn't come back up. He wanted to be a Navy SEAL..." His voice broke and he trailed off, his eyes watering and his lip quivering.

"Okay, kid. We'll take good care of him." I pasted on a reassuring smile as a Fort Sperry police officer started to question him.

Over the years, I've learned to wear a number of convincing masks designed to calm and reassure people. My Reassuring Smile is pretty convincing. Sometimes, it's even real.

I turned my attention to Mary, and she was having problems. She tilted the kid's head back and tried to ventilate with the BVM that Bobby handed her. She squeezed the bag...nothing. She cursed under her breath and tried again. Still nothing. She looked up at me.

"Try a jaw thrust," I told her. "I'll get the laryngoscope."

"I can't even get it open with a jaw thrust!" Mary hissed to me urgently. "His teeth are clenched!" At this point, Mary's teeth were pretty clenched, too, and I couldn't blame her. This kid was just getting more purple.

"Just keep trying," I hissed back, handing her the laryngoscope as I reached into the bag, digging for a bite stick. Mary tried once more to open his mouth to slide in the laryngoscope, but no dice. Still clenched.

I gently butted Mary out of the way and tried to bag him myself. Still no chest rise. This kid had a world-class overbite, and he was trismic. We couldn't open his airway or ventilate him. I wedged a bite block between his molars and twisted. Damn, this kid was clenched!

*Come on now, kid, open up. I'm even asking nicely.*

Amazingly, the plastic bite block snapped in half. My Reassuring Face was rapidly giving way to the Purposeful Determination Face. The expression isn't much different; there's still an occasional smile when needed, a little lighthearted banter, maybe even a joke or two to cut the tension. But the orders are just a little more clipped, and I tend to adopt an exaggerated politeness. The unspoken message everyone seems to get is "Do what I tell you, and do it now." They usually do, without question. Those who know me well will tell you the Purposeful Determination Face is really more like a High Pucker Factor Face. They're right, but I think I hide it well.

Someone, a bystander, was trying to hand me something. "Thanks for your help, ma'am, but we have this under control. Please step back," I told her firmly.

"Kelly, it's me, Dana." Surprised, I looked up to see Dana Sellers, who was one of our medics and A. J. Sellers's stepmother. She was handing me an oral screw, kind of a threaded ice-cream cone designed to pry someone's mouth open. I took it, tried to find an opening in the boy's bite, but couldn't find a purchase.

*Of all the people in Chennault Parish, I find the only one with a full set of teeth! Screw this, let's just go. We'll try to ventilate him on the way.*

"Okay, everybody, we gotta go. Let's get him on a board and get him to the truck." Bobby Grisham and Andy Sellers, Dana's husband, positioned the board under the boy as Dana and I rolled him over. Mary was hurriedly gathering up our equipment. We quickly rolled him back over and strapped him down. The sprint back to the rig was far tougher carrying a teenager, even when splitting the load among four people. Bobby got in the front to drive, while Andy, Mary, Dana, and I piled in the back.

As we hit the highway, I was still working on an airway. Andy was getting an IV while Mary was attaching monitor leads. Dana was sitting in the attendant's seat getting vital signs. I knew what she'd get for a respiratory rate. The kid had stopped trying to breathe a couple of minutes ago.

I briefly tried bagging without success, then desperately tried to wedge the laryngoscope blade between his teeth. He relaxed ever so slightly, allowing me to advance the blade a couple of inches, and then clamped down like a pit bull with lockjaw. I had to work at it to get my laryngo-scope back. I looked up at the cardiac monitor. It was sinus bradycardia at 40, and I'd have trouble believing anyone could get more cyanotic.

*Damn, this kid is going to die. I can't get an airway, and he's going to die before we get to Fort Sperry. I have got to ventilate this kid!*

I flipped the laryngoscope around, grasping the handle like a hammer. I was fully intending to bash this kid's teeth in to get his mouth open. I caught Mary's gaze and she looked horrified, shaking her head. I call it her Jiminy Cricket Face; it's the one she uses when I'm teaching class and my humor gets a little off-color. Between Mary and my conscience, I can usually keep my ego from talking me into doing something stupid, so I lowered the laryngoscope.

*So what do I do now? I can't drop a nasal tube. He's not even breathing to give me some sounds to shoot for. Talk about a shot in the dark. Okay, I'll probably get my ass chewed for this, but...*

"Dana, get me the obstetrical kit." She looked at me as if I'd just spoken Kurdish. I asked her again, and still got the blank stare. "Dana. Scalpel. Betadine. From the obstetrical kit. NOW."

Her eyes looked like saucers as realization dawned on her. She scrambled through the cabinet as I felt the truck swerve a bit. I turned around in the seat and caught Bobby's eyes in the rearview mirror. He wanted to be back there so bad he could taste it.

*Bud, right now I'd give anything to swap places with you.*

Dana found the obstetrical kit and promptly ripped it open, scattering its contents all over the place.

"Fuck!" she blurted, looking mortified. "Sorry about that." She looked scared.

"Relax." I grinned at her as I put back on the Reassuring Face. "I doubt we'll need the sterile drapes and cord clamps. I will need the Betadine, though, so if you'll get that off the kid's lap while you find the scalpel, I'd be grateful."

By the time she found the scalpel, I had the kid's neck prepped. Everybody—Dana, Mary, and Andy—was frozen, staring at me. I could feel

Bobby's eyes on the back of my neck.

*Damn, it got quiet in here all of a sudden. Well, here goes nothing...*

I was just about to cut when an inspiration struck. "Hold on, everybody! I've got an idea." I quickly grabbed a 6.0 tube out of the airway kit and lubed it up. I gently inserted the tube in the kid's right nostril and it slid in easily. There was some slight resistance, which passed as I gently twisted and advanced the tube. I listened to the tube, and, as expected, there were no breath sounds. "Chest compressions," I told Andy. "Slow and easy." As he compressed the kid's chest, I listened again.

*Hot damn! It worked!*

I could hear faint breath sounds as I advanced the tube. As I slid it home, the sounds got much louder.

*Holy shit, I'm in! Talk about luck!*

As I inflated the cuff, I felt like doing a Snoopy dance. Mary was checking breath sounds as Dana bagged, and she was grinning.

"It's in," she said. "Equal on both sides."

"Piece of cake," I replied. "Just rock me a little bit to break the suction on this seat when we get stopped, okay?"

I busied myself with taping down the tube, and when I looked up we were stopping at the hospital. The kid had pinked up dramatically, and the cardiac monitor showed the most beautiful, regular sinus tachycardia I'd ever seen. Bobby threw open the rear doors and we quickly unloaded. He took a look at the tube as we rolled the kid through the door, examined the Betadine stain on the kid's neck, and looked back at me.

"I just knew I'd open the doors and see a tube coming out of his neck, but hell, I've never seen a nasal tube, either."

"Yeah, and you were just itching to be in the middle of it. I could read your mind."

He didn't reply, just grinned as we rolled into room one.

Our medical director, Dr. Mark Brothers, was there. Until the last year, there hadn't been an on-site physician. The doctors were called in from home when they were needed. The volume of ER traffic had increased dramatically over the past couple of years, so the hospital had hired full-time physician staffing for the emergency room. Their first hire was standing in the hallway.

Dr. Brothers motioned him into the room and introduced us. "Kelly, this is Dr. Khalid Khofan, our new ER doc. Dr. Khofan, this is Kelly Grayson, one of our paramedics. Watch him closely. Pretty soon he'll be talking you into giving him permission to do brain surgery."

Dr. Khofan looked a little surprised by the hubbub. No doubt they'd lured him there with promises of a sleepy little town and a slow, sleepy little ER. He'd find out otherwise pretty quickly. We didn't bring a lot there, but what we did bring was pretty bad, and he'd have to manage it with one registered nurse to help him, at most.

"Bobby told me you were doing a cricothyrotomy," Dr. Brothers told me. "Were you comfortable with doing that?"

"No," I answered honestly. "But I didn't think I had much of a choice."

"So you managed to get a nasal tube when he wasn't breathing?" he asked. "I'm impressed," he said. Dr. Khofan nodded agreement.

"Don't be. I just improvised and it worked out. It was probably fifty percent luck."

Dr. Brothers peered at the Betadine stain on the kid's neck and looked back up at me, eyebrows raised.

"Only fifty percent?"

"Okay, maybe ninety percent." I grinned back at him. "But I got the airway, didn't I?"

"Yeah, you did," Dr. Brothers allowed. "Are we sure this wasn't a diving injury?"

"All the kids with him said he wasn't diving. Besides, there's nothing out there for him to dive from. They told us he was just goofing around, ducking under and holding his breath, when one time he just didn't come back up."

"Okay," Dr. Brothers decided. "Chest film, lytes, CBC, and blood gases, and let's get Priority Air notified that we've got a patient going to Shreveport."

Bobby and I backed out of the room as the two doctors begin assessing the kid. His friends had arrived, standing wet and puddling outside in the waiting room, shivering under the air-conditioning.

"Hey, mister," one of them said, grabbing my arm. "Is he gonna be okay?"

"I don't know," I told him, "but he's better than he was. Is there anything else you can tell us about him?"

"Well, like I said, he was just ducking his..."

"Yeah, you told us that," I said, cutting him off. "I mean, does he have any allergies or medical problems that you know of? Where are his parents? For that matter, what's his name?"

"His name is Richard," one of the girls said. "He lives with his mom. We already called her."

I nodded to her and headed outside to clean up my rig.

Later, as Bobby and I were finishing up, Richard's mother arrived. She was understandably shell-shocked, but gave me all the information I needed for my report. I told her to have a seat while I found the doctor. I promised to have him come out and talk to her as soon as possible.

As I walked back into the ER, I heard the nurse shout for help. As I rushed back into the room, the nurse was standing at the head of the bed, squeezing the ventilator bag. The heart-rate alarm was beeping, as was the pulse oximetry alarm. Richard's neck was horribly swollen, bigger than his head. As the nurse bagged, the swelling crept down into his chest. "It just happened," she said desperately. "He got real hard to bag, and then something just popped. Everything went to hell right after that."

Brothers and Khofan rushed into the room, with Bobby and Mary right behind them. Richard's heart rate was down to 40, and his pulse oximetry value was only 78 percent. I felt for his pulse and noticed a hard bump in the soft tissue on the left side of his neck. I felt again, digging a little deeper.

*Is that what I think it is? Whoa! That's his thyroid cartilage!*

I motioned Mary closer and grabbed the stethoscope from around her neck. As I listened to breath sounds, I grabbed Mary's hand and placed it on the kid's neck. "Feel that," I told her.

His breath sounds were faint on the left side, and on the right side they were, well, weird. They didn't sound like breath sounds at all, more like somebody blowing up a balloon. There was subcutaneous emphysema all over the right side of his chest.

"Hey, is that what I think it is?" Mary asked. "Is that his trachea I felt?"

"Yep, that's what it is. He's got a tension pneumo."

"Yeah, he needs a chest tube right now," Dr. Brothers broke in.

"No chest film first?" asked Khofan. "Which side is it on?" The doctors huddled together, looking at the chest film taken twenty minutes ago. They weren't going to find much on it—this had just happened. I grabbed the IV therapy tray and looked for a 14-gauge catheter. They had only 16s, and they were all too short to penetrate this kid's chest cavity.

"Bobby!" I barked. "Go get me one of those swizzle sticks from the truck!" Awhile back, some genius bought a case of 2-inch, 14-gauge catheters. We kept the swizzle sticks around for the rare occasion when we might needle a chest. Bobby bolted for the door and was back in a flash with the catheter. He handed it to me as Brothers and Khofan began opening a thoracostomy tray.

"Hey, Doc?" I asked Dr. Brothers, holding up the catheter.

"Yeah, sure, go ahead," he said. Then, to Dr. Khofan, "See what I mean? He'll talk you into something before you stop to think what you've just given him permission for."

I inserted the needle into the kid's right chest wall, and it immediately popped out of the catheter. There was a sustained rush of air, sounding like someone deflating a tire.

"Sharps on the floor," I warned everyone as I checked the cardiac monitor. His heart rate was already coming back up, and the pulse oximetry was rising. Everyone looked relieved. By the time Dr. Brothers got the chest tube in, Richard's neck was almost back to normal size, and his vital signs had stabilized. The ER nurse gingerly retrieved my needle from the floor and disposed of it.

I grinned at Dr. Brothers. "My work here is done. I've got other lives to save," I said as I walked out the door.

"And don't come back! We've seen enough of you for one day!" Dr. Brothers said to my back as I left.

The grin disappeared as I came face-to-face with Richard's mother in the hallway. She had heard all the shouting and knew something bad had just happened.

"What's going on?" she asked. "What's wrong? When can I see him?"

"Mrs. Hampton," I told her gently, steering her back to the waiting room, "we just had a little scare, but everything is under control now. Remember how I told you we had inserted a tube to help Richard breathe? Well, one of his lungs just collapsed and we had to put a tube in his chest to reinflate it. That's all."

"But, but is he going to be okay?"

"Well, I can't tell you much more than I have, because I don't know. What I can tell you is that he is alive, and right now his vital signs are good. We've arranged for a helicopter to fly him to Shreveport, and it should be here any minute." As if on cue, the roar of a helicopter was heard as Bobby came through the ambulance entrance doors.

"Priority Air just landed," he announced unnecessarily.

"Mrs. Hampton? I have to go now to help them load Richard into the helicopter." She nodded absently as I left to do just that.

Fifteen minutes later, we paused in the hallway as she leaned over her son, sobbing quietly as she tenderly kissed his forehead. Richard didn't respond—he'd been paralyzed and sedated by the flight crew. We quickly loaded him into the bird and watched as it lifted off and turned west toward Shreveport.

In thirty-five minutes he'd be in LSU Medical Center, a level-one trauma center. I said a little prayer as the helicopter shrank in the distance. Richard hadn't moved or opened his eyes since he'd dropped his right lung.

A few hours later, Bobby and I were called back to Fort Sperry Community Hospital. Dr. Brothers wanted to talk to us. Looking grim, he motioned us into the doctor's dictation room. "Well, we just heard from LSU. Our boy has fractures of the second and third cervical vertebrae. What I want to know is why he wasn't immobilized."

I was dumbfounded. "I didn't think it was necessary. All the witnesses denied a traumatic mechanism of injury. Everybody said he wasn't diving."

"Well, one of them changed his story. Apparently, our boy was standing on his friend's shoulders in waist-deep water, diving in. Weren't you taught to assume spinal trauma in all near-drowning cases?"

"I didn't think it was necessary," I said defensively. "Yeah, I know to immobilize near-drowning victims, but that's because you're not sure of the mechanism of injury. Everyone here told us he wasn't diving! I guess I shouldn't have believed them."

"The kids tried to tell the surgeon at LSU the same story. His buddy only fessed up when the doctor told them he knew their story was bullshit, and had the X-rays to prove it," Dr. Brothers said tiredly, rubbing his eyes. "Either way, we are probably going to get sued over this, so each of you needs to write up a formal incident report on it."

"Yeah, sure, Doc. We'll write it up as soon as we get back to the office. Look, I guess I screwed up. I'm sorry." He just smiled ruefully.

"Well, I should have shot neck films, and that wasn't your fault. Relax, guys. You didn't break Richard Hampton's neck—he did. And if you hadn't taken some pretty extraordinary measures, he wouldn't be alive to complain about it. In the future, just don't take a bystander's word at face value." Dr. Brothers dismissed us and we drove back to the station in silence.

For a change, Bobby didn't have much to say. On July 3, exactly one day short of a year later, Richard Hampton sued us for malpractice. Dr. Brothers and I were named as primary defendants in the suit.

# Leon and the Man-Eating Car

"UNIT TWO, DISPATCH. Respond Priority One to 2354 Highway 808. Man trapped in a car."

Shelly Sanders whooped excitedly as we pulled out of line at McDonald's to take the call. It was two in the afternoon, and I hadn't gotten my burger yet. This was not good—I needed my burger.

We hadn't eaten since the night before, and at this point my belly button was rubbing a blister on my spine. Well, not quite. My belly button hasn't been within a foot of my spine in five years, but you get the idea. I was hungry, and in no mood for the bullshit we were about to encounter.

We hadn't been all that busy, but we'd started running transfers before breakfast that morning, and every time we'd had a chance to stop and eat, Satan had chimed in with "Dispatch to Unit Two..."

To top it off, I hadn't had time to take a shower, so I was driving around with a serious case of bedhead and trying to cover it with a ball cap. Shelly looked at me quizzically as I groaned in despair and banged my head repeatedly on the window.

"What?" she asked. She didn't know who lived at 2354 Highway 808, but I did.

Leon Jones was one of our frequent fliers. He was an alcoholic and a chronic malingerer, but he had enough legitimate medical problems that you couldn't just dismiss whatever he was saying. For some reason Leon liked me, probably because I treated him with respect and listened to what he had to say. Some of my coworkers had a hard time hiding their exasperation with Leon. Not me—I found it easy to smile on the outside while I was mentally strangling the life from his body.

Shelly was still a fairly new EMT, and this was her first Leon Jones call. She was envisioning generators humming, the Jaws of Life snarling, and a life-or-death battle to snatch an innocent victim from the Grim

Reaper. She had a sparky little grin on her face, and obviously was loving this. She'd gotten kind of possessive of the siren and lights, as if the console were her personal domain, the exclusive realm of Queen Shelly the Sparky.

I didn't really mind—I let her have her fun. As long as she woke me up when we arrived at the scenes, she could do whatever the hell she wanted. She still had the naïve idea that the dispatch information actually had something to do with what we'd find at the scene. She was about to discover otherwise. I didn't know what we'd find at 2354 Highway 808, but I was betting it was going to be unusual. Leon Jones calls were kind of like "vujà dé"—you got the feeling that nothing like this has ever happened before.

When we got to the scene, there were no fire trucks, no generators, no Jaws of Life, and no excitement. Shelly deflated before my eyes. What we did have was one bemused sheriff's deputy, and one very drunk Leon Jones. The deputy, Danny Harmon, was smiling and shaking his head.

"Well, he's been there since this morning," Danny said, nodding his head toward Leon. "Watch your step when you go over there. He's sitting in a puddle, and it ain't water."

Leon greeted us cheerfully, giving us a bleary, alcohol-fogged grin. "I sho' glad y'all here. I'm real thirsty, and I cain't get loose!" He had his left arm jammed in the glove compartment of his car and apparently couldn't pull free.

On closer inspection, I could tell he had shoved his hand behind the back wall of his glove compartment, wedging it between the dash and the back of the compartment. Whenever he pulled his arm back, the glove compartment opened fully and the back wall pinched his arm against the dash. If he tried to push it farther in, the glove compartment door closed, pinning his arm.

He'd apparently been there awhile—at least long enough to finish a twelve-pack of Schaefer. Apparently he'd had to urinate as well, and since he couldn't get loose to go to the bathroom...

"Uh, Leon? How in the hell did you get your arm caught that way?"

"Well, ya see, I dropped my blood pressure pills. They done fell back behind the box. When I tried to get 'em, I gots my arm hung up! I been out here all day, and it's so hot. I done drunk all my beer..." he trailed off, his voice breaking.

He looked pitiful, sitting there with tears in his eyes, with his arm caught in the man-eating car, sitting in a big urine mud puddle. It was a real tragedy. Danny Harmon stifled a giggle.

"Well, Leon, you certainly called the right people. Did Wanda call 911 for you?"

"Yessuh, she did. She ain't mechanical. She don't know what to do 'bout this stuff."

"Well, this young lady here is our finest EMT," I said, pointing to Shelly. She shot me a dirty look. "Shelly will get you out of there. She's mechanical."

I motioned her over to the trunk of Danny's cruiser. I smacked a Phillips screwdriver into her palm, just like in the movies where the surgeon asks for an instrument. "Your extrication tool, madam. Now go over there and save a life." Danny nearly swallowed his dip of Copenhagen.

In a few minutes, Shelly had the glove compartment dismantled, and a grateful Leon Jones was rubbing his numb but uninjured arm. Shelly didn't look quite as fresh as she had a little while ago. Apparently, it was a bit hot in that car. I doubt she wanted to snuggle up next to Leon to dismantle the glove compartment, so she probably had to lie across the front seat to do it. Leon's front seat held enough dirt to grow a respectable garden. Danny and I sauntered back over.

"Ooh, my arm numb!" Leon wailed. "I cain't feel nothin'!"

"Well, Leon, my man, that is to be expected. It'll wear off. Now all you need to do is sign my form and we'll let you get back inside." I was sending out the most powerful refusal-of-care vibes I could generate. It usually worked—my Refusal Mojo is powerful.

"Do you think it might be broken?" Shelly asked, concerned. "Would you like us to take you to the hospital?"

*Nooooooo! She didn't just offer to take him to the hospital! What was she thinking?*

Leon brightened up considerably. "Yes'm, as a matta fack, I would like to go to the hospital. I think I needs my arm X-rayed." Not coincidentally, Leon's house wasn't air-conditioned, but the hospital was. If he milked it long enough, he might still be in the ER when the meal trays came around.

"Okay, Leon. To the hospital it is. Shelly will take care of you till we get there," I told him, concealing my dismay.

I motioned Shelly closer, so I could whisper in her ear. "I think you should take this one. Leon doesn't normally cooperate with us like this. Apparently, you've built quite a rapport with him. Can I trust you to ride in with him if I drive?"

Shelly puffed up considerably at the prospect. She was actually honored that I'd entrusted her with such responsibility, bless her sparky little rookie heart.

"And while you're at it, you'd better splint that arm. When you're done, you can even do the run ticket. You write it, I'll sign it."

When we got to the hospital, Shelly had Leon's arm splinted and in a sling, just the way she was taught in EMT class. Leon was happy, Shelly was proud, everybody was happy.

Well, everybody except the nurses. We were kind of on their shit list. Before we left, Leon gave Shelly a hug. He reeked of urine and alcohol, and if he'd bathed that week I'd be surprised. But Shelly didn't shy away, and the smile on her face was genuine. "No problem, Leon. That's why we're here."

Bless her sparky little rookie heart, she may actually have what it takes.

# Hoppy Doll

NOTHING WRONG WITH him as far as I can tell," grunted the fire captain. "He's got a crick in his neck, that's all." He pointed the way to a young man curled on the concrete stoop of a ramshackle frame house. His head was oddly canted to one side, and one side of his body seemed to be contracted. The First Responders from the fire department were standing around looking bored, convinced that it was a bullshit call. No one had even checked the kid's vital signs.

"What seems to be the problem?" I asked the kid.

"You gotta help me!" the kid slurred, his tongue thick and unwieldy. He was drooling, and his mouth was drawn to the right. His head was cocked over at a painful angle, and his eyes were crossed. The entire right side of his body was contracted into a painful ball.

"He crazy," a young black woman offered. "He on drugs."

"What makes you say that?" I asked curiously, as Rob started to check the kid's vital signs.

"'Cuz he take all kinda shit, and don't know what it do," the woman answered. "Same shit happened to him yesterday. He took some bad shit."

"Do you have any kind of medical problems?" I asked the kid. He just lay there on his side, jerking and spitting.

"You gotta help me!" he repeated.

"No, he ain't got no medical problems," the woman answered for him. "He my brother. Ain't nuthin' wrong wit him 'cept he crazy!"

"Does he have a history of mental illness?" I asked. "Does he normally act like this?"

"Naw, he just took some crazy-people medicine, that's all. He bought it from my uncle. He dumb enough to take crazy medicine that ain't scribed to him, he must be crazy," she opined.

"Hey, kid, what did you take?" I asked him. He just writhed on the stoop, trying to shake his head. "Come on, kid. I'm not a cop. If you want me to help you, man up and tell me what the fuck you took."

"Hoppy doll," he spat. "I took Hoppy doll."

*What the fuck is hoppy doll? I've never heard that street name before.*

I looked at the sister blankly.

"Hoppy doll," she repeated, rolling her eyes as if I were stupid. "You know, crazy-people medicine?"

Ah, the picture is clearer now...

"Haloperidol, you mean?" I asked the sister. "He took haloperidol?"

"Yeah, that's what I said," the sister confirmed. "Hoppy doll. Same shit happened to him yesterday when he took it."

"Is that right, kid?" I asked him. "You took haloperidol yesterday and it did the same thing to you?"

*Dumbass. Your gene pool obviously needed some chlorine.*

"Yeah, I went to LSU and they gave me a shot," the kid said, sitting up on the stoop. "I need another one." The muscle spasms and slurred speech were rapidly disappearing.

"Fucking faker," I heard the fire captain mutter under his breath, just loud enough for me to hear. "He's drug seeking."

I turned to the firefighters gathered behind me. "Any of you guys ever see a dystonic reaction?" I asked mildly.

"A dis-*what?*" the fire captain asked, one eyebrow cocked skeptically.

"Dystonic reaction," I repeated. "It sometimes happens when you take certain antipsychotic medications, like haloperidol. This is what it looks like. It is not a 'crick in the neck,' like some people seem to think." I looked pointedly at the fire captain, then turned my back on him.

"What's your name, kid?" I asked the boy on the stoop. "How old are you?"

"Tyrone," he furnished, speaking normally for the first time. There was no evidence of the spasms and slurred speech at all now. "I'm nineteen."

"Your sister says you took this before, and the same thing happened. Is that right?"

"Yesterday night," he confirmed. "She took me to LSU."

"Jesus Christ!" I said in disgust. "You didn't learn your lesson the first time, and you went out and bought some more? You're not real smart, are you?"

The kid said nothing, just sat on the stoop, staring sullenly at his shoes.

"All right, Tyrone," I ordered, "get your stupid ass off the porch and go get in my truck. Rob, go with him and get him strapped in, and set me up a line." Rob nodded and led Tyrone to the rig.

"Hey, look," the fire captain told me quietly once they were out of earshot. "I didn't know. Hell, I've never even seen a whatever-you-said-it-was reaction before. How was I supposed to know?"

"Because he's a nineteen-year-old black kid in this part of town, he just had to be faking or drug seeking, right?" I asked nastily. The guy said nothing, just looked apologetic.

"Look," I said, softening, "he's obviously stupid as hell, and I'm half-way tempted to let him suffer through more of this, but just as obviously he was having more than a 'crick in the neck.' Assess more thoroughly next time, okay?"

"I will," the captain promised. "Now, what exactly did you call that again?"

"It's a dystonic reaction," I repeated patiently. "A whole cluster of symptoms like he was having. The ten-dollar words are oculogyric crisis, torticollis, lordosis, and tardive dyskinesia."

*Now say all that ten times really fast. Drop those into casual conversation at the fire hall next chance you get, and you might make chief.*

The captain's facial expression conveyed quite clearly that my impromptu lesson had flown ten feet over his head, despite the fact that he wore a paramedic patch just like mine.

*Just go look them up, genius. Assuming, of course, that you can spell them.*

I climbed into the back of the rig to find Tyrone in the midst of what appeared to be a full-blown reaction—apparently, the "hoppy doll" hadn't worn off. His eyes were crossed comically, his tongue was protruding from his mouth and cocked off to the right side, and the entire right side of his body seemed to be trying to tie itself into a knot. A trickle of drool trailed from his right cheek, forming a puddle on the pillow.

"Blood pressure and breathing are normal," Rob told me, pointing to the notations he had made on the stretcher sheet. "Pulse is a little fast." He looked at Tyrone and shook his head. "I wonder what the hospital gave him to make it stop."

"Benadryl," I told him. "Fifty milligrams should clear it right up."

"You gotta give me some!" Tyrone slurred. "I'm hurtin' here!"

*I don't have to do anything but give you a ride to the hospital, you little dumbass. I can pretend to be as dumb as the fire captain and watch you jerk and spit all the way to LSU.*

"Don't worry, Tyrone, I'm going to make all the bad stuff go away," I told him soothingly as I nodded to Rob that I was ready to go. "As soon as I get this IV, you'll be as good as new. You'll probably be home in a couple of hours, back to wasting oxygen and scoring diarrhea medicine from your friendly neighborhood dealer." Tyrone was much too busy drooling and tying himself into a knot to appreciate the humor.

I started an IV and slowly pushed fifty milligrams of Benadryl, and within a few minutes Tyrone was back to normal.

"Thanks, man," he said to me gratefully, offering me his hand. I ignored it.

"So tell me something, Tyrone," I said. "If this happened to you before, why in hell did you do it again?"

"Don't know." He shrugged. "I just wanted to get high, you know?"

"Did you?" I asked pointedly.

"No," he admitted. "I thought it would be different this time, though."

My definition of *insanity* is doing the same things over and over again, and expecting a different result. But I didn't think Tyrone would understand that philosophical observation.

"How many times did you piss on the toilet seat before you figured out that you had to raise the lid? You keep doing dumb shit like that, and you're gonna get into some really bad drugs that can hurt you."

"Come on, man, don't be like that," he said, half-warningly. "You 'bout to piss me off."

*You're five and a half feet tall and you weigh 150 at best. That threat doesn't scare me much, Tyrone.*

"You can always get out of my rig and walk the rest of the way to the hospital," I pointed out. "Or walk home. Either way, it's a long hike." Tyrone said nothing, just glared at my reflection in the rear window, his arms folded across his chest.

At LSU Medical Center, the resident looked at Tyrone with interest. "Weren't you in here last night, kid?"

Tyrone played dumb.

"Dystonic reaction to Haldol," I told the resident. "I gave him fifty of Benadryl."

"You were in here last night," the resident accused, "for the same thing! Damned kid, don't you learn?" The resident shook his head tiredly and pointed down the hall. "Put him in triage," he ordered.

"What, I ain't going to a room?" Tyrone asked indignantly. "When you come in by ambulance, you go straight to a room!"

I lowered the stretcher and helped him stand up. I swept my arm at the fifty or so people still waiting to be seen. "Sure, you're going to a room, Tyrone!" I assured him. "The waiting room. Have a nice night!"

# Ice Storm

"Y OU KNOW, IT does no good to get only halfway to the scene really fast," I reminded Mickey as our wheels lost traction yet again. "They'll have to send somebody to come get us! It is considered bad form for the paramedics to need an ambulance for themselves, remember?"

"Shit!" Mickey snarled in frustration, steering into the skid. "By the time we get there, the kid will be born, weaned, and potty-trained!"

It was mid-December, and we were in the middle of an ice storm. Chennault Parish had come to a standstill. We normally got a bad ice storm every couple of years, but it usually happened in February, not December. Only two weeks earlier I was still wearing shorts!

The entire parish was without power, and quite a few people were without phone service. Our Mason Ferry station was dark and freezing cold, and since the town's water system required power, we had no water, either. Mickey and I had spent the last eighteen hours evacuating one wing of Mason Ferry Nursing Home and distributing blankets to the rest of the residents. There were tree limbs and power lines down everywhere we looked.

The only wreck we'd worked was a woman who'd slid her minivan off the road into a deep ditch. She and her two children were uninjured, but I got wet all the way to my crotch while standing there in the ditch and handing the kids up to Mickey. To add to my discomfort, I'd been unable to dry my pants because the power was out all over town. My nuts were only now beginning to defrost.

We were going to a call for a woman in labor in the Liddieville community, up near the Arkansas line. For the past thirty minutes we'd been picking our way north through the ice and fallen pine trees at a hot five miles an hour.

"Look at it this way," I said. "Women have delivered babies for millennia without the help of an EMT. She'll probably be fine."

Mickey just snorted and rolled his eyes. "Transport is gonna be a bitch," he pointed out. "We have less than half a tank of fuel, and at the rate we're going, the trip to West Oneida will take two hours. We'll be lucky to make it on the fuel we have."

I hadn't thought of that. The gas stations were all without power, as was the bulk fuel plant. The only gas stations likely to be open were forty miles away, which might as well have been four hundred miles with the current road conditions. This could indeed be a problem.

"Oh, shit," Mickey groaned. "This is a problem." He was looking at a large pine limb lying across the road, its needles encased in a thick crust of ice.

"Maybe we could move it," I suggested. "It might not be as heavy as it looks." Mickey rolled his eyes at that assessment, but put the rig in park and got out.

*Me and my big mouth. Damn, it's cold out here! That limb looks a helluva lot bigger now that I'm out of the rig, too.*

"Well, it's not going to move itself," he said. "You get that end, and let's see if we can pull it off to one side." Predictably, I was on the heavy end. Sighing, I grabbed a couple of sturdy branches and struggled to pivot the limb far enough that we could squeeze the rig past. By the time we were through, my back was aching and my hands were scraped raw, and I'd managed to slip down and bang my left knee. We moved the limb about three feet, however, and Mickey wanted to try squeezing past.

"Spot for me while I try it," he said, heading for the rig. I grabbed his arm, stopping him.

"Uh-uh, partner. You EMT, me paramedic. Plus, I'm still soaking wet. You spot while I drive." Mickey gave me a look that would curdle milk, but moved around to the passenger side of the rig.

"Ready when you are, asshole!" he yelled. "I'm freezing out here!"

Grinning, I inched the rig forward. I could hear the branches scraping against the passenger side, and the wheels bump over something big, but I made it past. Before Mickey could climb in the passenger side, I hit the door locks.

"Hey, goddamnit!" he yelled, banging on the window. "Quit kidding around! It's twelve degrees out here!"

I gave him an evil grin and pretended I couldn't hear him. "What was that?" I yelled back, cupping my hand next to my ear. "I can't hear you with the heater going full blast like this!"

Mickey just continued beating on the door. "Open up, asshole! This ain't funny anymore!"

*Nonsense. It's hilarious! And you stood up on the road shoulder while I froze my nuts in that ditch, remember?*

"Excuse me?" I ask. "What did you say? All I heard was 'asshole' over the heater..."

"Okay, please let me in," he pleaded. Chuckling, I unlocked the doors and he scrambled into the rig, glaring at me and holding his hands in front of the heater vents.

Five minutes later, we pulled up in front of the house. I tried to pull the rig up the steep dirt driveway, and nearly wound up sliding into the ditch. "How about we leave the rig parked on the road?" I asked Mickey sheepishly.

"Yeah, why don't we," he retorted. "Unless you want to hike all the way back to town." We gathered our gear and carefully made our way up the driveway, slipping and sliding on the frozen ground. The house was dark, but there was smoke coming from the chimney. Mickey knocked on the door with his flashlight. "Chennault Ambulance!" he called, then opened the door.

A woman was sitting in a recliner near the fireplace, telephone pressed to her ear. Her face was glistening with sweat, despite the chill in the house. The only illumination in the room came from the fireplace and a few candles.

"They're here," she groaned gratefully into the phone, then hung up. She managed a tired smile. "That was your dispatcher. We were beginning to think you weren't going to be able to make it up here."

"The roads are really bad," Mickey said apologetically. "Plus, once we get north of town, our communications get real spotty. One of the towers must be down. How far along are you, ma'am?"

"Eight months," the woman answered. "I'm not due until January fourth. Ooooooohhh crap, here comes another one!" she groaned, gritting her teeth.

I checked my watch. "Has your water broken?" I asked.

"About an hour ago," she said, nodding, while panting through her contraction. "At first I thought I had wet myself. I called right after that." She visibly relaxed as the contraction eased. I checked my watch again.

"You didn't realize it was your water breaking?" I asked, curious. "And where is your husband?"

"He works on an offshore rig," she told us. "He comes back in on the seventeenth. And this is my first pregnancy," she explained.

Well, that was a relief. She might be in labor for quite some time. Her contractions were only fifteen seconds in duration.

"Any complications with your pregnancy?" I asked as Mickey checked her blood pressure.

She shook her head. "My blood pressure was a little high at my last visit, but my doctor wasn't too worried. I was working until two weeks ago. He said to just take it easy for a while, that it would be better if I didn't work."

"Her pressure is 150/84," Mickey told me. "Pulse is 116."

"Still high," the woman says, shaking her head. "Do you think this will hurt my baby?"

"It shouldn't." I smiled reassuringly. "All the same, though, a dark, cold house is no place to have a baby a month early, so why don't we get on our way to the hospital?"

"I hope West Oneida Regional is your hospital"—Mickey grinned—"because anywhere else is probably going to add another hour to the trip."

"Actually, it's St. Matthews, but right now the closest place that has lights and heat is fine with me," the woman said as we helped her out of the recliner. "I think my doctor goes to West Oneida as well, anyway."

"Normally, we wouldn't ask the pregnant lady to walk to the rig," Mickey chuckled as we walked her to the door, "but considering the conditions, a stretcher ride down your driveway may be more excitement than you bargained for." The woman laughed and walked gingerly between us, holding on to our arms.

It was bitterly cold outside, and the lawn and driveway were coated in ice, but we made it to the rig without any embarrassing slips. I climbed into the back and helped her aboard, and Mickey closed the door behind us.

I applied oxygen and wrapped a tourniquet around the woman's arm. "Ma'am, I'm going to start an IV on you and give you some fluid," I informed her as I spiked a bag of saline.

"My name is Kate," she grunted, then doubled over and grabbed my knee. "Here comes another one!" she announced as she unconsciously dug her nails into my thigh. I checked my watch yet again.

Just under ten minutes since the last contraction. Not too bad. We might even make it to the hospital before she squirted this kid out on the cot. Of course, if she didn't let go of my leg soon, I was going to have a baby.

I waited until she was through panting and gently detached her fingers from my leg.

"Sorry about that," she apologized. "That was a hard one."

"No problem, Kate," I lied, as I inserted a 16-gauge catheter. She had those great veins common in pregnant women. They stand out like ropes. "So what are you having? Boy or girl?"

"It's a boy," she announced proudly. "My husband carries the ultrasound picture in his wallet."

"Well, if you haven't decided on a name"—I grinned at her as I opened up the line—"Kelly is a good name. It means 'warrior' in Gaelic."

"Sorry, Kelly," she laughed, "but we've already decided to name him Bryce Daniel. Listen, with my pressure as high as it is, should I be getting all this fluid?"

"Well, your pressure is high, but it's not *high*, if you know what I mean," I assured her. "The amount I'm giving you shouldn't make that much of a difference. I'm trying to slow down your contractions."

"How does it do that?" she wanted to know.

"I trick your body into thinking it has too much fluid, and it stops producing certain hormones," I explained. "One of them is a twin sister to the hormone that stimulates uterine contractions. They come from the same gland. Sometimes this works."

She nodded and leaned back on the stretcher, closing her eyes. I had nothing else to do, so I amused myself by trying to hear fetal heart tones. It took some listening, but I eventually heard a heartbeat over the sound of the engine. The rate was fine, about 140 or so. I sat back and watched the road pass slowly beneath us as Mickey crept back toward town.

Kate had several more contractions, and I encouraged her to breathe but to avoid pushing. I felt the ambulance make a slow left turn and looked up to see the darkened windows of the shops along Main Street in Mason Ferry. Thirty minutes had passed, and Kate's contractions were now six minutes apart. I'd given her a 500-milliliter bolus, and I wasn't comfortable giving her any more.

"Hey, Mickey, can we step it up a little?" I asked hopefully, sticking my head through the window into the cab.

He shook his head ruefully. "No way, man. The tire chains aren't giving us that much traction. Any faster than this, and I start sliding around."

"We may wind up delivering this baby before we get there," I told him quietly. "The trip to West Oneida may take an hour and a half."

"Want me to divert to Fort Sperry?" he asked. "I got through on the radio a little while ago. They've got road crews out spreading salt and clearing trees off the road between here and Fort Sperry."

"What are they going to do that we can't?" I pointed out. "Go through Fort Sperry just the same, though. Don't take any of your shortcuts. Those back roads will be the last to get cleared."

Mickey nodded and said, hopefully, "Maybe the main highways will be in better shape than this. I might be able to make up some time."

I pulled my head back through the window and checked my watch again. We'd made ten miles in slightly less than forty minutes, and we had another forty-five miles to go. I was starting to get a bad feeling. There was nothing to do but sit in frustration and check vital signs. Kate's labor seemed to be progressing normally, but I wasn't thrilled about delivering a thirty-six-week preemie in the back of my rig in the middle of nowhere.

Thirty-five minutes later, we were entering the outskirts of Fort Sperry. The roads were clearer here, and Mickey took the opportunity to put the hammer down, accelerating us to a whopping thirty miles an hour. We'd passed a number of utility company and highway crews, busy trying to clear the roads of fallen trees and restore power. With the exception of the hospital and Chennault Ambulance headquarters, most of Fort Sperry was still in the dark.

"Uh, how much longer is it going to take?" Kate asked, grunting as another contraction hit. They were four minutes apart now.

"Just passing through Fort Sperry, and the roads are getting better," I said brightly, trying to be reassuring. I was not very convincing.

*Thirty more miles, and another hour at this speed. We were not going to make it.*

"We're not going to make it," Kate echoed my thoughts. Tears formed in her eyes as she asked me fearfully, "I'm gonna deliver before we get there, aren't I?"

"Probably," I answered honestly. "But every mile we go is another mile closer to the hospital. Try not to worry."

"Please tell me you know what you're doing!" Kate panted, grabbing my hand.

"Lawdy, Miss Scahlett, I don't know nuthin 'bout birthin' no babies!" I said in my best imitation of Butterfly McQueen.

"That's not fuuunnnneeeee!" she half-cried, half-laughed, as the contraction peaked and began to subside.

*Damn. That was forty seconds by my watch. Not good.*

I got the obstetrical kit from the shelf and opened it, spreading its contents out on the bench seat. "Okay, Kate," I directed, "let's get ready, just in case. Lift up your hips."

She elevated her hips and I quickly pulled down her underwear and slid an absorbent pad and a pillow under her buttocks. There was no crowning yet, thank God. I quickly draped her legs and abdomen and lay the receiving blanket and stocking cap on the seat. I was ready to go, except for the sterile gloves. There was nothing to do now but wait. I occasionally peeked under the drapes to look for crowning.

I looked up to see Mickey's eyes in the rearview mirror. He'd been watching. He said nothing, but I could hear the engine change pitch and feel the acceleration as the rig picked up speed. "Good roads south of town," he called out reassuringly. "They're practically clear." I nodded my thanks.

Thirty minutes later, Kate's contractions were less than two minutes apart, and close to a minute in duration. I lifted up the drape to look, and immediately wished I hadn't. I saw baby hair.

*Well, at least it's not a baby's butt. Look on the bright side.*

I looked out the windows to see that we were entering the outskirts of Oneida Parish. West Oneida Regional Medical Center was fewer than ten miles away, but right now it might as well be ten thousand. I sighed.

"Mickey, find a good place to pull it over!" I called out. "We're not gonna make it!" I could hear him cursing to himself, but I couldn't quite make out the words. Another minute passed, and I felt the truck turn to the right and come to a stop. Presently, the rear doors sprang open and he clambered into the back. We were parked at a convenience store just outside town. It didn't have power, either.

"What do you need?" Mickey asked uncertainly.

"First, squeeze past me and get into the jump seat," I ordered. "Switch her oxygen to a non-rebreather mask, and get the Pitocin out of the drug box. Other than that, just hand me stuff when I need it."

I scooted down to the end of the bench seat and kneeled on the floor next to the cot. "You ready, Kate?" I called out. "When the next contraction starts, you can push, okay?" She just nodded her head and grunted. I didn't have to wait long.

"Aaaaaaahhhhhhh shit!" Kate screamed, grabbing Mickey's hand in a vice grip. His face went pale and he shot me a dirty look. Kate screamed through her contraction as I encouraged her to keep pushing. The baby's head came tantalizingly close to delivering, then receded like a turtle withdrawing into its shell.

"Next contraction, Kate, and we'll be in good shape. Now puuuuuuuuusssh!" I found myself unconsciously pushing with her, and a tiny fart slipped out. Nothing horrendous, mind you, but just enough to make its presence known. I prayed that nobody would notice.

"Oooooooohhhhhhhh God!" Kate screamed, and all at once, the baby's head popped out. He looked like a little blue Shar-Pei with a cone-shaped head.

"Bulb syringe," I ordered curtly, and Mickey smacked it into my palm. I suctioned the baby's mouth and nose, noting that his airway was agreeably clear of fluid.

"Okay, Kate, there's the head! You're doing great! One more big push and we're done, okay?" She complied, grunting and swearing like a sailor, and the baby turned slightly and the upper shoulder delivered. Kate relaxed, sobbing in relief.

"Uh, Kate?" I said. "I lied. Make that one more big push, and we're done!"

"That's what you said the last time!" she snapped. "And what's with this 'we' shit?" Nevertheless, she strained mightily and the baby immediately popped out into my hands.

"Towel," I told Mickey, then I looked up at Kate, grinning. "You did it, sister! One big baby boy! Congratulations!"

I took the towel from Mickey and vigorously dried the little boy off, and was immediately rewarded with an irritated wail. His color improved rapidly, as if someone had swiped him with a pink paintbrush.

I jerked my head at Mickey. "Slide down here for a minute." Once he did, I nodded my head at the umbilical cord clamps and sterile scissors lying on the seat. "Clamp and cut the cord," I directed, pointing at where the clamps should go.

He grinned and clamped the cord while I held the baby. A few spatters of blood hit me on the neck as he cut the cord, but I didn't mind. I finished wrapping the baby in the receiving blanket and put a stocking cap on his head.

"Hey, Kate," I said quietly. She was lying back on the stretcher, exhausted, but she opened her eyes when I called her name. "I present to you Bryce Daniel...what is your last name anyway?"

"McMillan," she laughed, taking him from me. "Bryce Daniel McMillan. We named him Bryce after my grandfather, and Daniel after my husband's grandfather." Glowing, she looked quietly at her son as he squirmed and wailed.

"Uh, that all you need me for?" Mickey asked gruffly. If I didn't know better, I'd say those were tears in his eyes.

"Yeah, sure, tough guy," I told him wryly. "Get us back on the road. We still have a ways to go."

# Varices

I WAS WORKING with a new guy at Med Star. His name was Seth Barnes, and he worked full-time as a Sherwood Parish sheriff's deputy. Already a First Responder, Seth had just completed his EMT training, although he had yet to take the National Registry exam. He was a bright guy, agreeably free of the naïveté seen in most EMT students, a fact due largely to his law enforcement background. Now, if I could just get him to stop conducting his patient interviews as if they were interrogations, I'd be happy.

It was Christmas Eve, and the night promised to be cold and clear. I had holidays off, but Mary had drawn an ER shift and I didn't relish spending the night at home alone. Seth was working overtime to pay hospital bills. His baby girl was in the NICU at St. Matthew's, and his wife was on unpaid maternity leave. They were struggling.

"So how's the munchkin?" I asked him. "Have they said when you can expect to bring her home?"

"End of the week, hopefully." He sighed, holding up crossed fingers. "Melissa's going nuts."

"I can imagine," I sympathized. "But at least she can see her whenever she wants. The courtesy room is just down the hall from the NICU."

"I know," he said tiredly, rubbing his eyes. "It's still tough on her, though. She thinks it's her fault Mariah is sick."

"Why?" I asked curiously. I'd met Seth's wife only once, when the NICU transport team and I picked up his little girl from Sherwood General Hospital.

"Well, my wife is diabetic," Seth explained, "and they're having problems managing the baby's blood sugar. I keep telling her that it wasn't—"

"Central to 256," the radio interrupted.

"That's us," I said, gesturing to Seth to answer the radio.

"Unit Fourteen, go," he said, blushing, as I shook my head in amusement. Unit 14 was his number with the Sherwood Parish sheriff's department. Seth had answered the radio like that all day.

The dispatcher didn't miss a beat. "Ten-four, Unit 256. We have a report of a man vomiting blood at 1254 Frontage Road. It's room fifty-two at the Day's Inn." The laughter in his voice came through the speakers quite clearly.

"Unit Four-uh, Unit 256 responding," Seth replied as he pulled out of the Quickie Mart parking lot.

"Maybe they should just stencil the unit numbers on the inside of the rigs," I mused. "Might make it easier to remember," Seth answered with an extended middle finger.

"That is a decidedly un-Christian gesture to be using in this holy season, Deputy Barnes," I chided, mockingly stern. "So, what do we do for a man vomiting blood?" I asked, quizzing him.

"Stay out of the way," he replied automatically, grinning. I merely looked at him, one eyebrow raised. "Okay, we take orthostatic vital signs. We, uh....ask if they've had any abdominal distress. We look to see if the blood is bright red, or like coffee grounds."

"And what do those things mean?" I pressed.

"Bright red means upper-GI bleed, coffee grounds mean lower-GI bleed?" he guessed.

"Bright red means it hasn't stayed in the stomach long enough to digest, which may suggest a faster bleed," I corrected. "Faster, but not necessarily worse. People may ignore coffee-ground emesis until quite a bit of blood has been lost. When they puke bright-red blood, they usually don't waste time calling 911. And if it were in the lower-GI tract, they'd probably be shitting blood. Black, tarry stools and that sort of thing."

Seth nodded thoughtfully, absorbing the information. He hadn't been around a bad GI bleeder yet. I'd described the smell to him, but he'd never appreciate it until he'd whiffed it for real.

In the room, we found a man sitting on the bed, hunched over a wastebasket. There was a small puddle of bright-red blood congealing on the floor. His wife looked concerned.

"What happened, sir?" I asked as I handed the blood pressure cuff and stethoscope to Seth.

"Puking blood," the man groaned. "Twice now in the past thirty minutes."

"Ever have something happen like this before?" I asked, noting his jaundiced skin and distended abdomen.

"Plenty of times," the man confirmed, "but not since last year."

"What other kind of medical problems do you have?" I asked.

"Hepatitis C," the man told us, hanging his head over the wastebasket. "I got cirrhosis of the liver, too."

"He's a recovering alcoholic," his wife offered. "He has hypertension."

"Lie back, sir," Seth said. "I need to check your pulse and blood pressure once more." I motioned to Seth not to bother, earning a curious look.

*You start with 'em lying down, then you sit 'em up, partner. Besides, I have an idea what the problem is.*

I reached over and placed my hand on the man's abdomen. His liver felt like a spongy brick, easily palpable below his ribs. I tapped the other side of his abdomen and felt an obvious fluid wave.

"Did they teach you about ascites in EMT school, Seth?" He shook his head. "Well, move around here and put your hand on this side of his stomach," I told him. "When you tap the other side of his stomach, you should feel a fluid wave. That means he has fluid collecting in his stomach." Seth complied, tapping the man's abdomen with a fascinated look on his face.

"I feel it!" he said excitedly. "What does it mean?"

Before I could reply, I saw the man's cheeks bulge and I grabbed Seth by the shirt and yanked him out of the way. The man vomited a torrent of bright-red blood across the room, right over Seth's shoulder.

"Did you get any on you?" I asked, alarmed. He looked himself over.

"No, I don't think so," he said shakily, his eyes still as wide as saucers.

"Let's get him on the stretcher and go," I ordered.

That had to be one of the stupidest things I'd ever done. I'd made an EMT student kneel down directly in front of a hep C patient with bleeding esophageal varices. *Dumb move, Kelly.*

In the rig, I checked the man's pressure again. It was a little low, maybe 100/60, and we were twenty minutes from the hospital. From the southern end of Sherwood Parish, it was a toss-up as to which hospital was closest. Mainly I was concerned with avoiding projectile vomiting of infectious blood.

"Head to St. Matthew's, Seth!" I yelled. "Run hot!" I added as an afterthought. Seth dutifully hit the light and sirens and turned south onto Highway 154.

I started a 14-gauge IV on the man and hung a bag of saline, keeping the flow at a KVO rate. I couldn't remember what raising the blood pressure did to bleeding varices, but I suspected it wasn't good. Right now, I was happy with the pressure he had, so I contented myself with hollering at Seth to drive faster.

We made it to St. Matthew's with no more puking, and only a few false alarms. Every time the man would retch, I'd press myself against the wall in the extreme front of the rig, well behind his head.

"Room seven," the nurse told us, barely taking her eyes off her newspaper.

"I don't think so," I disagreed politely. "He needs to go to one of the trauma rooms."

"Is he a trauma patient?" she asked me, looking at me over her glasses as if I were some species of interesting insect.

"No, he's got bleeding esophageal varices," I try to explain. "I just think—"

"If he's not a trauma patient, he doesn't go to a trauma room," the nurse interrupted imperiously. "Take him to room seven." Having straightened out the foolish, panicky ambulance drivers, she turned her attention back to her newspaper.

Before I could protest, our patient turned his head to the right and let loose another torrent of blood, splattering the four holding beds and the linen cart. There was blood on the ER desk, not two feet from where the triage nurse had her feet propped up. It looks like someone has exploded a gallon of red paint.

"Holy Christ!" the nurse exclaimed, nearly falling out of her chair. "Put him in a trauma room!" She scrambled from her perch and hollered for help.

*Thank you very much, madam. Maybe next time you'll listen.*

Seth and I quickly slid our patient over to the ER bed and gave report to the doctor. He listened to our brief report, nodded brusquely, and shooed us out of the room. Our guy's vomiting episode had ignited a flurry of activity, and it was rapidly getting crowded in there.

"So those are bleeding varices," Seth observed wonderingly. "They did teach us about those, but not much. What causes them, other than alcoholism?"

"Kinda the same thing that causes the ascites. With liver failure or cirrhosis, fluid leaks out of the capillaries in the hepatic portal system. That's ascites. The increased pressure also causes veins in the esophagus to dilate. Eventually they rupture. Basically, they're varicose veins in the esophagus. They pop, the patient vomits, causing more to pop, patient vomits more. It's a vicious cycle."

"Can it kill you?" Seth asked.

In answer, I gestured at all the blood. "What do you think? And by the way, never kneel down in front of someone who has been puking. That was stupid of me to tell you to do."

"I won't," Seth promised. "And thanks for pulling me out of the way."

"You have a new kid." I shrugged. "Somebody has to look out for you. Speaking of kids, though..."

His eyes lit up. "Yeah, what about 'em?"

"Well, since we're at St. Matthew's"—I grinned—"and the NICU is right upstairs...why don't we go visit one?" Seth whooped and sprinted for the elevator.

# Silent Night

WE COOED OVER Seth's baby girl for nearly an hour in the NICU. Med Star called us twice on the radio, asking us when we'd be back in service.

"We're out of service for OSHA cleanup," I lied. "My rig is a mess. We'll let you know when we're ready to go." I winked at Seth and his wife as he rocked his little girl.

"We may get to bring her home tomorrow," Seth whispered. "Some Christmas present, huh?" I nodded and look pointedly at the clock on the wall. "I know," Seth said, sighing. "We gotta go."

"Sorry, Melissa," I apologized as he handed the baby over. "There are little old ladies out there who have fallen and can't get up." She said nothing, just smiled and hugged Seth with one arm.

Later that night, we got called to stand by while the local police dealt with a hostage situation. Seth parked the rig on a side street several blocks away, turned off the lights, and settled back into his seat. After a while, he turned to me and asked, "How long you been a medic, Kelly?"

"Ten years," I sighed. "It feels like more. It seems like I've always been a paramedic."

"What did you do before you got into this line of work?" Seth asked curiously.

"I was a professional retriever trainer, if you can believe that," I laughed. "Some switch, huh?"

"I'll say," Seth chuckled. "What keeps you doing it?"

"The great pay and the chicks, of course," I said, deadpan. Seth just frowned.

"Come on, man, I'm serious," he said. "I mean, here we are sitting in the dark on Christmas Eve, waiting for some guy to either shoot someone or get shot by the cops. Today an alcoholic nearly puked blood on us. You deal with drunks and derelicts and drug users. You pull broken bodies out of wrecks. You do boring transfers, shuttling little old folks back and forth between the hospital and the nursing homes. How do you do it without getting burned out?"

"Why are you a cop?" I asked him. "You see most of the same things, and you just took an EMT class. Why do you do it?"

He paused, reflecting. "I guess I just want to help people. But I've only been a deputy for two years. I haven't even taken my EMT exam yet. But you've been a medic for ten years. So stop avoiding the question."

I stayed silent for a while, unsure how to answer.

Why do I do it? Not for the money, certainly. I make good money for a paramedic, but it's hardly what I'd make as a nurse or physician's assistant. I dropped out of college, and I keep finding excuses why I can't go back. So why do I do it?

"I've been burned out," I began, not sure of what I intended to say. "Maybe six years ago. The job just wasn't fun anymore. I didn't feel appreciated, I wasn't getting paid much, and I didn't feel as if I made a difference. I took some time off, and I got over it."

"How?" he pressed, unsatisfied by my answer.

"I figured out that I don't save lives," I explained. "Sometimes I get lucky, and we resuscitate someone successfully. Mainly it's luck and good timing. I came to realize that what we do isn't lifesaving. My job isn't about blood and guts. It's about helping people just like you do as a deputy. Your job isn't all car chases and armed standoffs. You may go your entire career and never fire your weapon. There's more to it than the adrenaline rush." I looked at Seth and saw that he still didn't get it.

"Look, two weeks ago I delivered a baby in the middle of the ice storm. It wasn't fun. The fun part was seeing the mother's face after I handed her the kid.

"Two days ago, I took an old lady to the clinic for wound care on her bedsores. They stank, Seth. She stank, and she knew it. But I cracked a joke or two, made fun of her nurses, and I made her laugh. I held her hand on the way to the clinic, and she smiled at me when I dropped her off.

"I started an IV on a six-year-old kid yesterday, and he didn't even cry. He was more scared of the needle than of his broken arm, but I talked him through the stick, and he figured out that the needle wasn't so bad.

"We picked up a combative Alzheimer's patient this morning, and the nurses were sure we'd have to restrain her, that she'd fight us. We talked to her for a bit, and she went with us without a fuss. We earned her trust.

"Today I got to teach you something. That's why I do it, for stuff like that."

"And what about the ones without happy endings?" Seth asked darkly. "What about the ones who you can't do anything for—the ones who die?"

"Well, you remind yourself that it isn't your disease," I answered. "You do the best you can. And you don't let the things you see harden your heart."

"Base to all units, stand down," the radio crackled. "Repeat, stand down. Suspect is in custody. Channel is cleared for nonemergency traffic." Seth grunted in surprise and flipped on the headlights.

"But that stuff will just eat you up," he protested as we drove back to our station.

"I didn't say let it eat you up, Seth. I said don't let it harden you. You know those big, tough paramedics who don't let anything bother them? They never last, or they stick around but nobody wants to work with them. They never cry, but they forget how to smile, too.

"Keep looking for the good stuff," I advised. "You can always find something good, if you just take the time to look."

Just then the radio crackled, and an anonymous voice floated over the airwaves. "'And lo, the angel of the Lord came upon them, and the glory of the Lord shone round about them, and they were sore afraid. And the angel said unto them, Fear not: for, behold, I bring you good tidings of great joy, which shall be to all people. For unto you is born this day in the city of David a Savior, which is Christ the Lord.' Merry Christmas, everybody."

The radio clicked again and again as units around the parish keyed their microphones in response. I looked at my watch. It was just past midnight. The dispatcher transmitted a moment later, adding only a quiet "Amen."

"See what I mean?" I smiled. "Merry Christmas, Seth."

# Grief Sponge

I DROVE BACK through DeVillier the other day, a detour from the route I drive every week to EMT class. That place holds a lot of memories for me. I met the woman who would become my wife there. Randy Stanton and Lasson were both groomsmen at my wedding. I've been back in this area for six months now, and Monday was the first time I had ventured off the main highway in ten years.

Not that I don't notice things as I pass through every week. The Death Tree has two more crosses hanging on it, and the trunk bears a few new scars. The field beyond it where we landed the helicopter now bears a row of miniature storage warehouses. The local seafood joint is still open, albeit in a new location just down the street. My old ambulance station is now someone's house. I hope they got the wiring fixed. It's a bitch when you can't run the air-conditioner and the microwave at the same time.

Monday I had time to kill before picking up KatyBeth, so I turned left instead of right on my way home and cruised slowly through town. The ambulance service that covers this area now has their station in a strip mall downtown, but their rig wasn't in the parking lot. Maybe they were on a call. The medic who used to work this station, one of my former students, died of cancer a few years ago. I don't know the crews who work here now.

The town itself really hasn't changed all that much; there are a few new businesses, a few less old ones. The local convenience store probably still gives free fountain drinks to the cops and EMTs. I stopped at the local Popeye's and ate. I asked the manager, and she confirmed that they still send their leftover chicken and sides over to the police department after closing. I doubt the local ambulance crews hang out there as much as we did, swapping lies and mooching free food. The crews these days are far too busy to be up at midnight eating a midnight snack at the police department.

On my drive through, I found myself continuing onto the highway west of town. What used to be timberland and pastures has sprouted new neighborhoods and businesses like so many weeds. Not even the small towns are immune to urban sprawl.

The place just doesn't have the same feel anymore.

Without conscious thought, I turned off the main highway through a brick archway into an upper-middle-class neighborhood. Ten years ago, the archway wasn't there. There was no artfully manicured shrubbery, no wrought-iron fencing, no neighborhood community center.

Back then, there were just a few nice homes on tree-shaded lots, separated by acres-wide tracts of hardwoods. It used to be quiet, peaceful. Now every lot is taken up by very large, ostentatious homes on very small lawns. Most of the trees are gone, and there is traffic on these streets. No doubt soon they'll form a homeowners' association, maybe gate the community and hire a security guard to keep out the riffraff. You know, the same riffraff they were ten years before.

On a quiet street in the oldest part of the subdivision, a house sits at the end of the cul de sac. The garage door is closed, but the lights are on inside. I slow down as I pass, wondering if the people who live there now know the history of this house. Did they meet the couple who built it, maybe shake their hands when they closed the sale? Did they wonder why a young couple would want to sell a home they'd built only a couple of years before? Or did the neighbors fill them in on the whole story through neighborhood gossip?

I scan the mailbox as I inch past, and the name stenciled there stops me cold.

The Websters.

They still live here.

I stop my truck next to the curb and clench the steering wheel, breathing hard as my eyes cloud over. Through the rearview mirror and my tears, I can still see the house, but the image is of the same home ten years ago. It's the same image I see in the occasional nightmare, the one that makes me call my ex in the wee hours to ask if Katy is okay.

\* \* \* \* \* \*

"Dispatch to Medic Six, DeVillier Police are on scene. CPR is in progress."

"Thank God," murmured Randy Stanton. "Maybe there's a chance."

I said nothing in reply. I never liked these calls, especially when the patient's age was measured in months rather than years. I just leaned my head against the hot window, closed my eyes, and mentally went through my checklist: *Broselow tape in the side pocket of the trauma bag...Epi dose is 0.1 ml/kg...first dose will be Epi 1:1,000 down the tube, then I'll get a line, probably intraosseous...*

Because I was outwardly calm, because I taught pediatric advanced life support thirty times a year, because the more tension and chaos on a scene, the more placid my demeanor got, Randy thought I was all over this. He thought I was unaffected.

*No one is ever unaffected when they're doing CPR on a six-month-old baby. Not ever.*

*It's simply that I don't do my praying out loud, and I don't do my crying in public.*

And so I continued running this call in my mind as he navigated the winding roads on the outskirts of town. It would take us close to ten minutes to get there, all told. The address was outside town limits, well out into the parish. DeVillier Police Department shouldn't even be responding.

It didn't matter.

When you hear the call go out for a baby not breathing, you go. And you do not worry about petty shit like jurisdiction. Chillicothe Parish sheriff's office understood this as well.

*Tom will be there doing CPR...I'll get EP to set up a BVM and oxygen, and have him take over ventilation...once Tom can talk I'll get the details of the arrest...try to question the parents if I can...I'll need a number 1 Miller blade for the laryngoscope, maybe the pediatric Magill forceps...lots of calls for kids that age are chokings...*

Randy made the right turn from Parish Road 214 into the housing development. It was quiet and peaceful. The sound of a siren was obscene there, so I leaned over and switched it off. Randy pulled into the driveway at 112 Mockingbird Lane directly behind the DeVillier Police cruiser sitting there with the driver's door and trunk lid ajar.

We bailed out of the rig and started fetching equipment, resisting the urge to rush headlong into the house. The front door was open, and we could hear a woman wailing in there, but these calls got even more chaotic when you started sending people to your rig for equipment you should have lugged inside in the first place.

Plus, I could focus on process rather than the fact that a six-month-old baby was dead and would likely stay that way.

Newly laid flagstones led us to the front door. The sod in the yard, while obviously professionally done, had yet to fill in. You could still see the faint lines where it was rolled out. This entire place was brand-new, no doubt the dream home of a young professional couple just starting a family.

Inside, we followed the wailing through the foyer and living room, past a Fisher-Price activity gym set in the middle of the floor. Just off the living room, a young woman close to my age knelt just outside the door to the nursery, sobbing into her hands.

Her crying had waned to a ragged, soul-rending moan, and her blond hair was plastered to her tear-streaked face.

*"No, no, no...God please, please, please...nooo...Oh God Jesus please God..."*

She rocked back and forth, shoulders shaking as she sobbed her mantra over and over into her hands as if the words had the power to blot out the horror of finding her son facedown and lifeless in his crib.

Words just don't have that power. Mine least of all.

I ducked past her into the room as Randy gently took her by the shoulders and scooted her aside.

She had decorated the nursery with loving care. Winnie the Pooh and friends adorned every surface. Eeyore was decoupaged on one side of the bureau, looking back forlornly over his shoulder, and Kanga and Roo were on the other side. One wall was a cheery fireplace, Christopher Robin sitting cross-legged in front of the hearth, Pooh at his side with his arm deep in a big jar labeled "Hunny." The wall opposite the crib was a mural of the woods, Owl in his tree and Piglet and Tigger frolicking outside. Bees swarmed around a hole high in the trunk of the tree, and a little door was cut into the base of the trunk.

I could envision the mother lovingly tracing this mural on the wall, filling in the colors as the days passed and her first child grew in her womb. There were a few of Daddy's touches here, too. The Tigger doll on the bureau was wearing a miniature Saints helmet, and there was an Atlanta Braves banner pinned to the wall above the crib.

Amid the cartoon cheer of a small child's bedroom, Tom Tate knelt on the floor with a small body cradled tenderly in his arms. It was a little male child, clad in yellow Winnie the Pooh jammies with feet, dwarfed by Tom's burly frame. His body was limp, but his neck and hands were stiff with rigor mortis.

The automated external defibrillator case lay open on the floor beside him, the pads not even removed from their backing, the CPR mask not even torn from its wrapper. Both of them were far too large for the baby.

Tom was chanting his own mantra, but his voice was quavering.

*"One and two and three and four and five and breathe...one and two and three and four and five and breathe..."*

He looked up at me, and I could see the horror in his eyes, the horror that comes with being a father and being forced to do this job.

When you're a father as well as a cop or EMT, your particular curse is that you see your child's face in every tragedy. You see your teenager in the bloody, broken face you pull from the wreckage of his graduation present. You see your wife's face when you knock on a stranger's door at three-thirty A.M. to tell her that her daughter has died. And you see your infant's face somewhere in that purple, mottled face of a baby wearing fuzzy yellow pajamas, and you start CPR even though your rational mind reports that you are far too late in coming.

I could see all of that and more in Tom Tate's eyes as he looked up at me mutely, still silently mouthing his CPR cadence, hands still moving on the baby's chest. For all intents and purposes, he'd been doing CPR on his own child.

"Tom," I said gently, putting my hand on his shoulder as he once again lifted the infant's stiff little body to his mouth. His muscles were corded with tension. He was literally shaking.

"*Tom,*" I said again, more forcefully this time, but my voice was quavering, too. "*You can stop. He's dead.*" I reached out and pried his hand away from the baby's chest and took the stiff infant from him as he let out an explosive, shuddering breath and rocked back on his heels.

He sat there silently, chest heaving and hands shaking, hollowly staring at the floor, and I sat beside him cradling this boy's stiff little body to my chest, both of us wondering if we'd ever be able to banish the memories of this day.

Behind us, the mother's cries began anew as she realized what our stopping meant, and Randy knelt on the floor behind her and pulled her back to his chest. She dissolved into a heap, burying her head in his chest, clutching at his arms, wetting his shirt with her tears.

He just held her and crooned in Cajun French, something I couldn't understand. This wasn't how we were taught to deal with a grieving family, but PowerPoint presentations and case scenarios in a sterile classroom cannot prepare you for days like these, and so Randy held this woman in his arms and crooned to her, professional distance be damned.

I stood up, still holding the infant against my chest, keeping my back to his mother in an attempt to shield her from the sight of him. It didn't occur to me that she had already seen what he looked like.

I walked on wobbly legs over to the crib and peered down into it. No thick blankets, no fluffy toys or pillows lay there. The only thing in the crib was a light, thin coverlet and a pinkish, foamy stain on one end of the mattress, forming an obscene blot directly under a mobile clamped to the headboard, brightly colored fish dangling from monofilament line strung on the ribs of an equally cheery miniature umbrella.

*They did everything right. Nothing for the kid to roll over on, nothing to bury his face in, not even a pillow. The mattress is firm enough, and there are no gaps between the mattress and the frame. No thick blankets or toys in the crib. No baby monitor, but he is a little old for SIDS.*

I pulled the infant away from my chest and noticed the same bloody purge dried on his face, marring his features. The rigor had started to set, and his face was flattened a bit where he had lain on the mattress, his nose and one cheek mashed a little out of shape. Dependent lividity rendered his face and chest mottled and purple. He had been dead for hours.

*No mother should ever have to find her child like that. No parent should have to live with that memory.*

Some of that purge was smeared on Tom's lips and cheek, and I gestured silently toward my face, finger pointing as if to say "Wipe that off before she sees." Tom absently wiped his lips with the back of his hand and stared at the foamy, blood-tinged smear.

I gently placed the baby back in the crib, away from the bloody stain on the mattress, and covered his body with the pale yellow coverlet with blue trim, the one with Pooh, Tigger, and Eeyore embroidered on it. Tom stood next to me, alone with his thoughts as he stared down at the body in the crib.

*Body in the crib. Even thinking it sounds obscene.*

Tom was the first to break the silence. "Call the coroner?" he asked softly.

"Yeah," I sighed. "Probably need to cancel anybody else who is still responding, too."

He nodded his head, agreeing. He took a few deep breaths. His hands were clenched on the crib rail so tightly I could see his knuckles whiten.

"You okay?" I asked, looking at his face. His eyes told me everything I needed to know.

"No," he said simply, "I'm not. But I can handle it." And his carriage told me that, too.

Neither one of us wanted to turn around and face the mother. That task fell to me, and I helped Randy pull the mother to a standing position in the hallway as Tom packed up his AED and gently closed the door to the nursery behind him.

We steered her into the living room and eased her into a chair. She sat there, arms wrapped across her chest, staring vacantly at the baby's activity gym still sitting on the living room floor. I knelt down in front of her, blocking her view.

She looked at me, eyes searching mine, and Randy gently brushed back wet hair plastered to her face. "Is...is he..."

"Yes, ma'am," I told her softly. "He's dead. He's been dead for a few hours."

Her eyes welled with fresh tears, and her lower lip trembled, but she sniffed loudly and held back the sobs. She nodded her head in affirmation, as if admitting to herself that what I'd told her was true. She looked back down at my face, and asked in a cracked, hoarse whisper, "Did he suffer?"

I shared a look with Randy, and Tom made a choking noise and turned abruptly away, walking quickly back into the foyer. "No, ma'am, I think he died in his sleep. What is your baby's name?"

"Bryon," she answered softly. "With an o. It's an old family name."

"Bryon," I said approvingly. "Good name for a little boy. Had Bryon been sick lately? Did you have any problems with your pregnancy? Was he premature, for instance?"

"No, none of that." She shook her head. "I was on bed rest for the last couple of weeks because I'd been having premature contractions, but I carried him to term. He's always been so *healthy*..." At that, her voice trailed off and the sobs began again and she buried her face in her hands.

I waited silently, kneeling there in front of her as Randy stood behind her, his hands on her shoulders as her body heaved with every sob. Randy stared mutely at a spot on the wall ten feet over my head, his jaw clenched and his eyes moist.

I put my hand on her knee and squeezed gently. "Ma'am? Is there someone we can call? A family member or a minister? How can we contact your husband?"

"Our minister, at First Baptist Church." She nodded. "You can reach him through the church directory..." Her voice trailed off, and then her head snapped up and she looked at the clock over the mantel. *"Oh, my God, my husband will be home any minute now!* He works at one of the plants, and he gets off work at four o'clock, and, *Oh, my God, what will I tell him?"*

"We'll take care of that," I assured her, not at all sure how. I flashed a look at Randy. He nodded in understanding, took his hands off the woman's shoulders, and turned toward the door. He made it only a few steps and then turned around. "Ma'am," he asked uncertainly, "what's your name?"

"Karen Webster," she answered. "My husband's name is Kyle." Randy said nothing, just nodded and walked outside.

"Karen, we'll get your minister down here as quick as we can," I told her gently, moving to a seat on the couch beside her chair. "I need to tell you what's going to be happening in the next few minutes, okay?"

She said nothing in reply, just looked at me questioningly.

"The coroner will be here asking questions. There may be sheriff's deputies here taking pictures and gathering evidence. Just try to answer the questions as best you can."

She just nodded vacantly, staring at the Fisher-Price activity gym on the living room floor.

*There will also be an autopsy, mandated by law in infant deaths,* I don't say. *A pathologist will be photographing and X-raying Bryon's body, cutting him open and examining his organs, doing toxicology tests and myriad other indignities in the faint hope of determining what killed him.*

I quietly asked her a few more questions and prayed that her minister would arrive before her husband. I didn't want this responsibility.

She had been working outside all morning. Her husband had left for work at seven-fifteen, and she had slept in until Bryon woke at nine. She had fed him, changed his diaper, and played with him in the living room until nearly noon. She read *The Green Mile* as she nursed him, and then put him to bed. She went outside to work in her flower beds, checking on him once before two o'clock. She said he had rolled over onto his belly and was sleeping peacefully, so she had gone back outside. Three hours later, she had gone back inside and found him dead.

I sat uneasily on the couch, looking around the living room. A cordless phone handset sat on the mantel in front of a family portrait: Kyle standing behind Karen, hands protectively on her shoulders, Karen holding Bryon in her lap. Everyone was smiling, even the baby. My pager buzzed angrily on my belt, jarring the silence even in vibrate mode. I tried to ignore it, but in a few minutes it buzzed again, reminding me that I had to pay it heed. I quietly slipped the pager from its case and checked the display: "10-21 dispatch."

I cleared my throat apologetically. "Karen," I asked, nodding toward the phone on the mantel, "may I?"

She nodded her assent and retreated into her thoughts, and I picked up the phone and walked around the corner into the dining room to call dispatch.

"306," I told the voice that answered. "You paged?"

"What's the holdup there?" Satan demanded nastily. "I got your partner on the radio and he said it was a Signal 61. You've been on scene for thirty minutes!"

"And we'll probably be here for a while longer. We're waiting for the coroner."

"Thirty minutes on scene for a natural death?" Satan snorted derisively. "There's a cop there to handle things, isn't there?"

*If I had worked this kid, I'd be tied up on the call for an hour, minimum. You can give me another thirty minutes, at least.*

I said as much to the dispatcher, trying to keep my voice calm and professional.

"You need to stop playing social worker and savior and get your unit back in service," he told me curtly. "I'm logging you as available in the computer right now. Advise when you get back in town limits."

I carefully considered what to say next, and made the only response I could think of: "Fuck you, dispatch." I thumbed the button to end the call before he could reply.

I walked back into the living room, but before I could say anything to Karen, her husband burst into the living room. He was wild, frantic, desperately trying to shake Tom's grasp of his arm.

*"Get your goddamn hands off of me!"* he roared. *"That's my wife in there!"*

He pulled up short in the living room, looking first in bewilderment at his wife, then at me. Karen ran to him and collapsed into his arms, sobbing hysterically, and I edged between him and the nursery door. He reflexively wrapped his arms around her and stared over her shoulder at me accusingly.

Tom Tate moved closer behind him, and I could see Randy standing in the foyer with his back to us, talking urgently into the radio.

Never taking his eyes off mine, he grasped his wife by her arms and slowly, deliberately moved her to one side. I stood in front of the nursery door, hands at my sides and palms open. Tom lay a restraining hand on his arm and he shook it off.

"*Let me in there,*" he commanded, his voice low and menacing. "*Now.*"

"He's dead, Mr. Webster," I said softly, confirming what he already knew. "There was nothing we could do."

Kyle Webster's reply was to sweep an entire row of pictures from the wall in a frightening, splintering crash, then he buried his fist in the drywall just a few inches to the left of my head.

"*OPEN THE FUCKING DOOR AND LET ME SEE MY SON!*" he screamed, and I flinched as his spittle flecked my face.

"You don't want to see him, Mr. Webster," Tom said gently, wrapping him from behind in a bear hug. "Not right now."

Kyle Webster's face started to contort, and his voice broke as he said again, this time pleadingly, "You *have* to let me in there. He's my *son.*"

I just stood there mutely, not moving. I didn't know what to say or do. I knew only that he didn't need to see his son as he looked right now, and I would spare him that pain if I could. If he were to shake loose of Tom and swing again, I was not sure I would duck. His shoulders started to shudder, and I watched as he folded inward on himself, going limp in Tom's grasp. His mouth opened and closed, and his throat worked, but no sounds come out. His wife lay a trembling hand on his left shoulder, and Tom let him go as they both collapsed into each other's arms and sobbed out their grief together.

We stood there watching them, and presently we were joined by a dapper little man wearing black slacks and a light-blue polo shirt. Randy trailed behind him.

"Brother Combs, from the church," Randy whispered by way of introduction. "I already filled him in."

Brother Combs politely shook hands with each of us and whispered a word of thanks. His hands were soft and slightly moist, but his grip was firm. He nodded to us and turned his attention to the Websters, placing a hand on each of their shoulders and leaning his head close, talking softly to them.

"Come on, let's go outside and wait for the coroner," Tom whispered huskily. "I don't think I can be in here much longer." Randy nodded in agreement.

I said nothing, looking around at the Websters, whose world had all but ended, standing forlornly in their living room with their firstborn son dead in a room twenty feet away. Glass crunched under my feet as I turned and looked at the hole Kyle Webster had punched in the wall beside my head. I sighed and began picking up the shattered pictures Kyle had swept from the walls in his brief explosion of rage.

I picked up the biggest pieces of glass and gathered the remnants of the broken frames. A few were still intact, and I delicately picked the broken shards of glass from the frames, taking extra care not to damage the photographs they housed. Tom and Randy watched for a moment and then joined me, literally picking up the pieces of a couple's shattered memories. We deposited the broken glass in a can found in the kitchen and quietly stacked the frames on the dining room table. Brother Combs looked up from his prayer as we turned to leave, and smiled his thanks.

Outside, Tom slumped on the trunk of his cruiser and Randy lit a cigarette. None of us spoke for several minutes. I finished writing my run report sitting on the bumper of Tom's cruiser with my clipboard balanced across my knees, straining to see in the gathering dusk. Randy flicked his butt onto the pavement, ground it under his heel, and checked his watch.

"We should be getting back into service," he reminded me. "I've gotten three pages from dispatch in the past twenty minutes. The last one said to call the shift supervisor."

"I'll call him in a minute," I replied. "Frankly, they can all kiss my ass."

He nodded but said nothing. He knew I'd take whatever heat we had coming.

"Either one of you have kids?" Tom asked.

"Nope," I answered. "Just got married, myself. I hope to, one day."

"Me neither," Randy offered. "I'm divorced, and not likely to get married again anytime soon. How about you?"

"Two," Tom sighed, "both of them girls. The youngest isn't much older than that kid. She just turned one in March."

"Go home and hug them both tonight," I suggested, tearing off a carbon copy of my run report and handing it to him.

Randy grunted his endorsement, "That's what I'd do."

"Oh, I intend to," Tom said quietly. "Believe me, I intend to. You boys be careful tonight."

We drove back to the station in silence. The phone rang in the station not sixty seconds after we marked back at station with dispatch. Randy answered, and wordlessly handed the phone to me.

The shift supervisor wasn't quite breathing fire and threatening jobs as I'm sure the dispatcher had wanted, but he was not pleased. Mainly he wanted to hear my side of the story, and I told him, leaving out nothing. In the end, he was at least partially mollified, but chastised me for telling the dispatcher to fuck off.

"Next time, just call me and clear it first," he urged.

I lied to him and promised to do just that in the future, not bothering to point out that the dispatch supervisor was the one responsible for relaying those messages, and the only ones that got forwarded were the ones he wanted to forward, and since the company recorded only the 911 line, it was always our word against his.

I kicked off my boots and sat on the side of my bed, totally drained, unable to get Bryon Webster's mottled, lifeless face out of my mind. I could still hear his mother sobbing her prayers into her hands, kneeling in the doorway and rocking back and forth.

I checked my watch and noted that Mary's shift began in an hour. She was probably already awake. I dialed the hospital and asked for her room, and the tears started to flow before she even answered. By the time she picked up, I could only cry brokenly into the phone. I was making absolutely no sense and I knew it, but it didn't matter. In five minutes she'd be opening my bedroom door, and she would hold me until I fell asleep.

\* \* \* \* \* \*

I blink the tears away as I look at the house in my rearview mirror, and my vision clears. Even now, ten years later, the memory is still raw enough to make my breath catch in my throat. Mary and I eventually had a daughter, born twelve weeks premature. We divorced a couple of years later. After the fear surrounding Katy's birth had passed, after we thought we had put most of her health problems behind us, I could go months without thinking about it. But occasionally it surfaces, and the fear it engenders still chills me. Mostly it comes when Katy is in another room playing and I can't hear her. I'll get up to check on her, and invariably she'll be playing or watching a DVD, and she'll look up at me and smile, and the fear will pass. There are nights when I'll get up and tiptoe into my daughter's room and bring her to bed with me because *I'm* the one who had a bad dream.

Randy is remarried now, and he and his wife are still childless after years of trying. I know he has held her through long nights of disappointment, tears, and frustration, but they haven't given up. I wonder if, on the nights he holds his wife and comforts her, he remembers doing the same for Karen Webster the day she found her son dead in his crib. Would they have traded places with the Websters, if only to have a child for six months? Did the Websters think those six months were worth it?

I look up, and a neighbor's front door is open, a man framed in the light with a phone pressed to his ear. He's staring intently at me, no doubt calling the police to tell them there is a strange man parked in front of his house, crying and staring in his rearview mirror.

I wipe my eyes and put my truck in drive, and slowly pull away. A last glance in the mirror almost makes me stop again. Above the top of the privacy fence, silhouetted against the setting sun, I can make out a swing set in the Websters' backyard.

*I hope that means what I think it means.*